Sean Sennett is a music journalist and singer/songwriter. Between 1990 and 2008, Sean was variously editor, managing editor, owner and publisher of *Time Off*, a weekly music street magazine and institution since 1979. Sean has written for music magazines and newspapers such as *Rolling Stone*, the *Word*, the *Australian* and the *Age*. He now operates Time Off Media.

Simon Groth is a Brisbane-based writer and editor. His novels have been shortlisted in the Text Prize and twice in the Queensland Premier's Emerging Author Award and his short fiction has been published in *Meanjin*, *Overland* and *Island*. His fiction can go anywhere from rock music to narcolepsy. Visitors to his website at *simongroth.com* can download short stories and chat to a virtual writer.

OFF THE RECORD

25 YEARS OF MUSIC STREET PRESS

EDITED BY
SEAN SENNETT
& SIMON GROTH

UQP

First published 2010 by University of Queensland Press
PO Box 6042, St Lucia, Queensland 4067 Australia

www.uqp.com.au

Typeset in 11/15 pt Janson Text by Post Pre-press Group, Brisbane
Printed in Australia by McPherson's Printing Group

National Library of Australia Cataloguing-in-Publication Data
Off the Record / edited by Sean Sennett & Simon Groth.
ISBN: 9780702238635 (pbk)
ISBN: 9780702238314 (pdf)
Subjects: Rock music – Miscellanea. Rock groups.
Editors: Sennett, Sean.
Groth, Simon.
781.66

For Brenda, Melanie and Stella – SS

For Jo, who always knows what questions to ask. And for Xavier and Genevieve, who must endure a writer in the family. – SG

Contents

Introduction

For thirty years Australia's independent media have been developing a fine cache of street papers. Some titles were built to last, while others have come and gone. Leafing through the back pages of many of these magazines you'll find a healthy history of quality writing that reflects the sonic adventures of the subject matter and the shared experience of the audience.

Street papers as we now know them didn't arrive fully formed; the look and feel of the titles have been ever evolving. Their shape, size and editorial stance continue to match the temper of the times.

Time Off holds the mantle as Australia's oldest street paper. The magazine began life in 1976 at the University of Queensland. By 1980, *Time Off* was on the street reflecting – and occasionally helping to map – Brisbane's cultural life.

Early issues were tabloid size with Warhol-*esque*, screen-print-like covers. Editions were slim and the content, initially a little low on music when first off-campus, soon ran the gamut across rock, punk, new wave and jazz, as well as covering cinema and theatre.

The *Time Off* story isn't unique. It was the first link in a chain of unrelated magazines. Other titles devoted to exposing the art of working musicians appeared all over the country with *On the Street* in Sydney, *Beat* in Melbourne, *X-Press* in Perth and *Rip It Up* in Adelaide; all of which had their own identity and idiosyncratic feel. More magazines were to follow such as *Drum*, *Brag*, *dB*, *Rave*, *InPress* and others. Before homogenisation was the norm, each town had a distinct flavour to report on and each magazine had its own small team of writers to bring the weekly news, interviews and reviews.

For a kid hard-pressed to make the call between buying lunch and buying the latest issue of *Juke* or *Rolling Stone* (isn't that everyone's experience?), free street press was an easy choice.

In the 1980s, the discovery of new music or art was a linear process; the mosaic of information later offered by the internet was saved for science fiction plots. It was here that street press played a vital part in lifting the veil on new music, often espousing independent bands and securing talk time with artists that might have been too oblique or too local for *Countdown Magazine*.

Artist interviews, alongside the gig guide, are the bedrock of street press. Early on, the 'phoner' was established as the PR's weapon of choice. You'd be given thirty minutes on the telephone with national and international artists at all hours of the day. Sometimes, under pressure of a looming deadline or a communication breakdown with the record company, the phone would ring out of the blue with an artist awaiting his or her 'scheduled' chat. What usually followed was a broad line of questioning about 'the current single' and whether it was indicative of 'the album'. One writer for *Time Off* – who should probably remain nameless – struggled in such a way for a full twenty minutes before finally plumbing for: 'Before you go, where did the band name come from?'

By the dawn of the nineties, Australian street press had settled into its familiar focus and there was barely a major artist – local or international – who wasn't interviewed in its pages. Once seen by the establishment as mildly leftist arts papers run by students, street press had become a vital part of the fabric. Sure, flyers, word-of-mouth and radio worked, but people wanted to read about artists and hear what they had to say, and, frankly, the benefit of having very little advertising meant street press could devote reams of text to its favourite performers. These magazines presented an expanse of blank pages writers could fill with an artist's musings, often with little editorial interference. Working for a street press magazine was like being given a key to the city and its writers relished the sacred words: 'My name's on the door.'

The nineties were a special time for street papers around the country. In Brisbane, we'd shift a thousand magazines a week at the Pancake Manor alone. More street papers popped up and each capital city carried two, three and sometimes more titles. Running a free paper can be a tough gig and a lot of magazines fell by the wayside, but others dug their heels in.

At the time, street press relied on relationships with record companies and writers in various states to bulk up their pages and secure hard-to-get interviews. The fax machine became an essential part of the street press armoury, and magazines were making connections with writers everywhere and running their copy.

A big part of street press was to reflect what was happening on stage, on campus, in the clubs and on the street. We weren't spinning records and we weren't too snooty – we'd talk to pretty much anyone that was coming to town – and there was an obligation to our readers to cover all bases. The brief became, for *Time Off* at least, that if Kylie was on the cover, you could still read about the Celibate Rifles inside.

As publishing and music trends diversified and digitised through the nineties and into the new century, street press adapted and reflected the times. Street press titles were among the first publishers to go online in Australia – websites for *Beat* and *Time Off* first appeared in the early nineties. An interesting subtext to *Off the Record* is the rise and rise of the internet from complete mystery to part-time curiosity to all-encompassing delivery platform for bands and publishers alike. The challenges in reaching an audience for Hunters & Collectors in 1986 may be different from those facing Angus & Julia Stone in 2010, but the passion they inspire provides a common thread through the twenty-five years between.

For a contemporary audience permanently plugged into iTunes and Google, street press remains a credible and local source. The problem once was that not enough happened in the local scene. Now a bewildering number of bands vie for the limited attention of a furiously diversifying audience. Street press remains a vital and powerful tool to connect audience with band and vice versa. Today, street press is often still the first stop for a new band struggling to receive radio support. Every capital city in the country has a band or five championed in street press papers before radio has even had a whiff. You'll spot some of them in the accompanying pages.

Though much has changed over twenty-five years, the fundamentals remain. A successful street paper relies on teamwork. For every writer getting face time with a rock star, there's a person distributing the magazine or another pulling an all-nighter to meet a print deadline. While advertising is essential to their success, the first question that begins the working week at the better magazines comes from editorial. Who is on the cover, how many pages are mapped out for interviews and reviews?

This happens week after week – images are sourced, interviews are transcribed and magazines eventually hit the footpath. Some seriously committed people make that happen. The result of that commitment is evident not just in these pages, but on the street every week, rain, hail or shine.

Sean Sennett and Simon Groth

Hunters & Collectors

Sour record deals, the courtship of America and Australian ugliness

The kinetic energy that defined Hunters & Collectors mixed a near-unstoppable rhythm and brass section with one of Australia's more enigmatic front men, Mark Seymour. The band shared a groupthink philosophy loosely attuned to Western communism. This interview sees the band, on the cusp of commercial success with 1986's *Human Frailty*, reflect on hard times abroad, the rigours of the road and the difficulties facing Australian bands in the mid-eighties. There is even a glimmer that things might soon turn a corner, not just for H&C, but for the entire Australian music industry.

Mike Waters, trombone and saxophone player for Hunters & Collectors, has taken on the unlikely role of advising the Victorian government on the problems of young rock bands following the recent *Four Corners* documentary on the plight of young rock and rollers in tackling an industry that, although well established, remains unregulated. Mike said the aim of the program had been to show how tough it is in the rock industry. Hunters & Collectors had been approached because, after five years in the business, the band had experienced most of the frustrations of today's music industry.

Both the Victorian government and *Four Corners* chose wisely. On the long road to recent success with their fourth album, *Human Frailty*, and the single 'Say Goodbye', Hunters & Collectors have surely endured their share of hard luck. Determinedly serious in their earlier years together, the Hunnas were intent on 'changing the Western world's consciousness about music' says Mike, a little tongue-in-cheek.

When they first stepped onto a Melbourne stage, Hunters & Collectors became an overnight success. Their brand of rock incorporating a tribal primitivism took Australia by storm. They were deluged with press, raving fans, and even record labels. Virgin signed them up and everything looked perfect – for a second or two.

The relationship with Virgin lasted all of six months before the band was left stranded in a heartless London. The strain fragmented them, their line-up changed and changed again, and the media's praise drifted elsewhere. Mark Seymour, vocalist and songwriter with the band, recalls the period.

'Everyone just lost interest, though we didn't help. When the label signed us, they plied us with cash and champagne. They took us out to dinner at an Indian restaurant and we started telling their general manager that we considered him the capitalist – which made us the union – and we only wanted to rip him off. So there it was: the famous Curried Chicken Incident. They took it all seriously and suddenly washed their hands of us and we were pretty well stuck. Living in England is ridiculous for a serious Australian band anyway. You're never going to get past a tiny inner-city audience there and English punks hate Australian music – except Nick Cave. I don't know why people like the Laughing Clowns bother going there.'

'In Australia we became popular very quickly,' confirms Mike Waters, 'and we thought the same would happen in the UK. We couldn't believe it when it didn't happen. We couldn't work out why. Even the *Jaws of Life* album . . . it got favourable reviews, but it just didn't sell.'

Despite Britain's best efforts to do them in, Hunters & Collectors survived. They returned to Australia, refined their sound into a raw and ragged rock and made their live performances more powerful than ever. Waters says that, back home, the band rediscovered the crucial element in stage performance: to be entertaining and give people a good time. As Mark Seymour readily acknowledges:

'A great Hunters & Collectors gig is something few people forget, including the band. Maybe that's why the band have managed to survive for so long without any substantial chart success. The gigs are so intense that when the time has come to make a record, we haven't always had enough detachment to produce vinyl that sells. So, despite our massive live following throughout Australia, our record sales simply did not reflect our real popularity.

'I think we also suffer from the cultural phenomenon common to a lot of Australian bands like the Mentals. The people who can afford to see the band live don't seem to know that we have records out and don't buy them. What they do buy is records that are pushed out by the whole *Countdown* television thing: Cyndi Lauper, Bruce Springsteen. They may be great records, but the reason people buy them is because the artists are from *over there*. It's the same old problems.'

Perhaps, though, audiences are finally catching on that Hunters & Collectors are more than a live experience. *Human Frailty* has become their first long player to make an impact on the commercial charts as has the distinctive drums and bass rhythm of the lead single, 'Say Goodbye'.

Proving the Curried Chicken Incident is well behind them, the band have entered negotiation with American independent label IRS for the album's release and a tour across the Pacific. Strangely enough, Seymour thinks it is the Australian element in their songs that has created so much interest in the band from America.

'I think they like us because they think we sound a little bit exotic and non-American, which is heartening because we've always aimed to sound Australian, to get a sound that implies a sad mood that exists in an expansive space. I know that some Australian artists reject the idea of landscape these days, but I still think it has a profound effect on our consciousness.'

So just what is an Australian sound?

'There is a thing our drummer, Doug, calls the Great Aussie Tug,' says Seymour, 'that kind of "boompa boompa" feeling you get from people like Matt Taylor or Rose Tattoo – the kind of back beat that works in a pub. When we started, we had a flirtation with that kind of feel, but we stopped because we'd been reading *The Face* and we thought people might think we were ugly and rock-ist. But now we've realised we *are* ugly. What we do these days is simpler and more expressive.'

So, while the Hunnas are being lauded as the next big thing and are preparing material for their next album, they are still touring horrendous distances. When Hunters & Collectors next play Brisbane, they will have spent the weekend before gigging in Adelaide, travelling between the capitals *by car*.

'We had a chance to come back through Melbourne and stay over,' explains Waters with a shrug, 'but we decided to come through Broken Hill and on to Brisbane that way. The crowds see us so rarely up there, the gigs are always great. We really envy them.'

'In Australia, the pubs are the places where people experience rock and roll,' says Seymour, 'which isn't what happens in America or England. There's a whole cultural thing that interests me about pubs, a whole language you can draw on. There's a lot of ugliness and violence – boys bashing each other up, girls getting raped – in those places, but maybe there's a kind of truth there too.'

Seymour's rather romantic notion of Australia's pubs, though, does not extend to its clubs and discos.

'People who go to those places might like to think they're keeping their hands clean, but they have scurrilous little thoughts, they grope at each other in dark corners. The other thing about clubs that interests me is the people who treat going there as their job, their work ethic. They'll preen and look gorgeous and stand in a corner and not even drink. Those are the kind of people who'll endorse anything that anyone tells them.

'All those people just buy into it voluntarily, but the emotional spin-off from that kind of thing is very short-lived. In a pub, you can hold someone, you can laugh, you can fall in love. You can't do that in a club.'

January 1986 to July 1986. Original text: Shar Adams.

The Triffids

Feted and nauseous

Led by David McComb, the Triffids never scaled the pop charts, but their influence runs deep. Starting life in the late seventies, the group compiled eighty to ninety songs on crude cassette albums before they ever cut any vinyl. Music industry stalwart John O'Donnell recently described their early seven-inch singles as naïve gems, 'full of pop smarts and sharp lyrics but with a clumsy, awkward charm'. Truly great songs like 'Beautiful Waste' and the seminal 'Wide Open Road' were to follow, and, with their masterpiece LP, *Born Sandy Devotional*, the group fulfilled their 'widescreen studio ambition'. By the end of the eighties, the Triffids were no more.

There it was, headlined across the front of the *NME*: '1985: Year of the Triffids'. Other British media followed suit with the *Guardian* running a review of the Australian discovery, comparing the band with sixties American sounds, though their 'pugnacious instrumental drive and sense of enormous distances suggest the scorched earth of the bush outback'.

It's true the Triffids have an extraordinarily unique sound. Australian rock writer Clinton Walker described it in *Rolling Stone* as 'a new bent-dry, indigenous light and air to Australian rock'.

How has all this lauding affected the Triffids and where has it taken the band? From major songwriter and vocalist David McComb's perspective, it's all been a bit much. He views the press cynically, but concedes there were advantages.

'All those magazines like *The Face* . . . if nothing is coming up from the street, they have to invent something by this Thursday's deadline. I think that'd be the biggest reason we didn't stay there. After that magazine [*NME*] came out, we could have made a killing, squeezed it for every cent, but we just felt embarrassed with the whole idea, nauseous over it. One good thing though is that we can travel to Europe and the promoters have heard of us.'

The Triffids returned to Australia 'hoping everyone would have forgotten about it', but of course the ball was already rolling. A few months later, they were off to Europe where they played England (including a set at Glastonbury) and a host of continental countries, including Belgium to a crowd of fifty thousand, sandwiched between Midnight Oil and OMD.

They also used the time to record in London and mix in Liverpool their best record to date, *Born Sandy Devotional*. Described by Frank Brunetti from *RAM* as 'a shimmering multi-faceted jewel of a record', the album is the first example of the Triffids' studio work, with many of the songs never destined to be played on stage. McComb sees the album as a natural progression.

'Our first record was kind of orchestral with strings and stuff like that. *Field of Glass* was meant to expose a completely different side of the band. Once we'd done that, the trick was to keep the intensity of that and combine it with something more orchestrated and ambitious. So it was in with the vibraphones and keyboards and cellos and stuff like that. It was enjoyable, especially in the midst of this so-called resurgence of guitar bands – another load of meaningless hype. A lot of the songs were written with strings or whatever in mind. A good half – maybe six out of the ten – we'll never do live. It's a real studio album.'

Although David McComb's deep hollow voice clearly provides the focus, the Triffids' celebrated sound comes from the sum of all their members: Alsy MacDonald's intelligent and creative drumming, Martyn Casey's striving basslines, Robert McComb's electric strokes on guitar and viola, Jill Birt's haunting keyboards and vocals, and Graham Lee on pedal steel guitar, whose influence led the band back to their original emphasis on strings.

'When I joined,' says Lee, 'we never wanted to use slide guitar in any sort of conventional way. I think Dave's idea in the first place was to use the pedal steel to make the overall sound more grand and orchestral.'

'I think we'd already decided this album would be very much like that,' adds Jill Birt. 'On Dave's part at least, when he was writing the songs, he was obviously making a conscious effort not to follow *Field of Glass* too closely. He wanted to do something quiet and I think that might have been a reaction against what people were expecting.'

The Triffids are presently touring the east coast of Australia, before returning to Britain to, they hope, clinch a big record deal. Though they won't say which major label is courting them, any deal will not mean an end to their relations with Hot Records, their independent Sydney label.

'There are good reasons for staying with Hot,' says Rob McComb. 'They are interested in us as artists, not just money spinners.'

While determined to 'make it' in the industry, the band are adamant they will do it on their own terms.

'We're getting there,' says Rob McComb. 'What we would really like is to stop spending the money we make in Australia on jaunts to England, but we'll do it again if necessary. We like to work hard. We've learned that we have to be on the ball twenty-four hours a day. We don't have the attitude of just taking a holiday while we are here. We are all very committed. After all, we've been at it for seven years.'

February 1986. Original text: Shar Adams.

Stevie Wright

Moving back into easy street

Stevie Wright tore apart the Australian music scene as front man for the Easybeats in the sixties. It's Wright's voice that punctuates the band's classic material on tunes such as 'Friday On My Mind', 'Sorry', 'Good Times' and a host of others. Originally a writer in the band, he opted to concentrate on his singing while the Harry Vanda – George Young partnership built a head of steam. Later Wright became a solo star when his old Easybeats pals Harry and George penned the 'Evie' trilogy. Check out Wright's mannerisms on old footage and you'll see where Bon Scott took his cues. Sadly, much of Wright's life has been dominated by drug addiction. For years, many music fans wondered if he was still alive or just missing in action. This piece from 1986 shows Wright still on the hard road.

Stevie Wright was only sixteen when he hit it big time with the Easybeats. Now thirty-eight, his voice crackles down the phone line from Sydney. He calls me 'babe' and 'darling' as only the die-hard rock and rollers do even when we broach the subject of heroin addiction.

'I don't like to talk about my addiction,' Stevie says wearily, though he continues. 'Basically it was introduced to me the last week of *Jesus Christ Superstar* [where Wright played Hess for the show's two-year run]. I was at a party and it was given to me in aluminium foil. I accepted it that way. There was no shooting up then. It didn't take long before I was addicted.'

Although Stevie said heroin was never around when he was in the Easybeats ('we didn't even drink then'), he was interested in the drug primarily because of Ray Charles.

'Ray Charles was a very big attraction for me then and I knew he used heroin. It was brilliant, but what I didn't realise was the brilliance was me, not the drug.'

Stevie Wright has had it pretty rough since those *Jesus Christ Superstar* days.

'I have undergone shock treatment, sedation, two years of rehabilitation treatment with Salvation Army, and two lots of six-month treatments at a rehabilitation centre called Westmount. I was dying really. But then someone suggested that I do this gig. They said I could have anyone I wanted to play with.'

So some one thousand people packed a small suburban hotel to see a one-off gig. Wright was backed by some of Australia's best musos: guitarists Kevin Borich and Chris Turner played along with former Sherbet bassist Tony Mitchell, drummer Greg Hanson and Peter Kerkel on keyboards. And ironically, after twelve and a half years, rock and roll was the one thing that worked for Stevie Wright.

'All the bad things went away. I just flick 'em when I come across them now.'

On the back of his national tour with a top-notch backing band, Stevie Wright will soon be releasing a new solo album called *Facing the Music* before an Easybeats re-formation tour later this year, which will include *all* members (including Vanda and Young).

'We already have half a million dollars' worth of work for the re-formation,' said Stevie. 'Now all we have to do is get together and practise so we don't end up with egg on our faces.'

Until then, punters can check out the mix of old Easybeats material with newer numbers in Wright's eclectic set. If you go by Stevie's word, it's something to see.

'I'm totally over the top right now. The crowds love it. I have to play country and western numbers so they'll let me off the stage.'

July 1986. Original text: Shar Adams.

The Residents

The responsibility to be one step ahead, if not more

Starting life in 1969, the Residents mixed *avant-garde* sounds with equally curious visuals and were, to cop a phrase, way ahead of their time. After decamping from Louisiana to San Francisco, the band have been releasing music since 1972. The group's members have worked at concealing their identities from the public with costumes that often feature top hats and tails capped off with a giant eyeball helmet. With little regard for Western composition and a love for the surreal, the Residents' story has never been short of intrigue.

Weird, zany, outrageous, ugly, experimental, fierce, innovative, arty-absurdist-pop, *avant-garde*, off-beat, inventive, the biggest little cult band in America: slap a thick crunchy paste of adjectives around the Residents and maybe you'll get some idea of what the band are about.

The four band members wear giant eyeball masks and top hats to conceal their identity, which inevitably leads to speculation on who they are and why they feel the need for such anonymity. But, then again, who cares? The music is often brilliant and occasionally – as evidenced in the cover of James Brown's 'It's a Man's Man's Man's World' – sadistic.

The Residents themselves never speak to the media, so present to discuss the band's music and current activities by telephone is Hardy Fox from the Cryptic Corporation, an organisation formed by friends and fans of the Residents early in their career, around 1970. Hardy doubles, incidentally, as the Residents' recording engineer.

The Residents rarely play live. On this, their *13th Anniversary Tour* (now stretching well into the band's fourteenth year), the Residents will play music from across their recording career in what amounts to a retrospective show. Guitarist Snakefinger will join them on tour as he has done on several of their records making a five-piece band.

'Snakefinger will play what he always does with the Residents: a very strange guitar.'

The guitarist has, in fact, become an integral part of the show, involved in the entire process from arrangements to rehearsals.

And, in this day and age, what's music without video? A grab bag of computer graphics, animation, puppetry, props and costumes, along with a myriad of lighting and special effects has taken the Residents' videos all the way to the Museum of Modern Art, New York. For the *13th Anniversary* shows, audiences will see a selection of their work in the video form, but, alas, there will not be a showing of their feature-length film *The Mole Show* or the now legendary (and permanently shelved) project *Vileness Fats*. Even in the short form, though, the band's videos offer an example of just what is possible with the visual medium, a stark contrast to the average commercial rock video that remains marginally worse than the average toothpaste commercial.

So what else does the Residents' performance have in store?

'The show itself is live,' says Hardy Fox, 'and the band use sophisticated computerised equipment on stage to generate the kind of sound they put out. It's pretty high-tech equipment.'

The band's interest in computers is evident in their videos and this enthusiasm for technology continues into the recording studio. The Residents have their own studio setup that they continually update, improve and extend. Even the instruments they play are computerised and the band claim they can't do anything on paper anymore.

The Residents probably have more in common with contemporary experimental composers than with the pop music they parody and reinterpret. Their latest recording interprets the works of country legend Hank Williams and John Phillip Sousa, American composer of famous military and patriotic marching tunes. The new recordings add to the band's composer series already featuring George Gershwin, James Brown, the Beatles and the Rolling Stones.

'They're very interested in music in general, not just in playing music but in the basic philosophy or concept of what music is and why it is. Their approach to making music is dissection, trying to comprehend what it is about this collection of noises that makes it music. They study a lot of other composers and, in particular, people who may have been into music in a much more traditional sense, the kind of people who wrote music simply for the sake of writing music without any thought to the implications of what they were doing.

'Really, the Residents are romantics. They take an intellectual approach, but they never deny the music its essentially emotional sense. They find a lot of contemporary American pop music uninteresting, although they did recently buy a Michael Jackson record. Until recently, they haven't even listened to top forty radio.'

Perhaps the Residents' boredom with present day rock and roll culture makes sense when you consider how little popular music has changed since the Beatles (or even before). Melody, structure and arrangement have all remained more or less static. And it's this withering (and not uncommon) assessment of current musical form that has seen the Residents hailed as a cult band.

But is success the price of notoriety? Hardy says if the Residents were to become massively popular, they would almost certainly turn a completely different direction.

'They would feel they must be behind, that people are catching up with what they're doing. And if that's the case, they are not doing enough. The Residents feel they have a responsibility to be one step ahead. If not more.'

The Residents have released the majority of their material on their own label, Ralph Records. They have been independent from the outset of their career, though perhaps not entirely out of choice. Major labels may not show the slightest interest in them, but the Residents maintain their own healthy disdain for the commercial record industry. That music such as theirs exists at all in an industrial market dominated by musical product sold to humans like dog food to pets is an achievement in itself.

'The American industry,' says Hardy, 'is based on selling advertising. Radio stations determine what they play based upon how many people will listen, which then dictates how much they can charge for the advertising slots between the music. The whole thing really comes down to advertising: they play music that will attract most people to listen to their advertising. That is not the kind of marketplace that will make room for the Residents.'

Whether you're a fan or if you've never heard of the Residents before, their upcoming performance at East's Leagues Club is a once-in-a-lifetime opportunity to experience a performance that is challenging, exciting and probably completely off the planet! I'll see you there.

August 1986. Original text: Joy Flights.

Painters & Dockers

Painters play their own brand of dock rock

With singles such as 'Nude School' and 'Die Yuppie Die', Painters & Dockers are what we once called an 'alternative' band who had a brief flirtation with the pop charts. In the mid-eighties, it meant something to be 'indie' and, for a time, Painters & Dockers were certainly that. Two decades on, the band still sound joyfully subversive. Here they reveal that the inspiration for 'Nude School' came from an article in *Playboy*. What's surprising is not that they had a copy of the magazine to hand, but the fact that they were *reading* it. Were they so distracted by the new Gabriel Garcia Marquez short story that they completely forgot about the centrefolds?

Painters & Dockers are a great band who play great fun-time songs, although with titles like 'ANUS, The (W)hole of My Love' and 'Pull Me Off' you could be forgiven for being a bit suspect about the band's priorities. In fact, to put it bluntly, wouldn't it appear that the band have something of a fixation about genitals?

'Oh look, I'd like to strongly disagree with that,' argues bassist Phil Nelson. 'Go on, name a song with genitals in it,' he challenges.

Well I've already mentioned two.

'Yeah, okay, maybe the first one, but if you listen to the lyrics the second one is all about pulling people off their pedestals. With our songs, there's always something a bit deeper.'

But enough of song titles, Painters & Dockers are augmented on stage by a three-piece brass outfit called . . . the Brass Holes.

'I'll blame all that on Paul,' says Phil resignedly, referring to Paul Stewart, the band's lead singer and not-so-lead trumpet player. In true *Sweet and Sour* tradition the band came together as a bit of a joke – a fact that has characterised their subsequent work – to pay off some accumulated parking fines. From there the joke grew, along with the band's line-up, as their brand of music became more quirky and fun.

'A few years ago, everyone in Melbourne was into Nick Cave,' says Phil, recounting the band's origin. 'No one clapped, everyone wore black and looked really miserable, and we came on determined to have fun at any cost.'

The fun included covers of 'The Little Drummer Boy' and 'My Favourite Things', as well as original compositions such as 'The Boy Who Lost His Jocks on Flinders Street Station', which was inspired by John Cooper Clarke's tour last year. Apart from the obvious source of inspiration, the Painters took their name to have 'a bit of a go at Hunters & Collectors' and also because the band came from Port Melbourne, the union's traditional stronghold. The band soon earned themselves a reputation as a no-holds-barred good-time dance band and accordingly pulled big audiences.

'People like something a bit wilder. Perhaps because we play rock and roll is an easy explanation of our appeal.'

Despite their relaxed attitude, the industry quickly took Painters & Dockers seriously, something the band themselves welcomed.

'Even though we have humble origins, we have a lot of ambition,' says Phil.

The Painters' 1984 debut album, *Love Planet*, topped most independent charts around Australia, and since then the band have released *Kill Kill Kill*, a twelve-inch EP of covers and a live LP.

'We've definitely dug our heels in and we're going to be around for a while. Certainly it's better than being public servants. Not that we would have been. Paul was a rock journalist before he joined the band, and the rest of us all have degrees of one sort or another. There's even a lawyer in the band.'

Being taken seriously by the music industry is one thing. Being taken seriously by punters is quite another. Admittedly it doesn't help when your lead singer claims that people love the group because they're 'basically a bunch of dickheads'. Do the band ever tire of their image as a bunch of boozy good-time jerks?

'The fun times tag gets a bit annoying, but one day everyone's eyes will be opened and they'll see there is much more to us than that,' Phil claims.

And to help open people's eyes to their real talent, the Painters recently bought their own pressing plant, which is really taking an independent stand. The plant presses records on the band's own Dock label, but so far only two other bands have signed up. While the band plan to release their third album sometime in the next ten years, they have recently completed a new single titled . . . wait for it . . . 'Nude School'.

Phil groans as he admits the subject matter of the song seems suspiciously similar in theme to their earlier work.

'One of the band members happened to be going through an issue of *Playboy*, when he read about this school where all the students and all the teachers turned up every day nude. Look, I know what you're going to say, but it's just a nice, silly song about everyone turning up to school nude.'

Sure thing, Phil. Who said these boys aren't fixated?

December 1986. Original text: Gavin Sawford.

Warumpi Band

Why the bush band did a bunk

Formed by 'whitefella' Neil Murray in 1980, the Warumpi Band hailed from Papunya in the Northern Territory. George Rrurrambu from Echo Island and Gordon and Sammy Butcher were at the core of the group whose line-up would vary over the ensuing years. Often mixing a Chuck Berry rhythm with Aboriginal folklore, the Warumpis tore up the stage when playing live. In 1983, the band recorded 'Jailanguru Pakarnu' ('Out From Jail'), the first song using an Aboriginal language in a rock and roll format. Inspired by their close friendship, the Warumpis and Midnight Oil embarked on the legendary Blackfella/Whitefella tour into the outback in 1986. The tour took its name from the song of the same name that featured on 1985's *Big Name, No Blankets* LP.

After an impressive 1985 debut album, *Big Name, No Blankets*, national success seemed assured for the Warumpi Band. With the possibility of spots on *Countdown*, single and album launches, and general fame and fortune, how did the band respond? They did a bunk and took off back to the bush, playing sporadically around places as diverse as Alice Springs, Darwin and Kalgoorlie, before taking a break throughout most of 1986.

When they next emerged in a joint outback tour with Midnight Oil, it was with a major personnel change into a tightened-up four-piece line-up.

'It was a problem trying to reconcile being a successful rock and roll band with traditional tribal and family values,' explains guitarist and songwriter Neil Murray, the band's sole whitefella.

'Money is not that important in traditional Aboriginal culture. I mean, we'd all like to make our living from the band, but it was a matter of having a line-up change in order to keep going.'

The tour with Midnight Oil proved a curious experience and in many small towns and settlements it was the Warumpis as the support band who drew greater applause than the mighty Oils.

'We were playing to places we'd been before and the people knew us, but the response to the Oils varied. In places where they didn't have television, they were curious as to what this tall guy with a bald head was doing. But at least it was good entertainment. They got a laugh out of it, but more importantly they appreciated the fact that the band had made the effort to go out there because entertainment is pretty thin on the ground in these places.'

Neil was originally a Sydney resident who 'went bush' four years ago.

'I went north looking for adventure and excitement. I went to art school, so while my peers were planning to go to Europe I wanted something different. I was into music and wanted to find out about the Aboriginal people. I learned a lot of things I wasn't expecting. In fact, I underwent a massive re-education and went through a long period of disillusionment. In essence, I went there with a lot of romantic ideals that had to be shattered. I had this idea that I'd spend two years out there, get myself together, and then go back to the city. I never dreamed I'd get involved in a band out there.'

Apart from changing his own perspective, Neil encountered a variety of outback attitudes to Aboriginal culture.

'There are those in the pastoral community who feel they've known Aboriginal people longer than most because they've given them jobs and they're responsible for their welfare. At the same time, I think underneath that, they recognise they couldn't have got their damn pastoral industry off the ground without Aboriginal labour. On the other hand, there are a lot of good people who understand the culture and how to work within it. Basically, the people with power in rural areas – the ones in business and stuff – tend not to have a lot of time for Aboriginal people because their whole culture seems diametrically opposed to Western values.'

Neil's solution to overcoming cultural differences is simple and the music of the Warumpi Band is only one element of the solution.

'I don't consciously try to write a song with a message, but if I'm moved by something it'll come out. If you're honest and true to yourself when you're writing, the message will be implicit in what you create. In our case, action speaks louder.

'There has to be a reconciliation with the Aboriginal people. They have a civilisation as great and profound as anything in Europe or the Mediterranean and so much of it still isn't fully appreciated. Australia Day celebrates the founding of a white settlement, which suggests that there was nothing here before.

'The important thing is to give trust. Aboriginal people generally are very fair and all they need is to be shown some trust.

'Being in the bush was an experience. Those experiences are the things that have come to me through my re-education with the Aboriginal people.'

April 1987. Original text: Gavin Sawford.

Weddings Parties Anything

The wedding of country and rock

Weddings Parties Anything were one of this country's great bar room bands. With the dynamic Mick Thomas out front, the ensemble may have only enjoyed commercial success with the reflective 'Father's Day', but the Weddos had a swag of fine songs and thousands of great gigs now committed to the collective memory of anyone who ever caught them live. From bars and festivals to opening for U2 in entertainment centres, WPA fused folk and rock with a piano accordion and violin. 'Away Away' was a fine template for the band, while their early days boasted such stellar albums as *Scorn of the Women, Roaring Days* and *The Big Don't Argue.* The band released more records during the nineties and never fail to woo an audience when they regroup. Contemporaries of the Pogues, WPA took their name from a Clash song, though they remain quintessentially Australian. If they ever play near you . . . do not pass 'Go'.

On stage, they sweat copiously as they thrash their distinctive sound from a surprising variety of instruments. This instrumental strength is matched only by the power of their lyrics and, wherever they tour, they play to capacity audiences who pack into halls and clubs to hear . . . a piano accordion and violin (among the more contemporary fare).

While most bands are grubbing around in a post 1966–76 vacuum, Weddings Parties Anything have successfully welded Australian folk music, country and blues with punk into a vital and legitimate form that combines the lyrical relevance of the former styles with the ferocious accessibility of the latter.

Like the Pogues – to which they are often compared – Weddings Parties Anything use traditional styles as the core around which they build their music. There though the similarity ends and, while they have no objections to general comparisons, the Weddos eschew any lazy references to them as an 'Australian Pogues'.

'It's a complicated thing,' says singer and songwriter Mick Thomas. 'I suppose we both sing about Brendan Behan and we both do drinking songs, but we don't want anyone accusing us of jumping on their bandwagon. I mean, we were already off and running long before they broke.'

Far from any bandwagon jumping, a number of bands from around the world began exploring the rich catalogue of traditional music at roughly the same time.

'It's a matter of us being part of a visible genre with bands like Los Lobos and the Long Ryders. The machinery of the music business has become so big and so international that it's feeding everyone the same thing. Whatever Prince or Madonna does, it sells in just about every country around the world. I'm pretty turned off by that synthetic sound and I ask myself what it says about me in 1987 in Australia.

'I prefer to look back into our heritage for something that is more Australian, that feels somehow *warmer*.'

To this extent, Weddings Parties Anything's debut album, *Scorn of the Women*, rolls turn-of-the-century *Bulletin* graphics, bush politics and urban social concerns into a package that, while undeniably Australian, avoids any chest-beating jingoism or simplistic polemic.

'There is a strong sense of identity built into what we do. People sense that identity in what we do, rather than in being overtly political. There are ways and means of being political without being tiresome.'

Speaking of music and politics, the band recently supported Billy Bragg in Sydney.

'We'd just done two weeks of university gigs and I was depressed at the end of it, looking at this new breed of university students who were going to be released into the world in a couple of years' time. But then, at the Billy Bragg concert, they were chanting and singing along and I couldn't believe that these were the same kids. A week later, there was a well-attended anti-fees rally, so maybe there was some correlation. But music can't change a person's politics. You can't take a conservative and turn them into a radical, but you can make them think a little more carefully.

'What music can do is act as a rallying point for people of similar views so that ten people may come together and be made aware of each other's views through the music. Maybe then something can be achieved as a group.'

Thomas and co-writer Dave Steel spent their childhood in rural Victoria in places like Colac and Geelong.

'Dave's a real farm boy,' says Thomas. 'He didn't get to Melbourne until he was twenty-two. I spent the first ten years of my life moving around the bush and I can remember school singing being really strong, but instead of the usual stuff, we were taught Tex Morton and Slim Dusty numbers.'

In 1976, Mick moved to Melbourne, in time to catch the great rock-and-roll revival courtesy of punk, though Thomas never forgot his roots.

'Country music is a really valid form because its roots are in working people. Anyone can grab an instrument and have a go. It's the same do-it-yourself ethos as punk.'

Hearing two forms together, courtesy of Weddings Parties Anything, should dispel any doubts at their successful merging.

May 1987. Original text: Gavin Sawford.

Midnight Oil

Oils search for the perpetual sound of true Australia

Deeply etched in the memory banks is a Midnight Oil performance from the ABC Saturday morning show *Recovery*. It was 1998 and a slew of young Australian bands were on the playlist that morning with, possibly, the odd overseas name in the mix for good measure. Each artist played live a tune or two from their most recent album. The Oils, by this stage, were collectively in their forties. Opening with 'Redneck Wonderland', they destroyed everybody else on the bill. Garrett moved like a man possessed while Hirst and Bones fired up the engine room and guitarists Rotsey and Moginie churned out the last great Australian riff that Malcolm Young failed to find. It was awe-inspiring stuff, but hardly unexpected. After a number of years on the bench, the re-formed group conjured up the same magic at Wave Aid and Sound Relief. Midnight Oil were that rarest of beasts that could fuse politics with rock music and make it work. This piece was written around the time of their international breakthrough record, *Diesel and Dust*. Forget the ARIAs, the band deserve no less an accolade than 'national treasure'.

With the national publicity machine just starting to crank up enthusiasm for the bicentennial 'extravaganza', it's easy to forget that only one short chapter of this country's history is being celebrated. But not everyone is caught up in the euphoria of state-sponsored nationalist sentimentality, and the conscience of the Australian rock industry, Midnight Oil, have spent the last year trying to discover the true Australia – something that better reflects the country as a whole than the celebration of the last two hundred years of white habitation.

'There are a couple of things that sadden the band about the bicentennial,' says drummer and songwriter Rob Hirst. 'First of all, we're going into the bicentennial with a flag that's not our own. Secondly, we're celebrating only a couple of hundred years of white man's existence; the same white people whose forefathers virtually annihilated a forty-thousand-year-old culture.

'No part in the celebrations has been afforded to the original Australians to express their version of the last two hundred years, which shows you how far we still have to go. I've never felt a greater sense of shame going into the bicentennial year when the residue of misplaced and malevolent bureaucratic white policies towards Aboriginal people have left groups of them living under corrugated iron and other bits of white man's trash eating white man's trash tucker.'

In their tenth year, Midnight Oil's power and passion continues unabated, and, while the energy of their music is still apparent, it has been channelled into more specific Australian concerns. To many people, Midnight Oil are a political activist band – little more than sloganeering rabble-rousers. But while there's no denying the political content of a lot of their material, the band are motivated primarily by a deep love of Australia that transcends any chauvinistic nationalism.

This is reflected as much in the Oils' musical style as in their lyrical concerns and what emerges is probably the closest thing any band will come to producing a distinctively Australian 'sound'.

'People have grappled with this idea of an Australian sound for a long time,' says Hirst, 'and it's something I'm particularly fascinated with. I've always felt embarrassed by the fact that perhaps we've only just touched on this, but I'm certain now that some of the music we've made, and Hunters & Collectors and Mental As Anything, is distinctively Australian. It's to do with space and time, a combination of the accents and singers, and that quirkiness and dry sense of humour. I think we've got it and people are able to appreciate it after years of cultural cringe.'

Like generations of Australian painters, writers and film-makers before them, Midnight Oil found inspiration in the natural splendour of the country – in the Oils' case it was the sounds of the outback.

'The first line off the new album is fairly obviously sung by an Australian and the whole subject matter is big and really centred very much in the western desert of the continent. If what we've done defines an Australian "sound", it's because we've attempted to take some of that sense of perpetual motion and infinite space that you get in the country and put it into the music. I'm not one to judge whether we succeeded, but that was certainly one of our motivations from the desert tour with the Warumpi Band. For example, "The Dead Heart" starts off with a beat that's relentless for about six minutes and it's that sort of perpetual sound of travelling long distances in the desert. The motor hum of the diesel in your Toyota at that pitch that goes for hundreds and hundreds of miles until you run out of fuel.'

Listening to Hirst, it is clear that last year's desert tour has left a strong impression on the band both personally and musically and the experience has influenced the content and feel of their latest album, *Diesel and Dust*.

'I think the main things you remember are things like lying on your back in your swag in the middle of the night and looking up at the brightest heaven you're ever going to see. You realise why the sky and the signals from the sky are so incredibly important to Aboriginal people because you've never seen a sky that bright before. It scared the shit out of me!

'The people from Gondwanaland call it the "big quiet" and I've never heard a greater quiet than being out there. I felt that people living on the east coast in concrete and brick boxes and driving the latest car didn't realise just how incredibly fragile that way of life is. Here we are, stuck on the east coast, run by time and mortgages. And there, people live their much less fragile lives without all the fabrications. Out there for the first time, white people feel as misplaced as Aboriginal people must have felt when they were herded into missions. It was so valuable to have the experience from their side of the fence.'

Aside from the physical impact of playing with the Warumpis, the desert tour exposed the band to more traditional forms of Aboriginal music, which has had a considerable influence on the new album.

'That's partly how the songs of *Diesel and Dust* evolved, because we had to slow down. We had to change the big city talk sort of music – that adrenaline rush – and we had to make it "motor". It was a great learning experience. We came in on a whirlwind and left on a cool breeze.'

While anger is still part of Midnight Oil's music, it's not nearly as overt as on their earlier work. But Hirst draws the line at the suggestion the band might be mellowing.

'We've got families,' he says, 'and you do get a sense of dearly wanting a future and dearly not wanting your children to die in a war or in someone else's war. But I don't think we've mellowed. We're as angry as old men as we were as young men. And we're not that old either.'

October 1987. Original text: Gavin Sawford.

Do Re Mi

Avoiding the pitfalls of pinball and Twisties

You could feel the static bristle on radio waves all over the country when Do Re Mi's breakthrough single, 'Man Overboard', was released. Maybe it was to do with the lyric 'pubic hair on the pillow'. The first signing to the Australian arm of Virgin Records, Do Re Mi plotted a course for the UK to record their second album. Nothing went according to plan, and the band eventually found themselves back in Australia. This interview was conducted at the time of the release of their highly anticipated second album. Deborah Conway stayed with Virgin for some time after the band went belly up in 1988. This move led to her collaboration with Pete Townshend and even the recording of a Badfinger cover for a possible single, all of which amounted to little. Thankfully, a fruitful solo career at home with Mushroom Records was to follow.

It's been two and a half years between albums for Do Re Mi, but the band have hardly been idle during that period. Though the fabulous debut album, *Domestic Harmony*, sold a pathetic four hundred copies in the UK (talk about casting pearls before swine), it went top five in Australia. The album's local success at least vindicated Virgin Records, who chose Do Re Mi as their first Australian signing.

'I think *Domestic Harmony* didn't do as well in the UK because the record company there didn't know what to do with it,' says Deb Conway. 'They had this hot potato: a new album from an Australian band about penis envy, anal humour, and staunchly anti-pubic hairs on pillows and of course the BBC wouldn't touch it.

The company tried to blame [producer] Gavin MacKillop for not picking up enough songs as singles, but I've always thought that Do Re Mi are an albums band rather than a singles band and the English market is geared so much to singles.'

After touring Australia throughout most of 1985 in support of the album, Do Re Mi settled down in early 1986 to begin writing material for the follow-up, before flying off to the UK – ostensibly to promote *Domestic Harmony*, but also to check out a potential producer for the new work. From there, things started to get confused and the band failed to find anyone they felt they could work with.

'We tried a couple of people who didn't really work out,' Conway continues. 'One of them was Jamie Lane and the other was a complete and utter creep. I can't even remember his name. Jamie was okay, but he didn't want to produce us unless he could also do the final mix. It is understandable, I suppose, but we didn't want that. With the other bloke, whatever his name was, there was a real personality problem. Apart from being a no-talent bum, he was extremely obnoxious. So we came back home and things were suddenly all acrimonious with Virgin. There was a fair amount of pressure put on us to record with Jamie.'

Back in Australia, the band cut the 'Guns and Butter' single with producer David Courtney to maintain their profile, although Deb maintains it was a bit of a mistake.

'I never liked the song very much and the rest of the band were split. I was so surprised when Virgin loved it, because I thought we had much better songs. But we recorded it and I was proved right. I'd hate to say I told you so . . . '

Following the release of 'Guns and Butter' in 1986, the band found themselves back to square one – still with a bundle of songs for a new album and no producer – and things didn't look like they were going to get any better.

'We had approached so many people who were either uninterested or unable to do it or they were just too expensive.'

Just when it looked like the second album was fated never to get off the ground, someone in Virgin's London office came up with Martin Rushent, the producer responsible for the Human League's 1981 hit album *Dare*.

Having done little subsequent production work and currently in the throes of a messy divorce, Rushent was perhaps not the most obvious choice, but Do Re Mi immediately hit it off with him and he relished the prospect of a fresh project to devote his energies to.

Originally to be recorded in Australia, the second album ended up being laid down in the UK after an ugly scene where Rushent's wife prevented him from leaving the country just hours before he was due to depart.

'Martin just has a natural sway towards the commercial, towards the accessible,' says Deb. 'Which isn't to say that he's a sell-out or anything like that. He's just brought out what's best about Do Re Mi's songs. He brings the good parts together and chucks out the unnecessary rambling bits.'

The end result, *The Happiest Place in Town*, is brimming with a sophisticated and mature but still earthy sound, from a band which have largely replaced their early funk sound with a more passionate outpouring.

'We were once called a funk band, but I think we've become a lot heavier since then. On *The Happiest Place in Town* we cover a wide variety of sounds from hard rock to the title track, which I think is one of the most beautiful ballads ever written. With *The Happiest Place in Town*, we really kept up the intensity, especially in the early stages. We were all so desperate to do the album and Martin was so inspiring. We'd had two weeks of pre-production and we leapt into it straightaway.

'But you can't help but be clinical. You become so sedentary when you're recording an album and I think *Domestic Harmony* suffered from that. You really need to make an extra effort to do something physical because it's too easy to just sit around. Time just slips by and it's very easy just to sit on your arse and not do anything: just play pinball and eat Twisties and not even be involved in the recording.

'So when it actually comes time to record, you have to plunge deep within yourself to find the kind of emotion you're looking for.'

To find that emotion, Deb looked to her musical heroes, particularly Patsy Cline and Hank Williams, whose tortured passionate vocals she captured best on 'Adultery'.

'I've always thought they were fabulous – Dolly Parton, Crystal Gayle, Brenda Lee – but, as I've always said, the influences of Do Re Mi are totally eclectic: from AC/DC to Joni Mitchell, from the *Brandenburg Concerto* to Dead Can Dance. There are just bits of everything that you take, whether consciously or subconsciously, from all of those sources.'

The result is a unique blend of sounds and styles that results in something far more memorable than the sum of its parts.

'I don't think we sound like anyone else in the world. I don't know if that's a good thing and I don't say it in the same way that Morrissey says the Smiths are the best band in the world. I just honestly believe that Do Re Mi don't sound like anyone else: it's a unique sound and very hard to pinpoint.'

February 1988. Original text: Gavin Sawford.

Crowded House

The curse of the second album

From Split Enz through Crowded House to his solo work and back again, Neil Finn is an artist who appears regularly in the archive. This 1988 interview offers a glimpse into Finn's songwriting inspiration and process. It's interesting to note the very real anxiety and pressure Finn felt having to follow up Crowded House's phenomenally successful debut. As he feared, the album would not prove as commercial (at least in the United States) as its predecessor; however, no album with 'Better Be Home Soon', 'Into Temptation' and 'Sister Madly' could be considered in any way a failure.

Crowded House would again hit commercial paydirt with the hugely successful *Woodface* album, which saw Neil's brother Tim join the band. In the years since, between the break-up and re-formation of Crowded House, Finn has launched a solo career, recorded acclaimed albums with Tim and even joined the occasional Split Enz reunion.

Since the demise of the legendary Split Enz nearly four years ago, guitarist and songwriter Neil Finn has gone on to achieve remarkable success.

Forming the Mullanes immediately after the Enz folded, Finn worked hard writing new material and producing demos before finally flying to Los Angeles, New York and London in the hope of securing a record deal.

A few months later, the band landed a worldwide contract with Capitol. The group then boarded a plane to record in Los Angeles, changing their name to Crowded House.

Their self-titled album became a dream debut for Crowded House, boasting five singles and phenomenal sales not only in Australia, but across Europe and America as well.

Next month will mark the release of the band's follow-up. After initially giving it the title *The Mediocre Second Album*, the band later settled on the somewhat more optimistic *Temple of Low Men*.

'We started it in Melbourne, we finished the actual recording in Los Angeles, then we mixed it in New York so we sort of went on a journey eastward,' explains Finn.

Finn believes the first single released from the album, the acoustic-oriented 'Better Be Home Soon', is hardly indicative of what fans should expect.

'It's probably the least representative track on the album, in a way, because it's the straightest. It's the one that people got to know last year through the live gigs. We thought it was almost like one off the last album, so we'll stick it out now.

'The album in general is probably a lot darker than that song. Not gloomy at all – the playing is quite spirited – but some of them are . . . well I suppose even that one's not all beer and skittles either. The album's more melodic and less rock. I think it's a more interesting record. There are more extremes in every way.

'In some cases it's more sparse than the last record. We've done a couple of songs in the three-piece format with orchestration, but with the rhythm being all acoustic with Paul on brushes and snare drum and just a simple bass. That's all that propels a couple of songs.

'There are songs that are more complicated than on the first album too. We're not going to go out and do a Yes on anybody or anything like that. But it's good to stretch out a little bit in instrumentation.

'We used Mitchell Froom again on production. He's pretty cheap going because he only drinks tea!'

Contrary to strong rumours in the press, elder brother Tim didn't perform a duet on the album.

'There were a lot of rumours around,' smiles Neil, 'none of

which were true. Tim actually did almost the whole album, doing backing vocals with Paul. I'm going over to play on Tim's record pretty soon. We're building up to doing a record together. He's definitely got the motivation and I think that's half the battle with songwriting. I've heard a couple of his demos and they sound really good.'

Despite writing some of the most memorable songs of the eighties, Finn hardly regards himself as a prolific writer.

'I'd like to be,' he laments. 'I have plenty of ideas, but I don't finish much. Every year, I complete about ten or twelve songs. I'd like to think that the ones I write are of a reasonable standard.

'I think I could churn out a lot more if I just applied the craft to it. Inspiration is still ninety per cent of the songs, even if it's only ten per cent of the workload. You just wait around for that; there are no laws.'

With initially only an album's worth of material behind them and not wanting to be overly reliant on the Split Enz catalogue, the band found themselves including some surprise cover versions in their live show.

'It was a case of having to really,' muses Neil. 'We found ourselves playing one or two. We liked them so we'd play them live. We never learned any of them properly. I don't even know the lyrics to most of them. Now we even do "Whole Lotta Love", both acoustically and as heavy as we can off the cuff. We did it once and really enjoyed it so we decided to do it again. And I only know half the lyrics to that one.'

Regardless of Crowded House's large-scale success, Finn hasn't closed his mind to obvious problems in the Australian music industry.

'It's my impression here that radio has taken a bit of a turn for the worse. In Sydney, people seem to be complaining about it and I noticed it too. Like up here with FM104, people seem to be going for the classic rock format. They're playing a lot of older hits and that seems pretty negative.

'I also believe – though I could be wrong – that, in the main, major record companies haven't signed up anybody for the last two years.'

With *Temple of Low Men* being released worldwide in early July, the immediate future for Crowded House is hectic, with several weeks in Europe during July, a full Australian tour in August, and dates in America at the end of the year.

'That's as long as somebody doesn't decide to chuck it in in the meantime,' Finn adds ominously. 'You never know with this band.'

June 1988. Original text: Sean Sennett.

Paul Kelly

Bicentennial blues

Paul Kelly is one of the most gifted writers of his generation. Equally at home with a band behind him or solo with an acoustic guitar, Kelly is an artist who has continued to push his own musical boundaries, flirting with everything from folk and bluegrass to his later, more experimental, projects Professor Ratbaggy and Stardust Five. As a singer/songwriter, Kelly has remained consistent and challenging. An acolyte of Bob Dylan, Kelly has kept his musical backdrop evolving. Whether fronting the Dots, the Coloured Girls, the Messengers or one of his many touring outfits, Kelly has built a catalogue that is uniquely Australian. *Gossip*, recorded in 1986 with the Coloured Girls in tow, was the follow-up to the critically acclaimed solo work *Post*. *Gossip* was released in Australia as a double album and contained Kelly's breakthrough single, 'Before Too Long'.

Paul Kelly is a man who wears his heart – and his social concerns – on his sleeve. His music is passionately powerful and tenderly reverent in turn, but more importantly he believes in backing up his beliefs with actions. It's the sort of stance that leaves you wide open for criticism: not major pot shots, but snide little suggestions that somehow you're selling out if your actions deviate from your beliefs, or, more precisely, other people's perception of your beliefs.

Kelly recently copped criticism for appearing at an event that had been partly funded by a bicentennial grant, criticism he replied to spiritedly in the music press.

'Yeah, and I'm playing at the Biennale and that's been supported with bicentennial money too,' Kelly laughs. 'It's a fine line to draw. We didn't want to play at Expo because it's so closely tied in with the bicentennial. There were other reasons too, with the housing problem I thought there wasn't enough care taken with the residents of South Brisbane.'

There is an intrinsic Australianness about Kelly's work, a sense of the environment in which the music was created, evoked without obvious references to tying down kangaroos, calling Australia home or yearning for a home among the gum trees. Kelly's music leaves an indelible impression of a man very much in love with his country and its lifestyle, but not blind to its problems. It's something that emerges naturally in his music, Kelly explains, and it comes from a variety of sources.

'I think if you try to do that consciously it becomes self-conscious or trite. We get English influences and American influences and influences from other Australian bands, so I think a lot of bands in Australia have a fairly distinct sound that comes probably as a result of that mix. I don't sound like an American when I sing, I don't sound like an Englishman. I don't know what I sound like . . .'

Kelly doesn't think that there is an easily definable Australian sound, but recognises a commonality between his music and certain other Australian bands.

'There's a definite style of, say, the Go-Betweens that I've probably used a little. But with other bands like Died Pretty or the Triffids, it's probably more a case of similar influences rather any direct influence on each other. Bands like the Triffids I think have an original Australian . . . I don't think "sound" is quite the right word . . . "idiosyncrasy" maybe?

'We get a chance to become a little more idiosyncratic here than American bands. American radio tends to be very specialised, which makes the bands specialise. The reviews we got in America said we were playing so many different kinds of songs and they thought that was strange, that one man should have such a wide range of styles.'

Kelly has returned from an extensive tour of America following the release of *Gossip*, which attracted a lot of attention and even radio play. Despite the lyrical content and overall feel of the album, Kelly says he encountered no problems with American comprehension of such an Australian album.

'Funnily enough our first single there was "Darling It Hurts", which is an Australian pun – they didn't get it, obviously, but it didn't seem to make much difference. So I've never really seen a problem. We've always heard songs about Kansas City and Memphis and, even if you've never been to those places, you still understand what they're about.'

Although it was sold as a single album in America, *Gossip* was originally released as a double album in Australia, only the third double album ever to be recorded by an Australian band. Kelly's response to being asked why he chose to release *Gossip* as a double album is typically forthright.

'Because everyone told me not to do it and when they said that I knew it was a good idea!'

Packed with a variety of material, the album marked a transition for Kelly from his last days with the Dots through to his current band, the Coloured Girls.

'There was a backlog of a lot of songs going back over a few years that I just wanted to clear. Some of the songs that appeared on *Gossip* were played by the Dots so it was a link in that way. It's also our first album, which was another reason to make it a double. We wanted to show the range of the band; we wanted to prove what we were capable of.'

Kelly has spent years performing around Adelaide and Melbourne pubs and up and down the country, first on his own, then with the Dots and now with the Coloured Girls, but he doesn't subscribe entirely to the belief that constant touring improves musicianship.

'I think too much is made of it. I think it can be quite destroying touring without a record. It's a nice little myth, but I guess I'm as guilty as anybody else when I talk to the Americans about it.

The Australian pub scene is so exaggerated, especially when the Americans ask questions about a lot of the songs being up-tempo, implying that these are songs to be played live. When you play live, you've got to deliver and I've seen too many good bands break up under the pressure.'

For Kelly and the Coloured Girls, the days of struggling for a living have passed and Paul is now free to concentrate on developing his songwriting style and proving to critics there's more to his art than the oft-quoted Dylan/Guthrie/folk comparisons.

'In one sense, we're a pop band with hit singles on the radio. Then we're a . . . .' he pauses to sigh, ' . . . a folk band. But sometimes they meet: folk and pop. I mean, folk music once *was* pop music.'

July 1988. Original text: Gavin Sawford.

Hoodoo Gurus

Faulkner looks to music's bargain basement

With *Stoneage Romeos*, the Hoodoo Gurus released one of the great debut albums. Originally from Perth, key songwriter Dave Faulkner had already demonstrated his talents on the Victims' classic, 'Television Addict'. As the Gurus' line-up evolved, collecting a couple of Hitmen along the way, the band established themselves as masters of the three-minute radio single. By the time *Blow Your Cool* was released in 1988, the Hoodoo Gurus were firing on all cylinders.

And the reference to grebo rock . . . you've never heard of it? You're not alone.

As the music of the *six-tease* gets pounded into the dust of the national subconscious through radio overkill and misplaced, idealised nostalgia, it must seem all a bit of a giggle to Dave Faulkner. As head honcho of the Hoodoo Gurus, Faulkner officially declared the sixties open for pillage with the band's debut single, 'Leilani', in 1982, a song that set the stage for subsequent acts like the Stems.

An ode to tacky mid-sixties American girl pop played at ten times the speed, 'Leilani' later resurfaced in extended form on the Gurus' pop pastiche debut album, *Stoneage Romeos*.

'A lot of things that influenced us very early on – psychedelic music and things like that – weren't big with anyone at the time,' ponders Faulkner. 'Now every city's got its own bunch of snotty-nosed garage bands doing all the psychedelic greatest hits, so we really had to step away from that. We never really saw ourselves as a psychedelic band anyway, it was just something we liked and it reflected in our music, but we've grown away from our influences as much as grown towards them. We really think it's what we sound like to ourselves that matters more than what we listened to when we were growing up.'

By the time *Stoneage Romeos* was released, the band's personnel had changed radically with guitarists Roddy Radalj and Kimble Rendall replaced by Brad Shepherd and Clyde Bramley, and drummer Mark Kingsmill later replacing James Baker. It was this line-up that consolidated the band's success with 1985's *Mars Needs Guitars* and last year's *Blow Your Cool*, which proved to be the last album to be recorded by that particular combination of the Hoodoo Gurus with the recent news that bass player Clyde Bramley has called it a day with the band.

'Last year was a hard year for us,' explains Faulkner. 'Lots of touring. He didn't feel up to doing much more of that. Touring is hard on everybody – Mark has got two kids and a wife and it's very difficult for him being away from them – but some people feel it more than others and Clyde just wanted to spend some more time around Sydney.'

Bramley's decision is understandable, particularly when you consider that the Hoodoo Gurus have been touring America and Europe for more than six months of last year and four of this year so far. In the UK, despite attracting new fans and opening up for a number of U2 concerts, the band copped the wrath of the fickle British music press. The *NME*, then hopelessly besotted with its Next Big Thing discovery in the form of 'grebo rock', lambasted the Gurus for supposedly betraying their grebo roots on *Stoneage Romeos* with the more polished sound of *Blow Your Cool*.

'That's bullshit, isn't it,' says Faulkner exasperatedly. 'Nothing in the English press ever surprises me, it's pathetic really. They are so fashion conscious, it's just one more thing in a long line of things I have against them. If you're from Australia, you've got no chance in the English press because automatically you're colonial upstarts and if you take them seriously you're a bigger fool than they are.'

But if the British press took offence at the Gurus, the rest of the country embraced them and the band found even greater success in Europe – so much so that in a couple of months' time they will be flying to France for a handful of dates in Paris before returning to Australia to commence work on the next album.

Released from a less-than-satisfactory record contract with Big Time, the band are currently enjoying a well-earned break, and although their popularity has increased, particularly in America, they are not about to bow to the pressures of a foreign market.

'We're not prepared to modify our sound for that. We just play the music we like for the people we like. You can't tailor-make your sounds for everybody because when you do that you lose the magic of what made it work in the first place. If you try to grow to fit your suit, you'll never be successful. It will always be a bit baggy here or a bit tight there. You've got to buy the clothes that suit you.'

So what tailor will Dave Faulkner turn to for his next piece of sartorial vinyl?

'The bargain basement of life has many riches to be offered for the plucking. We just have to rummage through and see what comes up.'

July 1988. Original text: Gavin Sawford.

The Go-Betweens

Waiting for the train that never comes

At the beginning of 1989, the Go-Betweens were preparing to release the album that would ultimately make good on their potential to cross over to commercial success without compromising their artistic credentials. At the time of David Burchill's interview with Robert Forster, such success was anything but a given. Burchill, however, maintains his faith and, in the process, proves his clairvoyant skills in the final paragraph of this article: Wayne Goss indeed occupied the position of Queensland's head honcho later that year, Queensland finally took out the elusive Shield six years later, and today the Go-Betweens have not only taken their place as an essential Australian band, they have been officially embraced by the city they once abandoned. After all, how many bands have a bridge named after them?

After ten years slogging it out in the music industry, any band could be excused for losing their inspiration or giving up in despair. Not so the Go-Betweens. Their most recent vinyl offering, *16 Lovers Lane*, has been hailed by many to be among their best work ever. And slowly but surely the mainstream side of the industry appears to be accepting them into the fold and, more importantly, rewarding them with the airplay they have so justly deserved for so long. In talking to him, it becomes easy to forget Robert Forster is an industry veteran, such is his almost childlike enthusiasm for the band.

'I'm very happy with it. The record seems to be known and accepted. We're very happy our singles are being played on the radio. We like the idea of walking down the street and hearing our song blaring out of newsagents or chemist shops.'

This album is the band's slickest to date, production-wise.

'Yes, that's because the studio we recorded in here in Sydney was the best we've ever had to work with. I think it's a happier record in a way and [producer] Mark Wallis is very good at getting clear, bright sounds. The songs were very good and the band played extremely well. Also what's to be realised about this album is that we did play every instrument on it. We didn't have tons of session musicians; there are no thick layers of touchy gossamer keyboards on it. It's very much just the band, recorded very well.'

In a recent interview, it was revealed that Amanda Brown and particularly Lindy Morrison were more than a trifle miffed about being left out of the pre-production sessions, effectively reducing their input towards the overall arrangements. Robert is decidedly cagey and defensive when I ask how they have learned to live with it.

'Um . . . I think they're living with it okay,' he replies, though not convincingly. 'The pre-production to every album can't always be the same. That's just the way it was this time. We had a producer we hadn't used before and we were recording in Australia for the first time in six years. There were a lot of new things being done around this album. You can't keep doing the same things over and over.'

Alright, we believe you.

It was interesting to learn that many of Robert's contributions to the album were penned here in Brisbane.

'When we moved back to Australia, I went up to Brisbane for six weeks before Christmas and stayed at my parents' place, which is something that I haven't done since 1978. I moved into my old bedroom. It was good, especially after London. We'd just done a tour of America so to fly back and be at The Gap with my parents going off to work and me just in my bedroom or sitting on the verandah with an acoustic guitar was quite a novelty. It was inspirational. I had no interruptions, I had a clear head, and I could just get to work.'

Forster's love/hate relationship with his home town has presented itself in various quotes and been touched on in some of his songs over the years. How does he feel suddenly living back here after so long?

'Well I live out at The Gap, which is where I grew up. I didn't spend much time in town mainly because I don't know it well and I just don't like the look of it. I know of no other city in the world that has changed so drastically over the last few years. I remember Sydney in 1978 and Melbourne in 1980. When I go and visit them now, they look roughly the same. Brisbane seems to be completely and utterly remodelled. I can imagine someone at the age of sixty finding that completely demoralising. People who've lived in a city for more than fifty years of their life, they know all the certain haunts to go to and where everything is and then in ten years the Gold Coast real estate crowd and the mob in the Queensland Parliament decide to completely destroy the city. I miss turning a corner and seeing something familiar. I'm not anti-change or anti-progress, which is what's hurled at someone who tries to stand in front of a building about to be pulled down, but I'd hate to think what would happen if the people responsible for pulling down all the buildings in Brisbane were elected into power in Venice. Imagine, they'd floor the place in two years!'

Love it or hate it, Brisbane is the place where four out of five members of the band came from, and the city is something of a recurring connection when you consider the most recent recruitment of John Willsteed on bass.

'That was a strange twist of fate. After we'd been overseas for so long, we came back to Sydney minus one bass player. And who should move in just down the street, but our old friend John! It's the stuff that movies are made of.'

Despite the originally temporary nature of his position in the band, Willsteed has not only slotted into the job perfectly, but has also firmly established himself as the vital additional musician, particularly in the studio sessions. The Go-Betweens are more akin to a family than the typical rock group. They have always been an exceptionally close-knit and self-contained unit to the point of incest.

'We've very much done things our own way. It's unconventional and yet somehow it's all turned out well. When you make the decision to join the Go-Betweens, it means taking up your entire life. Robert Vickers was the one reflective and introverted member of the band, but now with John it's all gung-ho. John played most of the guitar on the album. He's a very creative person.'

One gets the impression that one area of Willsteed's creativity considered unnecessary for the band is songwriting.

'We're encouraging John to be creative in the arrangement of the songs and the artwork of the sleeves, but there are already two established writers in the band and I think a third one could cause havoc. But you never know; John's full of surprises.'

A scribe from the *NME* once described the Go-Betweens as 'geniuses with the arse hanging out of their trousers', a reference of course to their dire financial position while living in London. Was it mainly financial purposes that prompted the band to base themselves in Australia again?

'Yes, it's much better over here. London was just manic poverty. You just don't seem to be able to escape that over there. So many people are living in very trying conditions. It's good to have left all of that behind us now.'

With dollars in their pockets and a welcome new addition to the family, it surely won't be too much longer before the Go-Betweens become not just local legends but universally recognised as one of the eighties' more important and intelligent pop groups.

Then again, having wrung out that tired but optimistic prediction, I may as well go all out and back Queensland to win the Sheffield Shield and Wayne Goss as Premier just to make the treble.

January 1989. Original text: David Burchill.

Sonic Youth

Preparing for future mania

Sonic Youth are another band well represented in the street press archives and for good reason: they are, after all, the critical darlings of the eighties underground. This 1989 interview with Thurston Moore, though, focuses more on the band's eclectic side-project, Ciccone Youth. Moore's mention of *Another Green World* is a reference to Brian Eno's album released in 1975. We considered editing out Sawford's transliteration of Thurston's laughs, but there was something about seeing *hur hur hur* in print that made it essential to the story.

Thurston Moore may play guitar for one of the heaviest, most intense groups to come out of America this decade, but you'd never guess it talking to him. Softly spoken and hesitant to the point of indecision, and with a rumbling wheezy laugh, the gangly six-foot-six Moore is one of the original members of Sonic Youth, one of the premier American post-post-punk bands, the so-called No Wave.

Their grinding, relentless wail of fuzz has drawn comparisons with artists from Phil Spector to the Jesus and Mary Chain (two camps who, when you think about it, probably aren't that far apart). But, amidst all this serious distortion, there is still time to laugh as Thurston readily confirms.

'I guess there is a certain sense of humour in our work,' he says. 'We're all fairly positive people, happy people. We're not like . . . uhhh . . . there's a lot of people who find a lot of humour in our music. I've heard people say *Daydream Nation* is a hilarious record, but I think that has more to do with where we are now looking back at our music history. It's like the Jesus and Mary Chain, in a way. They're actually a hilarious band, their stuff is so completely miserable and we really like them for that.'

But Sonic Youth's sense of humour shouldn't be judged completely on their work under their primary moniker. After all, the band is about to release the collected recordings of their alter ego, Ciccone Youth.

Ciccone Youth first came to public attention two years ago when they released 'Into the Groove(y)', a sampled homage to Madonna, who apparently wasn't that pleased. Thurston firmly denies the reports that the original Ciccone has considered legal action against her namesake.

'No, there was no lawsuit. When we first had that single out, I think it was played to Madonna and she said it was fine with her, although Sean Penn probably thought we were insane assholes, *hur hur hur*,' he laughs wheezily, taking a sort of perverse relish in the idea.

'We have a Ciccone Youth album with that single, but that's as far as it goes. The cover is a detail of Madonna's lower right-hand side of her face – where the mole is, *hur hur hur*, and it's like huge detail on the cover xeroxed a couple of times so it's pretty abstract. I'll be curious what kind of reaction we get, because there are really no Madonna affectations on the record at all. We kind of lost interest in her since she became so involved in aerobics, and the album is basically instrumental. It's a lot like *Another Green World* or something like that, going on that way.

'It was just a sidestep for us because we had toured and recorded, doing the same thing for a long time. We had some time off and we didn't want to sit back and watch television so we went into the studio with absolutely nothing, turned everything on and kicked the tape-heads around to see what happened. There was no plan at all. We just hoped something would come out. And we called it Ciccone Youth because the name already existed and it seemed kind of fitting.'

Thurston is adamant that Ciccone Youth has outlived its usefulness. Even the name tends to date the idea.

'Yeah, I mean it should now be called Tiffany Youth, *hur hur hur*. It probably won't be used again; that record was pretty much it. We finished it a while back and so it's been in the can for a while. It's a nice record to put out after *Daydream Nation*.'

Daydream Nation is probably Sonic Youth's most polished album to date, but listening to it one gets the impression that, as with most of Sonic Youth's work, it would sound so much better live. Indeed, like Henry Rollins, Sonic Youth tend to subscribe to the notion of the purity of the live performance.

'I agree with that, Henry's pretty right on,' says Thurston. 'Usually when you go in to record, the first thing you're trying to capture is the structure of what you're doing and I think a lot of records fail because that's all they're trying to do. Rollins is a good example because his records progressively get better, but when you see them live, they just kind of explode and you can't fit that into a groove. Performing live is also a highly visual medium and Henry is a very powerful performer. The records suffer because you're not watching him when you play his record. But then the Rollins Band is more of a live unit. We take that into consideration when we're recording and, in the studio, we'll come across in ways that can't ever be translated live. So we get things happening on record that are very trashy but can only be done with the technology. You don't plan on re-creating that live. There's so much else going on in a live show it's much more of a spontaneous gesture.'

Like the Rollins Band, Sonic Youth are very much located in the cultural surrounds of their native America, and even Thurston sounds bemused at their appeal outside the States.

'We've just been to New Zealand, which was very strange because it was so serene, a bit utopian. When we played, people were going nuts and we were singing these songs that were written in a whole different culture and basically they could only relate to the immediate visual thrill, which is fine. People always say they guess we'd play better in the States because the relationship is much more complete, there are certain nuances.

'I mean it's the same thing with Australian bands. Bands like the Triffids, I think, have a lot of nuances in their music that relate to living in Australia and there's a whole cultural backdrop that I can only guess is happening in their music, but it's probably definitely there. Somebody who would have lived the same kind of lifestyle as the Triffids is going to get a lot more out of it than I will. But then, I'm interested in that. Einstürzende Neubauten work very much in that way. A lot of what they do is so German – nobody really gets it, especially in the States – but they're an amazing band nevertheless.'

A critic once raised the idea that all bands at the heavier guitar end of the musical spectrum exuded much more sexuality than your average rock band, citing the Cult and Zodiac Mindwarp, as well as Sonic Youth, as evidence for this. While the theory is probably perfectly applicable to Zodiac Mindwarp, who seem to revel in lecherous lyrics and phallic posing, I find it hard to imagine Sonic Youth as love messiahs of the eighties.

'Yeah, I suppose,' ponders Thurston, 'but that's all kind of intuitive in a way. Sexuality is not a forced thing at all. Rock and roll tends towards that way, *hur hur hur*, but we don't try to cultivate that. We're definitely into the physicality of the music and I think that's where people get the vibe or whatever.'

Sonic Youth are pretty much on the cutting edge of innovative music as we hurtle towards the nineties and, ultimately, the twenty-first century. Like REM, their lineage and influences aren't immediately discernible and they have proven themselves over some six albums to be flexible and open-minded enough not to get stuck in the one groove.

Rather than following the current cry of 'Pop Will Eat Itself', Sonic Youth seem to embody Thurston's notion that 'Pop Will Ignore Itself'.

'I don't know. I think the whole thing is that people are going to totally block off the past. There's going to be total future mania.

The world is preparing to enter the twenty-first century; the whole of the nineties will be spent preparing for that. The Vietnam War will be totally forgotten. It's going to be very interesting. I am kind of excited about it in a way and it's going to be good working in these times.'

January 1989. Original text: Gavin Sawford.

Jello Biafra

Biafra versus the taste police

In the mid-to-late eighties, Brisbane was a tinderbox of political and cultural frustration fuelled by corruption and breathtaking hypocrisy at the highest levels. Taking a cue from the atmosphere, *Time Off* ran a series of searing social and political editorials on everything from licensing laws to the still ubiquitous venue closures to Expo '88. But, in 1989, just when it seemed that the worst excesses of the government had been consigned to history, came the pointless and farcical raid on a local independent record store. The raid was sinister enough to draw former Dead Kennedys front man and activist, Jello Biafra, into the fray. He offered what must have been – in that pre-internet age – a unique international perspective on Queensland's censorship laws and the people unafraid to abuse them.

When licensing branch detectives raided Rocking Horse Records last Tuesday and made off with five hundred dollars' worth of records, Queenslanders once again realised they were a race apart from the rest of Australia when it comes to basic rights like freedom of choice.

It's one thing for the state government to presume that we aren't morally responsible enough to view certain films (witness last year's banning of *The Last Temptation of Christ*), but quite another to confiscate, from only one particular store, records which are otherwise freely available in this fine city.

Among the albums confiscated were copies of the Dead Kennedys' *Give Me Convenience or Give Me Death*, containing the track 'Too Drunk to Fuck' (well known for its ability to whip virginal schoolgirls into a frenzy of untrammelled lust), so it was only a matter of time before the man himself, Jello Biafra, lent his personal support to Rocking Horse's plight.

Biafra is no stranger to the censorship battle and, in America, he has been at the forefront of the defence against the assault upon recording artists' rights by the religious right, who have operated through a variety of pressure groups ranging from the Moral Majority to the Parents Music Resource Center (an initiative of the notorious and influential Wives of Washington, a sort of politicians' spouses' moral freemasonry).

As front man for the sadly defunct Dead Kennedys, Biafra was a particular target of the religious right: an artist who saw it as his duty to alert his audience to the dangers of intellectual, social and political complacency. Biafra, through the Kennedys, was a gadfly on the Moral Majority's arse.

And he was a gadfly they resolved to swat when, in 1986, police raided a San Francisco record store and Biafra's own apartment, confiscating copies of the Dead Kennedys' third album, *Frankenchrist*, which contained a poster of surrealist artist HR Giger's *Penis Landscape*.

A year later, after a spirited but exhaustive defence by Biafra, the case was dismissed following a deadlocked jury. It was a hollow victory for Biafra, who was physically and economically exhausted after a prolonged court case largely responsible for the eventual disintegration of his band.

And now, halfway across the world, it's happening all over again. Is Biafra ready to do battle once more against the forces of evil and darkness? You'd better believe it!

No stranger to Queensland's peculiar political climate, Jello likens last week's raid to the Dead Kennedys' experiences when they performed in Brisbane during a blistering tour in 1982.

'It brought back some very ugly memories of when the Dead Kennedys were in Queensland,' he recalls. 'We got a really bad taste of the area's state politics. At the time, our drummer was arrested for public drunkenness for having an unopened can of beer in his hand when a cop car drove by. He was also the only black guy standing with a group of white guys. And then I ran into somebody who'd been arrested for carrying a concealed weapon – a pineapple!

'I felt terrified after a while. I've felt safer on the streets of Harlem or East Berlin than I have in Brisbane because the police state under Joh Bjelke-Petersen was so crazy. I realise Joh is gone now, but this current lynch mob mentality against record stores is doing nothing to ease Queensland's reputation with the rest of the world as Australia's own little South Africa.'

Biafra is in no doubt as to the real motive – or, more to the point, motivator – behind the raid and sees disturbing parallels between last week's Brisbane raid and his prosecution in America.

'I sense there are other forces at work in the form of one crackpot minister who runs a fundamentalist church outside of town.' Biafra is referring to Reverend Pastercamp of the Ipswich Christian Life Centre, who was responsible for a raid on Cosmic Records in Ipswich a week prior to the Rocking Horse raid.

'These same records have been on a blacklist circulated by the American religious right for quite some time and they openly admit that shutting down records and record stores is their first step and that what they really want to do is start attacking books, school libraries, and so on until they can slowly but surely tell the government what to do.

'Literature isn't banned so much as blacklisted. What will happen is that a group of vigilantes will organise, usually a small group acting on order from headquarters in some organisation in Washington, be it one of the religious groups or the Parents Music Resource Center in the case of rock music.

'They then quietly go to the store or the school library or the radio station or whatever saying, "We want these items on our blacklist removed or we are going to raise hell for you." And, most of the time, the retailer or the school board are so intimidated, they do it without informing the public.

'I'll jump at any chance I can to expose the religious right for the fascist crooks that they are. I get a great deal of enjoyment out of that.'

If the concept of the state government as puppet to fundamentalist religious pressure groups wasn't so sinister, last Tuesday's raid would have been laughable given that police not only picked up copies of the Kennedys' album, but also a Champs album with the track 'Do the Shag' on it and a Sonic Youth album that contained the song 'Master-Dik'.

'Well, many people addressed Richard Nixon by that very title and granted I think Nixon himself is obscene, but that's another story . . .' laughs Biafra.

'When I first heard about the Brisbane raid, I fell on the floor laughing. Not only did they bust Dead Kennedys records, they even went after the Champs, who'd have to be one of the most calculatedly harmless bands in the history of rock and roll. They don't even have any lyrics, it's all instrumental. The song that the minister didn't like – "Do the Shag" – I mean "shag" is a technical name for a type of carpeting!'

Biafra sees the raid as indicative of the hypocrisy rampant in the conservative establishment.

'Now I know if I'm a robber or a rapist in Brisbane, I should call the cops and report obscene records on the other side of town in a store before I go out and commit a crime that harms real people, because obviously the cops don't care about those kinds of crimes.'

Rocking Horse was issued with a summons to appear in the Brisbane Magistrates Court to show cause as to why they were stocking 'obscene matter'. They are appealing for an adjournment in order to prepare their case, but, should they not show proper cause, charges will be laid. Rocking Horse, however, is vowing to fight any charges, the only effective response according to Biafra.

Cosmic Records, though, agreed to withdraw their 'offending' items from sale rather than face a huge legal bill.

'That is slitting your own throat in the long run,' says Biafra, 'because once they're done purging the shelves of the first blacklist, there will be another blacklist and another blacklist until the church has become governor of the store because it has so much power over what they can do. I've seen it happen time and time again in America.

'The attempt to smash the Dead Kennedys and our label very nearly worked, unfortunately, and that's not lost on the religious right when they attack independent radio stations and record stores today.

'I would warn people in other parts of Australia that this probably isn't just an isolated crackpot minister in Queensland and there's probably a nationwide push. I expect the religious right will try this in many other communities just to see how far they can go and how much they can get away with.'

It's one of life's rich ironies that, in a country that prides itself as the bastion of democracy – 'the land of the free' – social intolerance and artistic censorship are rife. What is it that nurtures such reactionary tendencies?

'I would say primarily greed,' says Biafra without hesitation, 'greed and fear, because Americans are terribly insecure and paranoid of anybody with a different point of view, unless it's something they can understand by watching *The Cosby Show* or something like that. You would not believe how dumb people here have become.

'The one thing I found to be true about both the religious right and the far right is that they lie like crazy to get what they want. They have absolutely no morals. It's classic doublethink.

'And it will get worse before it gets any better because of who has access to the media. At present, eighty per cent of the media – from radio to TV and newspapers on down to record labels and school textbooks – is in the hands of only twenty-one corporations, all run by white conservative Republicans.'

So what can a poor boy do apart from play in a rock and roll band? In a recent interview, REM's Peter Buck suggested that politics in America was rapidly approaching the point where a couple of bullets in a few politicians was the only solution.

Admittedly, he was drunk at the time.

But, while Buck's suggestion gets the thumbs-down from Biafra, it's clear he's considered it.

'America is a nation of John Hinkleys and Sons-of-Sam, so these emotions run through my head at times. But then I have to gauge whether or not it's worth going to jail or getting killed on account of one person. I mean, I could never get close enough to somebody like George Bush or Oliver North to actually carry out an assassination.

'As far as what Peter Buck is saying, what REM could be doing is writing songs with harder-hitting lyrics and including inserts with the records that detail why they're writing these songs, kind of like what we have on our last few albums. It's very easy to use a record as a great journalistic tool. There's room for one or two newspapers apiece per album.

'I think it's important for people who are in the public eye like myself – even though I'm a pretty small potato in the greater scheme of things – to use our art as a way of informing people and not just entertaining. I think it's possible to do both at the same time and so inspire people to learn more and take action on their own. That's one of the reasons the Dead Kennedys and myself have been harassed over the years.'

Biafra is well aware that his message often falls on deaf ears, particularly with the increasing conservatism of youth, which he sees as a result of the years of reactionary federal administration.

'I think that is a trickle-down from the policies of the Reagan administration, where they sort of sent the unwritten message that it was cool to be a racist redneck goon and get violent again.'

Surprisingly, Biafra has no desire to enter mainstream politics, despite once running for Mayor of San Francisco – on a ticket that in part demanded all businessmen wear clown suits – and coming fourth out of a field of ten candidates.

'I think generally I do a better job with my art because this way I don't have to kiss ass to all those financial backers, power-brokers, gangsters and political action committees that own and operate most politicians.'

Since the Kennedys broke up following the *Frankenchrist* trial, Biafra has had little time to return to music: something he hopes to rectify in the future.

'It's just that I have so little free time compared to what I'd like that I really want to get back to isolating myself from the goddamn phone and write some real songs for a real band. If much more of these Queensland-type problems crop up though, I may have to turn up and start rattling some sabres – or, let's say, rattling some cages.

'Mind you, if these attempts to shut down record stores because an instrumental band mention a type of carpet on their record helps to galvanise people to vote out the present administration, then by all means let's see some more raids.'

February 1989. Original text: Gavin Sawford.

Malcolm McLaren

Punk, rock, Warhol and good manners

Malcolm McLaren was the one of rock's great impresarios. Long before he considered running for Lord Mayor of London, he built his legend managing the Sex Pistols, the New York Dolls, Adam and the Ants and Bow Wow Wow. Prior to the Pistols, he had a clothes store called Sex and was the partner of Vivienne Westwood. When he died in 2010, an obituary in *Q Magazine* described his voice as a 'pitch perfect blend of camp incredulity and condescension: Oscar Wilde's Lady Bracknell on twenty-a-day'. McLaren was also a recording artist. The singles 'Double Dutch' and 'Buffalo Gals' were hits and helped bring hip-hop into the mainstream. As McLaren had sampled African ideas, so too was his work later sampled by everyone from Mariah Carey to Eminem. Then there were more esoteric mash-up works such as the albums *Waltz Darling* and *Paris* that merged classical music, opera, electronica, spoken word and rap into one big melting pot. Here, before Madonna grabbed it for herself, Malcolm talks up the power of vogueing.

Malcolm McLaren, rock and roll's most flamboyant entrepreneur, woke up one morning four years ago to discover the magic had gone from his life. To help fill the void, every Friday night he would wrap a brick in the most elaborate coloured paper he could find and attach a small card to the parcel.

'I'd visit suburban churches and then – looking around to make sure nobody was around that late – I would toss the brick through a window hoping the priest would read the message on the card. It would always say, "The magic's back." I did it to feel alive, that's all.'

For the man who 'invented' the Sex Pistols purely so he could sell more trousers, the magic is indeed back, in the form of a new LP, *Waltz Darling*. The album is possibly McLaren's ultimate creation. Rich in texture, it superbly marries the likes of Strauss's *Blue Danube* with New York rap, while fully embracing the latest dance fad, 'vogueing'.

'New York is the home of it,' says McLaren. 'Vogueing came out of a strange part of black gay culture. It was invented in the twenties as part of drag balls. Back then, it was all big guys trying to look like big girls while trying to imitate a vogue mannequin. Seventy years later, it has been taken to the street and mixed with the notion of what rap and street culture are all about in New York. It takes *Vogue*, which is generally associated with wearing rich to look rich, and makes it the domain of the street.'

After three and a half years in America, McLaren compares his return to Europe to a thirsty traveller finding an oasis in the desert.

'I was actually living in Hollywood. I felt like I was living in a giant hotel for too long. It's a transient place. Sometimes it can drive you mad because it's such a "me me me" culture.'

Given McLaren's *avant-garde* leanings and entrepreneurial flair, it's hardly surprising that he cites Andy Warhol as one of his greatest influences.

'The idea of being a painter and not having to paint has always intrigued me. I was very influenced by Warhol because he managed to take painting out of the domain of sitting in the attic on your own, he developed the notion of a factory and the notion of teamwork and he was also able to embrace pop music with the Velvet Underground and so forth. I surrounded myself with very much the same mood and feeling, but I was more of an anglophile – less polite and much more vulgar.

'In some respects I have less to do with product than Warhol. I guess I'm a little bit more intellectual than he was. People will probably accuse me of being the exact opposite, but that's the way I see it.'

McLaren believes vogueing will become *the* essential form of the nineties, purely because it allows people to feel glamorous without taking away the flavour of the street.

'It's early days for vogueing in England. But then you know what the English are like. They're a very homophobic community. They're worried of looking like faggots. I don't know why. The Tories are fifty per cent faggot and we have a school mistress running the country and giving everyone a caning. It will be nice when that dictatorship ends so we can have a fresh approach in the nineties.'

McLaren believes vogueing revives the etiquette and manners of the twenties. One street gang now calls itself the House of Extravaganza in homage to the fashion houses. So is vogueing the antithesis of punk?

'It is and it isn't. Remember, punk was also something you could dress for and its attitude was very much around doing it yourself. Personally, I don't think the Sex Pistols could have sustained through the eighties because the mood of the country was so completely different. The eighties were the decade of pragmatism and career. Let's face it, that's what rap music is all about. It's a black version of punk. Vogueing is about embracing the notion of etiquette and charm. The rest of the culture doesn't want anything to do with vogueing. It's considered too down-market. So when it's rejected like that, you know you must be doing something very rock and roll. That was all I needed to know.'

August 1989. Original text: Sean Sennett.

The Ramones

Influential down to their jeans

These days you'd be forgiven for thinking the Ramones sold more t-shirts than records. Their emblem shows no sign of fading and the music they made has inspired a generation or two of bands. Emanating from New York, the Ramones fought like crazy, played like there was no tomorrow, and even had a staunch Republican in their ranks. Out front was the great Joey Ramone, who took his nom de plume from a moniker Paul McCartney dreamed up in his pre-Hamburg days. Joey was a so-so singer with attitude and a great enthusiast of the music that preceded him. With all that combined, the Ramones made music like no other. Hey Ho Let's Go . . .

Most rock bands come and go, but others seem destined for eternity, and among the immortals, thankfully, are the Ramones. And if you're to believe the whimsical rantings of hirsute front man Joey, these guys have only just begun, despite the recent loss of original bassist Dee Dee.

'We couldn't be any more hungry,' Joey blurts in a call from downtown Noo Yawk. 'It's the kind of people we are. As time goes by, we play harder and faster and we're never satisfied. That's how it should be.'

This is no idle chat. If you could hear this guy, you too would believe every word he says. I swear. The band's new LP, *Brain Drain* – their first under new label Chrysalis – continues recent moves away from bubblegum rock. Amazingly, in 1989, the Ramones remain contemporary. And at thirty-seven, Joey really does seem to still have that bug, the spark that got him going so many years ago.

'I'll play until I don't want to do it any more. I enjoy playing for myself as much as for the kids. It's very good therapy. It sounds like I'm seeing a psychiatrist! Things are only getting better. Our audience is getting larger. Our fans are crazier and the shows are wilder. Things are so bright, I have to wear shades.'

It is only in the brief moments between froths of boyish excitement that Joey shows signs of his bitter disappointment at losing an original member after so many years.

'Everything was going great, but Dee Dee had been doing side projects and his extracurricular activities got the best of him. You can do stuff on the side, but the Ramones are the priority. Dee Dee left without notice, like we'd only known him for twenty years. You'd think if he wasn't happy he'd have said so.'

In Joey's words, Dee Dee has gone on to become a 'Noo Yawk Rappa'. But despite one of the heaviest losses of their career, Joey and the rest of the band are going great guns at pushing on with the recruitment of new bass player Cee Jay, just twenty-three years old.

The story goes that Cee Jay was AWOL from the Marines or something when he was selected from around seventy-five hopefuls at an audition.

'Cee Jay just got out of the Marines. I don't even know him that well myself.' Joey says. 'He's perfect. He looks good and he's got that kind of street credibility, you know what I mean? He's really excited. Things can only get better because there won't be any tension any more. There was a bit of friction. Dee Dee believed he was some kind of genius: God's gift to the rock world.'

So one of the most seminal bands in rock history powers on. With this in mind, it's hard not to ask what Joey thinks of . . . gulp . . . the likes of Bon Jovi or Poison and the new crop of guitar outfits.

'They make me wanna puke. It's superficial bull. But there are other bands far more exciting, like Metallica, Anthrax and Guns N' Roses.'

Joey has no qualms admitting the Ramones have influenced millions and continue to do so.

'Rock and roll is bigger than it's ever been. We *know* we've had a major effect on just about everybody. Sometimes it's the music, the attitude or the look. Even Bon Jovi are wearing ripped jeans.'

November 1989. Original text: Richard Kwong.

The Stone Roses

Rebel without a vocabulary

With their self-titled debut album and single 'Fool's Gold', the Stone Roses virtually invented 'Madchester' and built a template for Brit-pop. Mixing guitar grooves with a little acid house, the Stone Roses were a band that influenced the future of British Rock. Their Spike Island gig in 1990, a pseudo Woodstock for the baggy generation, is still spoken about with an awe usually reserved for bands that achieved world domination. The Stone Roses fell short of that, but with their Jackson Pollock aesthetic and a combination that included Ian Brown, John Squire, Reni and Mani, the Stone Roses occupy a unique place in the British rock pantheon.

Manchester's Stone Roses topped all sorts of English readers' polls last year and were voted best indie act of the year by the ever-so-hard-to-please *New Musical Express*. But despite what can only be called super independent stardom, singer Ian Brown appears to have some sort of attitude problem. During a short and sharp-witted call from downtown London, Ian displayed all the signs of being the proverbial James Dean: an Ian without a cause.

The Stone Roses are Britain's independent darlings following the success of the eponymous debut LP and a number of singles. They may have such tomes as the *NME* waxing lyrical about 'chiming phased guitars, softly bruised vocals and more electricity than the national grid', but still Brown can't relax.

Question after question, the answers are blurted back, some accompanied by a snide snigger.

Are you living in Manchester?

'Anyone in their right mind would get out of Manchester as often as possible.'

Okay.

How would you describe your own music?

'It's Stone Roses music, innit?'

Okay.

Do you think you've managed to create a new sound?

'Yeah, it's new because no one has ever done an LP like we have before.'

Hmmm.

What are your influences?

'I'm influenced by everything I've ever seen or heard, but we're not following any role models if that's what you mean.'

Needless to say, I wish he'd lighten up a little.

Anyway, lately the guys from The Stone Roses have been recording yet another single, titled 'One Love', due for release in the United Kingdom around mid-April.

They have also been touring, with a series of gigs in Europe and Japan all in the space of only three weeks. Long tours are not the band's forte, it seems.

'We don't do long tours because they're a waste of time,' Ian blurts. 'I don't believe anyone can entertain anybody else for forty nights on the run.'

Future touring plans see Ian and cohorts in the United States and, if all goes according to plan, Australia later this year.

Of course before these guys go anywhere, they have to clear up a little legal matter. In early February, Ian, guitarist John Squire and drummer Reni burst into the offices of their old record company FM Revolver Records and splattered five litres of blue and white paint over managing director Paul Birch and his girlfriend, Olivia Darling. They then reportedly spilt more of the stuff over his rather expensive Mercedes and two other cars. All of this was in protest over the unauthorised release of a video for one of the band's singles.

Ian readily confirms the story but also assures us his actions were justified.

'I'd do it again. I thought we were right and still do,' he says.

As a result of the protest, the boys were charged with criminal damage and are expected to appear in court in March.

Let's hope Ian Brown can withstand the cross-examination.

March 1990. Original text: Richard Kwong.

The Church

Kilbey knows a good deal when he sees one

Seeing the Church on *Countdown* with their paisley shirts, pointy boots and Roger McGuinn haircuts was a call to arms for lovers of guitar music that mixed clever lyrics with a little electric jangle. Early in their career the band released a batch of terrific singles that included 'Unguarded Moment' and 'Almost With You', alongside fine albums like *The Blurred Crusade*, *Séance* and, later, *Heyday*. Near psychedelic at times, the band's music was a backdrop for Steve Kilbey's poetic lyrics. Success in America was to follow with 1988's *Starfish*, which spawned the hit 'Under the Milky Way'. The follow-up, *Gold Afternoon Fix*, saw the band record in Los Angeles and marked the departure of drummer Richard Ploog. Despite featuring the single 'Metropolis', commercially, the album wasn't the band's finest hour.

With the release of their latest LP, *Gold Afternoon Fix*, the Church have delivered their most eagerly awaited album to date. While once considered too esoteric for wide scale public consumption, the Church have now established a niche all of their own, both in Australia and around the world.

Recorded in Los Angeles, *Gold Afternoon Fix* takes its name from a stock market term used for establishing the overnight price of gold. To date, the LP has already spawned the single 'Metropolis'.

While the music was mostly composed by the Church as a whole, the majority of the lyrics remains the property of the band's engaging vocalist and bassist, Steve Kilbey.

When Kilbey wrote the lyrics for the *Heyday* LP in 1986,

he would swim daily, using the time to consider the themes and phrases that he wished the songs to convey. It wasn't until the music for the album was completed that Kilbey added lyrics to the songs. In contrast, the lyrics for *Gold Afternoon Fix* were prepared with far more haste.

'We had some time in an eight-track studio and we wrote millions and millions of pieces of music,' explains Kilbey, 'then I'd go back to my room and jot down notes really rapidly . . . like three minutes without any prior thought. I already had one or two phrases floating around that I'd picked up on my travels, but no real lyrics. So I just knocked 'em out quickly. The whole album was like that. I had to trust my subconscious. You should really give in to your subconscious and let it take over, it's always good. A lot of people so far seem to be complimenting me on this album, so I guess it was the right thing to do.'

With a volume of poetry published under the title *Earthed*, Kilbey has become widely regarded as one of this country's most influential underground poets, though the lyricist doesn't believe his written work is that indicative of the man.

'There's a song on the album called "You're Still Beautiful", which is a nasty sneer at a used-up kind of sycophant. The song before that is "Essence", which is about how the universe is female and all good things are female. I only expect a song to be a snapshot of the mood I'm in. I don't imagine most songwriters can stand behind every song they've written and say this song is me, it represents my feelings.

'I suppose in some of the songs, I'm a character. There's a song called "Terra Nova Caine", which is about a guy picked up by aliens and brought back. It's a comedy song – a scientific spoof – and I guess that isn't even me at all singing that song. I can't find the bottom of myself anymore to find the truth . . . '

When it comes to including a lyric sheet, *Gold Afternoon Fix* follows the same credo as the band's last LP, *Starfish*. Fans will have to listen to the disc and forgo the luxury of being able to see Kilbey's words in print.

'I won't ever be including a lyric sheet in anything I do ever again,' he says. 'I don't want people to read the lyrics. They were written to be heard not read. I find people read the lyrics and they read them for their own sake. I wanted to write lyrics that didn't have to stand the test of being on a page.'

When the group embark on a world tour to promote the album, they will be joined by new drummer, Jay Dee Daugherty. Jay Dee comes into the group in place of Richard Ploog, who has decided to take a year off.

'I'm not sure what he plans to do,' says Kilbey of Ploog. 'Jay Dee is the drummer from Patti Smith's band. I met him backstage one night. He's an intriguing guy. We were doing a tour and Tom Verlaine from Television was opening for us. Tom recommended him highly, even when we weren't looking for a drummer. When Richard's thing happened, he was the first person we turned to.'

Having Jay Dee in the band is something of a bonus for Kilbey, especially given that Patti Smith was, for a time, one of his main influences as an artist.

'I'm beyond a fan,' says Kilbey. 'The first Patti Smith record meant an awful lot to me. I thought it was a breakthrough. She was one of the first female artists I respected for playing real rock and roll.'

Co-producing *Gold Afternoon Fix* with the Church was Waddy Wachtel, who worked with the band on their two most commercially viable projects to date: *Starfish* and *Heyday*.

'Waddy was a good yardstick. He's a perfectionist. Waddy is good for discipline and for polishing ideas, good for having a joke between numbers. I thoroughly enjoyed making this album with him. One or two members didn't enjoy making the album with him at all, but that's the way it goes.'

Despite predicted sales for *Gold Afternoon Fix*, Kilbey has misgivings about the record.

'I reckon they've all got problems. I've got songs I particularly like but I've never been happy with a *record*. I'm always frustrated and disappointed. That's just the way it is. I would say this album is the end of the *Starfish* phase. Our next album will be the beginning of a new phase. This is a summing-up album.'

Despite the prospect of having to forgo solo projects and having to spend possibly up to a year on the road both promoting and touring *Gold Afternoon Fix*, Kilbey remains optimistic.

'I'm going to be paid to travel round the world,' he says, 'seeing all the hotspots with a bunch of my friends, strumming a guitar. Sounds like a good deal to me.'

April 1990. Original text: Sean Sennett.

The Celibate Rifles

Real bullets shocker

Led by Damien Lovelock and Kent Steedman, the Celibate Rifles were one of Australia's hardest working bands. Signed to small independent labels, their discography includes fourteen studio albums. They toured the planet consistently earning pockets of fans wherever they went. This interview was done around the time of 1989's *Blind Ear*. The band had signed to the True Tone Records label and their work was distributed by industry giants EMI. After grinding it out for years in pubs, they found themselves at Brisbane's Festival Hall supporting Diesel. But the big time wasn't meant to be, and as the song goes 'it's harder than it looks'. Here Damien Lovelock talks music, touring and daylight robbery.

Many bands vie for the title of Australia's hardest working pub act, but few can match the credentials of Sydney's Celibate Rifles. Recently returned from a three-month European tour, the Rifles make their way to the Sunshine State this weekend on yet another leg of their seemingly endless *Blind Ear* tour.

'We've toured *Blind Ear* for eighteen months now,' says vocalist Damien Lovelock from his Newport Beach home. 'It's now a six-week tour that's gone on for a year and a half. Every time we'd think that's it, there'd be another wave of interest or something. It's been amazing. I've been really happy about it.'

Although the Rifles haven't released any new material for quite some time, they are compiling a collection of all their old, hard-to-find singles to be titled *Platters Du Jour*.

'We realised a couple of years ago there are now thousands

of people who like the Rifles and who have missed the majority of our recorded work: all the early singles and that. If they wanted to buy a copy, they've got to pay somewhere between $50 and $300. All those old records have been deleted. So we decided we'd try to rectify it by making available all that old stuff as it was originally released . . . you know, the A- and B-sides. We investigated putting it out as a collection of singles, but it would have been so expensive, we felt it was prohibitive. It would have been forty or fifty bucks for a singles box.'

Apart from enthusiastic crowd response and encouraging record sales, the Rifles' European tour thrust the guys into a situation that left Damien feeling sore and guitarist Kent Steedman more than a little shell-shocked.

'It was the last show of the continental tour. We had a week's holiday before two London gigs and then home. We had all this foreign currency from all the different countries. There was me, Kent and our tour manager at the post office and the travel agent around the corner, booking everyone's holiday. We were supposed to be converting our currency into Dutch guilders to pay off all the end-of-tour costs, but they hadn't given us the right currency.

'Then there was a bang, like a firecracker going off. I turned around and realised *fuck!* It was a bank robbery! These guys ran in and did the number, sort of herding everyone into the corner of the room. They took Kent as a hostage, but I think it was really just a gesture; I don't think they were seriously going to hurt him. They have all this bulletproof glass in there, so the only way to get money is to take a hostage, see?

'They made everyone lie on the floor, but I lay my head against the wall and put my hands flat on top of my head. Suddenly, they were shooting everywhere and screaming in Dutch. One guy kept pointing his gun into Kent's ear while the other guy collected the money. Then as they ran out the door, this guy fired backwards into the post office, thinking he was shooting into the roof again, so no one would chase him. But he missed the roof. I was directly opposite the door with my face against the wall, hands still on my head. He shot me between my first and second knuckle. Half an inch lower and it would have gone straight through the back of my skull.

'But anyway, we did the gig that night and went straight on to Ireland for a holiday the next day.'

September 1990. Original text: Brent Hampstead.

Bob Geldof

Knighted and saintly, but no diplomat

Bob Geldof's 'pop' star had been on the wane prior to the release of the 1985 charity single 'Do They Know It's Christmas?' There'd been success with the Boomtown Rats prior to that, as well as a starring role as 'Pink' in Pink Floyd's film of *The Wall*. It was Geldof's charity work that brought him back into the global spotlight. Raising awareness and funds to fight famine in Ethiopia and Africa at large, Geldof, along with Midge Ure, was the driving force behind Live Aid. When the Rats (who took their name from Woody Guthrie's boyhood gang) were relegated to the past, Geldof penned a successful memoir 'Is That It?' and set about rebuilding his own career as a solo artist. In support of his second solo album – 1990's *The Vegetarians of Love* – Geldof made frequent trips to Australia to talk up his work and perform around the country. He even enjoyed a stint hosting his own radio show in Perth. Buoyed by a clever film clip and the single 'The Great Song Of Indifference', *Vegetarians* drew on Geldof's Irish roots, his love of Bob Dylan and a renewed sense of vigour to create what some consider a career highlight. As a solo artist, Geldof's output was soon overshadowed by a failed marriage to Paula Yates, tabloid headlines, more work in politics and a burgeoning media empire.

This interview took place at Brisbane's Park Royal Hotel. Geldof was alone by the pool, under a sun umbrella, dressed in black denim, jeans rolled up and his bare feet on the table.

As a child, Bob Geldof's sole interests were music and politics. In the 1980s, he managed to combine these twin passions while pricking the conscience of the Western world. With the global success of Live Aid, Geldof was dubbed Saint Bob then Sir Bob. Now he's back to Rockin' Bob, and in Brisbane as part of a promotional campaign to restart the chart life of his second solo LP, *The Vegetarians of Love*.

To date, Bob's promo tour has seen him inject a bit of spark into *Hey Hey It's Saturday* and Steve Vizard. He walked off Clive Robertson. He worked as a DJ for five days in Perth playing exactly what he wanted for two hours a day. He's had to put up with the endless media rounds, hosting the ARIAs ('one of the worst nights of my fucking life'), a run-in with a B105 rep about Madonna and Margaret Thatcher, and finally a rather enjoyable, if intense, dinner with *Time Off*, other media and record company types to talk further about the album.

His first solo venture since 1986's *Deep in the Heart of Nowhere*, Geldof's new album again makes use of the Rupert Hine's production skills.

'Since the last album he's been a friend of mine,' says Geldof. 'This sounds terribly name-droppy, but I was writing some songs with Dave Stewart from the Eurythmics, who was in Paris mixing Mick Jagger's single. Mick and I went out to dinner and he suggested Rupert would be perfect to do my record. I said if he's so good, why aren't you using him. He said he would but Keith didn't get on with him. It was a really good tip. I got back home and it was bizarre, because that morning Rupert had tried to contact me. He was the perfect guy for me at that moment. All the pieces seemed to fit together.'

The beauty of *Vegetarians* is its acute spontaneity. The record adopts a blend of Cajun (*à la* the Louisiana bayou) with a distinct Celtic flavour. As odd as that may sound, the material on the record works well.

'I went in the studio with about twenty-five to forty ideas, it was just me bashing on a guitar. There were only a couple of complete songs. About six songs that made the album were completely spontaneous; you can hear me asking if the tape is rolling.'

Despite his connections – legend has it he has the Pope's home number – Geldof steered clear of rock legend guests.

'It wasn't conscious,' he says. 'On the last record I didn't know any session guys. Dave Stewart, who's my friend, was helping me a lot. Then Annie Lennox came in and sang, as did Maria McKee and Alison Moyet. I knew most of them before they were well known, with the exception of Eric Clapton. He was obviously already famous when I was just starting. If Eric Clapton asks you if he can play on a couple of tracks, you don't fuckin' turn him down [laughs].

'With this album, I did it just up the road from my house and I wanted amateurs. I didn't want people overplaying. Rupert thought that was a bad idea. He suggested getting people who could improvise. He got some people from the Penguin Cafe Orchestra, an *avant-garde* classical group. That seemed a weird choice to me. I'm a great believer in John Lennon's maxim that *avant-garde* is French for bullshit. Anybody who assumes that label is usually a wanker.

'I play left-handed guitar and I don't change the strings around so they had to follow me upside down and backwards. I liked that because it was an impediment and they couldn't overplay. I wanted it to be scrappy. I wasn't going for sales. I wanted to hear the clanks and the fret noises. I wanted to hear the process of actually making music.'

In typical fashion, the album's first single, 'The Great Song Of Indifference', has already attracted controversy with Geldof declaring his disinterest at the demise of all nations and the Third World in particular.

Another track to raise eyebrows is 'Crucified Me', especially given Geldof's messianic image of recent times.

'I wrote "Crucified Me" last year,' Geldof explains. 'That was one track that literally popped out of my mouth. I'm not sure what it is. I'm not being coy; I actually don't have a clue where it came from. People were saying I can't be that much of a cynic and I'm not, I'm a sceptic. Cynicism is dangerous and unhealthy, an excuse to do nothing. Scepticism is necessary and vital: you should never stop asking why. That track is a song against indifference and apathy.'

Given Geldof's modest list of recent musical achievements, one can't but feel that sometimes the record-buying public expect too much of him.

'They did at the time of the last album. Even if I'd brought out *Sgt Pepper*, it would have been a dud because the expectations were so high. I went off and made a record about things that bothered me on a personal level. People would say, "why isn't he angry?" I'd been angry for three fucking years every night on television. I was exhausted emotionally and intellectually. Nobody wanted to understand that.

'The record did well anyway, so I was lucky. I think people still associate me with Live Aid – which is fine. I understand I carry certain baggage with me. If I had twenty number ones before the day I die, that's all they'd write about. Of course it wouldn't matter to me then. I'd be dead.'

Now, music is one of the many things that Bob is an expert on. And Bob likes to give his opinion on absolutely everything. Among others, he loves Van Morrison ('a terribly rude and disturbed man who writes beautiful music') and Bob Dylan. He saw the Beatles, the Stones and Bob Dylan play in the mid-sixties. He's glad he saw Sinatra and regrets missing Elvis.

'In Perth, on the radio, I played Robert Johnson from these 1936 field recordings, Louis Armstrong, Dr Feelgood and the Pistols. People loved hearing this stuff. I played "Crossroads" by Robert Johnston, followed by Cream's version and Hendrix's. People just don't get to hear this stuff because the programmers don't give 'em a chance.'

Like any music fan, Bob can't stand listening to the radio.

'It irritates me. Music should be fresh and exciting, not the drivel they serve up on radio.'

Ideally, Geldof would like music to start saying something again rather than drifting into 'Macy's music': tunes made for a department store to sell.

'I share the common global culture that started in the sixties,' he says. 'Music to me was absolutely critical. I didn't play sports; nobody was at home. The conversations I had were with the radio and with books. When I hear it being trivialised it upsets me.'

One of the great disappointments of modern music to Bob is rap. After embracing it because it was 'confrontational', Geldof soon became disappointed.

'I thought rap was dangerous and useful,' he says. 'I liked Public Enemy and NWA because they were a genuine black voice, though I dislike intensely their anti-Semitic crap and their racism. Then of course it turned into MC Hammer and Vanilla Ice.'

For his own music, Geldof has eyes only for the future. He sees his solo career as a long-term prospect; making it highly unlikely he will ever take the stage as a Boomtown Rat again.

'Why? If somebody came along and offered the band ten million pounds to do a world tour, I'd be on that stage like a shot. I don't know why people don't say that. Pete Townshend's a very honest guy. I don't know why he couldn't say that about the Who. They pretend it's for other reasons. I think it would be pathetic if bands like the Clash and the Sex Pistols got back together. It would be the very antithesis of what they talked about. The Buzzcocks got back together: they were crap then and they're crap now, they're just old.'

With time running short, there's time for one more question, is it true Bob has the Pope's home number?

'No,' he deadpans, 'he calls me.'

October 1990 to March 1991. Original text: Sean Sennett.

The Cure

Robert Smith and the cure for all ills

Mixed Up remains one of the stranger albums in the Cure's back catalogue: a remix record Robert Smith has described as 'fun after the doom and gloom of *Disintegration*'. By this stage in their career, the Cure were becoming a revolving door of musicians behind Smith. Now a global commodity, the Cure commissioned remix artists to have their way with the likes of 'In Between Days', 'A Forest', 'Close to Me', 'Caterpillar' and more. Spanning a double album, the work formed a bridge towards the group's next studio LP, 1991's *Entreat.* As the interview concluded Smith remarked that his listening tastes while driving were almost exclusively Charles Dickens's audio books on cassette.

Robert Smith is an enigma; it's that simple. The Cure front man is responsible for creating some of the most innovative popular music to come out of Britain in the last decade. Smith is a man who has refused to compromise. Once regaled as indie darlings, Smith's band are now as likely to grace the airwaves of Triple M as community broadcaster 4ZZZ.

Facts about the Cure are often unclear. As Smith admits, 'I lie a lot. I bore myself if I don't make things up.'

Of late, he claims to have written a series of short stories – all without endings – called *The Glass Sandwich*. He is also rumoured to leave his phone bell permanently switched off. He occasionally picks up the receiver to see if anyone is ringing.

Stories, lies and rumours aside, in the last decade, the Cure have managed to release a grand total of twenty-two singles and thirteen albums.

'That's a shocking statistic. I've never bothered to count them,' says Smith. 'I never thought we'd have kept going for this long, but I'm glad we have. Looking back, out of most of those records – every single one in fact – I'm glad that we did it. It doesn't seem like we've been doing it long enough to have twenty-two singles, though.

'It's like life,' he continues. 'If you look back in general, it doesn't seem very long. If you look at the little things, it seems much longer. I don't feel as old as I should. I've got such a bad memory. With drink and sleep, I feel like I've lived for only three years.'

Smith believes his records are 'little diaries', offering a perspective on the band that would otherwise have been lost.

Now, there's a new Cure chronicle available. Rather than opt for a straight 'best of', the group have released *Mixed Up*, a melange of re-recorded twelve-inch tracks.

'The whole point of the *Mixed Up* album, and everything that goes with it, is that it's different. I had all of these arguments initially. When it first started off, it was going to be an ordinary Cure compilation: all the twelve-inch mixes for the fans. People were requesting twelve-inch mixes of "Let's Go to Bed" and "Primary". Even at the time, I didn't think they were very good. I thought it'd be a drab album. Ultimately, this record is to do with music, not collectability. Musically, some of the old remixes don't stand up. They're drab. When we originally remixed "Primary", we were more interested in getting down to the pub. It was two minutes longer and it was awful. I'm not that proud of that.'

As well as including a new track, 'Never Enough', the album is essentially the work of DJs and producers such as Paul Oakenfold, Mark Saunders, Chuck New and William Orbit. Each took hold of a Cure classic and remixed to their heart's content.

'When we started, twelve-inches certainly weren't artistic statements like the singles themselves,' says Smith. 'We decided to set a precedent and get old songs remixed by people who do it now. It's turned into a dance marathon, really. It's a difficult record to talk about. It sounds brilliant. It sounds stupid me saying this, because I never say that about records. For me it's an instant Cure album, because I've had very little to do with the remixing process. I'm hearing it as a Cure fan would hear it.'

Smith is not entirely complimentary about some of the remixes offered to the band.

'Some of them were awful,' he admits. 'There was a version of "Love Cats" that sounded like UB40. That's not a compliment.

'If this was our first album, I wouldn't release it. I'd rather die than have it as a first album. We haven't run out of ideas, we're going into the studio in two weeks to record four new songs. We're doing this record because we think it's good. We're even thinking about doing some Christmas shows playing just these twelve-inch versions. That's how infectious it has become. But we won't end up doing endless dance remixes; this album is as far as it's going to go.'

Despite his appreciation of *Mixed Up*, Smith was never unhappy with the way the songs were originally recorded. Smith passionately defends his back catalogue.

'I'm not ashamed of anything we've done,' he says. 'The only thing I'd change would be the sound of the first album. If I was seventeen now and you asked what I wanted the Cure to be like in fourteen years' time, it'd be pretty close to what it is at the moment. I've devoted a lot of time to making sure it would end up like this. I wouldn't change how we've done anything. John Cleese said, when Monty Python started, they had to continually disregard everyone who told them it wouldn't work. We went through the same thing with *17 Seconds* and *Faith*. Everyone around us was telling us to do this or that and we'd be at the top of the charts. They couldn't see a long-term future. I guess I couldn't at the time either, but I knew what I wanted to do.'

November 1990. Original text: Sean Sennett.

Iggy Pop

Iggy builds a less dogmatic sound, brick by brick

At the forefront of the Detroit scene in the late 1960s, Iggy Pop, inspired by Chicago blues, the Sonics and the MC5, led the Stooges initially over three boundary-expanding albums: *The Stooges*, *Fun House* and *Raw Power*. What followed was an influential body of solo work, collaborations with David Bowie (*The Idiot*, *Lust for Life*), and a stage persona that lumbered him as both the prototype 'punk' and a true original. Early in his career, substance abuse and darker impulses took a toll, though they hardly diminished Pop's creative output. In the early nineties, Iggy found himself signed to Richard Branson's Virgin label. Deborah Harry, Kate Pierson from the B-52s and Slash were trotted out for collaborations. The single 'Candy' earned high rotation on MTV and a flirtation with the pop charts beckoned. With the *Brick by Brick* album it seemed there was a commercial opportunity to channel Iggy's baritone-rich, left-field appeal into something potentially ubiquitous.

In 1967, when most of middle America was bopping away to Lulu's 'To Sir With Love', Jim Osterberg, the son of a school teacher, formerly of Ann Arbor and later of Detroit, had different ideas. Debuting on Halloween, Jim unveiled his new band, the Stooges. That night, Jim became Iggy Pop and he's never looked back.

Branded the patriarch of punk, Iggy was 'metal before metal, punk before punk, a poet, a crooner, and a master of theatrical brinkmanship'. In short, Iggy never let the genre down. He was the wildest, the loudest, the most provocative, and probably the best of the lot.

As one reviewer pointed out, 'Iggy was drawing blood when Sid Vicious was still drawing on chalk boards'.

The night after playing his first ever gig in Mexico, Iggy spoke to *Time Off* over the line from San Diego. The Stooges influenced everybody from the Sunnyboys to Radio Birdman and, by their very existence, the Sex Pistols. So what was Iggy listening to ten years before the phrase 'punk rock' was coined?

'When I was in high school, I was a giant fan of the Stones and Dylan and a medium giant Van Morrison fan,' he recalls. 'The vocals on all those records by Them, you can cut grass with those vocals. All that stuff was seminal. I was also listening to the Kinks and the Kingsmen. The Kingsmen were a terrific American bar band who also had a lot to offer musically. Even though "Louie Louie" is a terrible recording, it's fabulous. Listen to what that drummer is playing.'

Something of a teenage musicologist, Iggy drew influences from far and wide. 'TV Eye', for example, is lifted directly from the blues.

'That's from Howlin' Wolf. It's a Muddy Waters–type lick. If you listen to "Mannish Boy", you'll hear it. If you listen to any old Alan Lomax Folkways recordings, with what they called "field hollers", you'll hear people doing these call-and-response hollers. That's the exact melody on "TV Eye". I knew quite a bit of music from around the world. Even on "I Wanna Be Your Dog", people would say it's only punk rock and it's only got three chords, but they never bothered to mention that the sleigh bells in there are just like the kind used on Tibetan records, the bells they use in their religious music.'

Iggy, now in his late forties, has done remarkably well to stay alive. After spending years battling drugs and his own sanity, Iggy decided nearly a decade ago to try getting his life on the rails.

'It's a tenet of modern psychology that thirty-three is the Christ age. I found it true. I was about thirty-three or thirty-four when I realised I wanted to change my orientation. There was a shift in my perspective. I thought it was imbalanced to just be a freelance cock-and-balls, basically . . . running around and having these adventures. It had been fifty per cent cock-and-balls, twenty-five per cent drug experiment, and twenty-five per cent boy's travel adventure. I wanted to learn some tolerance and have some order in my life.'

In 1990, Iggy has redefined his objectives and, in the process, has made the most accessible album of his career: *Brick by Brick*. Produced by Don Was, *Brick by Brick* features the current top ten hit 'Candy'. Admitting that he felt good about the album, Iggy was pressed on a recent quote where he described the record as a 'protest album'.

'That was somebody else's words. I wish the guy hadn't said that. It isn't meant to be a protest album, but a lot of the stuff I talk about on it disgusts me. You hear it in the tone of my voice on particular words.'

On the disc, Iggy sings about the plight of the homeless, social apathy, conformity and sex. But, despite its observations, *Brick by Brick* isn't a flag-waver.

'It's layered with acceptance,' continues Iggy. 'Sometimes you have to accept the way things are around you. I tried to report what I saw. Basically, if there's a concept to the album, it would be about being middle-aged with a kid's spirit.'

Brick by Brick is one of Iggy's more eclectic pieces. The bulk of the album rocks on, in fairly typical fashion, but Iggy is just as likely to croon, to dabble with reggae or to deliver a slab of power pop.

'I wanted it to be more varied than the last two albums I made. I felt they had too much of a party line to the sound: a little dogmatic for my taste. This one may stray too far for a lot of listeners. If you like one particular song, there may be another you don't like or find harder to accept. For me, it's satisfying to go in any direction I feel has heart to it.'

Having Don Was produce an Iggy album may sound an odd match, but the results are impressive.

'I didn't think of him as a future producer at the beginning.

We got friendly because of silly stuff. We're both from the same town. He just seemed like a cool guy when I met him. We were just hanging out. He wears jeans and flannel shirts. I like jeans and flannel shirts. It grew into something.'

Was brought some friends along for the ride: Kenny Aronoff (JC Mellencamp's drummer), Waddy Wachtel (everybody) and David Lindley (Ry Cooder's sidekick). Iggy's contingent included Charley Drayton (Keith Richards's X-Pensive Winos) and Slash and Duff from Guns N' Roses.

'That's where I really benefited from Don. He was more open-minded than I had been about guys I call "session players". I'd always resisted that sort of thing. I didn't want to catch that flight to Hollywood, go to the beauty parlour and get "processed" out there. So I met with the guys individually and played with them, jammed with them. It was a case of try before you buy.'

January 1991. Original text: Sean Sennett.

Chris Isaak

Save some waves

Chris Isaak got his buckled nose after a stint as an amateur boxer, but that hardly damaged his matinee idol looks. He learned to croon at an early age and had a fascination with Elvis Presley, Roy Orbison and Hank Williams. Like his musical taste, his considered quiff was almost out of place in the mid-eighties. Photographed by Herb Ritts, and cast in films by the likes of David Lynch and Jonathan Demme, Isaak's star had a steady rise, but the song 'Wicked Game' altered Isaak's career forever. Used by Lynch in the film *Wild at Heart*, the video, shot by Ritts, co-starred Helena Christensen and saw Isaak hit high rotation. Almost a blueprint for his future career, the song embodied Isaak's obsession with melody and unrequited love.

'The reason I'm calling ya man is because we're a little bit behind here in money. It'd be good if you could get on to the guys in Australia . . . we don't want to send somebody out. I mean . . . I don't want to talk too much on the phone, but some of the deliveries have been a little slow lately . . . what? Oh! You're talking about the record.'

Confused? Meet Chris Isaak.

With the purpose of our trans-Pacific call sorted out, it was time get down to business with one of the best rock voices in the world today. Six months ago, Isaak was relatively unknown to Australian audiences. That all changed with the release of the single 'Wicked Game'.

The track first appeared on Isaak's *Heart Shaped World* album from 1989, which sank without trace. It wasn't until the song popped up on David Lynch's *Wild at Heart* soundtrack a year later that the ball started rolling, eventually scoring Isaak a top ten hit.

Time Off caught up with Isaak fresh from catching an afternoon wave in California.

'It was great! I also went surfing this morning. It was beautiful; the water was sixty-two degrees. I only learned to surf in the past four or five years. I taught myself. I'm from a farm town, so there's no surf. It was like three hours from the ocean. Now I live in San Francisco, I just love it.'

To date, Isaak has released four albums: *Silvertone*, *Chris Isaak*, *Heart Shaped World* and his latest, a compilation titled *Wicked Game*.

One of the key figures in launching Isaak's career has been Lynch.

Apart from featuring his work on the *Wild at Heart* soundtrack, Lynch used Isaak's 'Gone Ridin' in his cult masterpiece *Blue Velvet*.

'That guy [Lynch] has followed me around Hollywood like a puppy for years,' says Isaak with tongue still in cheek.

Does he want to make you a star?

'Yeah . . . he had some tin foil and some scissors . . . he wanted to make me a star. I told him, let's just do this video and see how it works out. I've worked with him a couple of times.'

Since shooting the first 'Wicked Game' video with Lynch, Isaak has shot a much better clip in Hawaii with photographer Herb Ritts. No slouch in front of the camera, Isaak also has cameos in the Jonathan Demme films *Married to the Mob* and *Silence of the Lambs*.

His main asset, however, is his voice: an instrument reminiscent of a moody Roy Orbison. Like Orbison's, Isaak's music is sparse and elegant with deeply rooted 1950s sensibilities. Listening to Isaak rattle off his influences helps put his work in perspective.

'Marty Robbins, Bing Crosby, the Beatles, Elvis, the Everly Brothers. And I'm a nut for anything Jerry Lee Lewis ever did. What a cool style of singing,' he says. 'I believe everything he says.'

Initially brought up on a diet of country and western, Isaak was really only turned on to rock and roll after he heard Elvis's *Sun Sessions* in, of all places, Japan.

'I'd heard a lot of Elvis as a kid,' he says. 'My brothers and I used to listen to Elvis records before school. We'd get up at seven o'clock and play them. When I heard the *Sun Sessions*, I thought it was a style of music I could really relate to.'

Isaak was even lucky enough to jam with Orbison.

'We played together on stage – that was nice. But it was more fun when I went over to his house and played 'til one in the morning. We sat in his house with a guitar and we'd pass it back and forth, tell stories and just sing. When I walked out of the house that night, it was really late and there was nobody around. I got to the front door, said goodnight and split. I got about twenty feet down the steps and jumped up in the air and was going *yeah*! I gotta say he was probably the nicest guy I've ever met in show business.'

Like Orbison, Isaak maintains that the sombre refrains of his material are a direct reflection of the man within. This is the same quality that makes his work so appealing.

'I write a lot of the songs by myself. I do a lot of the writing at night . . . probably because I'm nervous during the day. Night is one of the times when I calm down enough to write. But I try to make myself as happy as possible and keep working. If you're happy, it's good for your work.'

Isaak isn't afraid to wear his creative influences on his sleeve either. *Wild at Heart* features the song 'Blue Spanish Sky' at some length. The trumpet solo towards the end of the piece sounds remarkably like the late Chet Baker.

'The trumpet on that belongs to one of the Los Angeles cats down here. That trumpet part was a weird thing. I wanted Chet to do that, so I wrote the song with Chet Baker in mind. Then, when he was gone, I just sang to the trumpet player the melody that I wanted and asked him to play in the style of Chet Baker.'

Isaak had met Baker before he died in dubious circumstances in Amsterdam. The pair cut an as-yet-unreleased song, 'Imagination'.

'I went into the studio and was hanging out. Chet and I were talking, and I didn't think I was going to play. Then Chet asked me if I knew this song. I didn't. Then he said I bet you do. The piano player played it for me and we cut it real quick. I'd like to release it on something – I think it came out real nice. He sings a verse and plays the trumpet. Then I sing a verse and he plays trumpet with me.'

At the moment, Isaak is working on a new album and so has no immediate plans to tour Australia.

'I'd love to come, but it costs so much money to fly down. We'd have to have a record out for the company to get us over there. As far as wanting to go, there's no lack of desire. I think everybody in the band would die to come over. Just tell everyone to save a wave for me.'

May 1991. Original text: Sean Sennett.

Jane's Addiction

Set to split . . . maybe

There was no 'maybe' about it. Richard Kwong's language here is guarded and careful. He wasn't convinced that this 'scoop' wouldn't turn out to be little more than a cynical ploy to sell tickets. While it might well have sold plenty of tickets, Dave Navarro's announcement was entirely accurate. Jane's Addiction duly went their separate ways following their 1991 Australian tour.

And as for the band's 'possible' re-formation? Currently on their second or maybe third reunion, the Jane's Addiction project is far from over.

Among the happiest raves this year have been those axe-slashing dynamos Jane's Addiction. Their nothing-short-of-brilliant third LP, *Ritual de lo Habitual*, has finally earned the guys a major following, with sales of previous LPs *Jane's Addiction* and *Nothing's Shocking* also skyrocketing.

Then there's the controversy still bubbling over singer Perry Farrell's artwork and lyrics, getting the US Moral Majority people in a flap at least, plus the highlight of a Grammy nomination this year for Best Hard Rock Performance. So now it's *tres hip* to listen to Jane's Addiction, hip if all your friends know you do and even hipper if you catch 'em stealing live.

But now there's the news that, if you don't see 'em this time around, then that's it, bucko! No more JA for you, unless they decide to re-form in the year 2012 or something, and do a Sea of Tranquillity gig on the moon, with We Remember Laura Palmer and the Sublunarkids in support (watch out for these guys too).

Yep, you got it. Jane's Addiction claim that shortly after the forthcoming stint down under, it's splitsville for all and sundry. During a recent chat with the guitarist *de lo* extraordinaire, Dave Navarro, *Time Off* was given an off-the-record and strictly unpublishable, but very specific date on which the said split would occur.

Let's just say it's not that far off.

But the band have so far punched out relatively few LPs and is now undoubtedly at its highest point. Why now? This gets one to thinking this split claim could just be a PR stint to bolster ticket and LP sales. I stress *could*. I'm not claiming that Dave was having us on in any way but when you take the Jane's Addiction equation and look at it logically, two and two should equal somewhere near four, right? But pursuing postulation, we asked the late Julius Sumner Miller (via ouija board) and he came up with 'two plus two here equals the square root of three recurring'.

Hmmm . . .

But Navarro makes things sound simple, making it more than believable that this split *is* the real thing, man.

We asked Dave why Perry was never on the blower himself for interviews anymore.

'I dunno. I don't talk to him.'

A pretty close-knit unit then, eh, Dave?

'We're all very different people. We're basically coming to a close now with the band. We've all got future plans and future directions and we're looking forward to that. We're splitting because we're finished doing this. It's what's we've been doing for five years. We're not only musicians, I'm not only a guitar player. And to tell you the truth, I would hate it if I ended up being a guitar player the rest of my life. That's not what I am. We are all creative and at this point I'm now playing guitar but it's not what I want to be doing down the line, you know. I'm not a rocker. I'm not a rock and roll guy forever. You know, I've been on tour for five years and it's time to move on. And just because this project, Jane's Addiction, is doing well, doesn't mean we're going to compromise what we want. We never have.

'I just think a lot of people don't understand what we are, but that's not why we're splitting. I think the original plan was to continue working until the end of this year and I went to my tour manager and told him I was leaving and we just want to do other things.'

Navarro says he is thinking of forming a new outfit with bassist Eric Avery, while Farrell wants to go solo.

'I also want to get back into my painting and writing,' Dave says. 'It's not only creative but it's an individual expression, whereas with a band you're working with others.'

But why was Navarro the first to officially declare outsville? Is Farrell that much of a pain or what?

'I don't know. Well, I guess it's been pretty well understood within the group for some time now. And I think that maybe I've been the first one to say okay, I want to do it on this day and give a date. But I think it's going to be the four of us sitting down and saying okay, well that's that. But there's no animosity between us. It's not like one of those ugly break-ups. That's why we can continue to play now because we all know this is coming up. We don't hate each other. We just don't want to stay doing this.'

And what's been the reaction from Warner Music?

'I don't know. I haven't told them myself. That's not for me to do. To tell you the truth, it doesn't matter what they think.'

But amidst all this, Navarro is just as keen to stress that Jane's Addiction *may* re-form one day.

'Who knows?' he says.

Personally, I wouldn't be surprised if they didn't split in the first place.

June 1991. Original text: Richard Kwong.

AC/DC

If you can listen to it at breakfast, it's no fucking good

When Bon Scott passed away in 1980, he left big shoes to fill. For three decades Brian Johnson has been AC/DC's new boy. With Bon gone, Johnson debuted on the group's memoriam for their fallen comrade, *Back in Black*. Johnson's high wail has underpinned such classic AC/DC tunes as 'You Shook Me All Night Long', 'Shoot to Thrill', 'Heatseeker' and 'Thunderstruck'. The latter was the lead single from the 1990 return to form, *The Razors Edge*: an album for which the band undertook a massive world tour. Here Stuart Coupe talks to Johnson as AC/DC prepared to embark on a long overdue trip back to Australia.

A reporter once asked Brian Johnson about the difference between him and his wife.

'I told him I thought I could sum up the difference in one sentence: she gets out of the shower to take a piss,' he chortles. Johnson is a funny bastard. The English lead singer of AC/DC, the most successful Australian rock band in history, is exactly like the band he fronts: basic, bordering on crude, unpretentious and extremely hard working.

It's night-time in Dallas and Johnson is doing the only print media interview AC/DC will do before arriving in Australia – and he's in a damn fine mood, thank you very much. Sounding happy to sit on the other end of the phone line, cracking jokes in his thick Geordie accent and answering any and all questions thrown at him.

The band have just started another American leg of *The Razors Edge* world tour, which began late last year. When they arrive in

Australia and New Zealand later this year, it will be their third return as performers since they left for London in 1977.

The band are riding on the success of their latest album *The Razors Edge*, their best-selling disc since 1980's *Back in Black*, which sold 12.5 million copies.

No one sounds more surprised than Johnson about the success of *The Razors Edge* – after all, they've made a lot of great rock and roll albums over the years that for some inexplicable reason haven't done well.

'We knew it deserved to do well, but with AC/DC we've never kowtowed to the flavour of the month, whatever it happens to be around the world. So with this one, as usual, we just held our breath and waited to see what happened,' he says.

'Then when the record went into the charts, followed by the tour, and everything just took off, it was great. I think the timing was really good for us with this one. The timing was just perfect. It's been wonderful. They even put our video clips on TV now,' he laughs, 'and all kinds of good stuff. In Europe and America it's just been a fantastic time, just absolutely packed out everywhere.'

Fans were initially concerned that *The Razors Edge* producer, Bruce Fairbairn, would take some of the hardness out of the AC/DC sound, especially given his track record taming a long line of supposedly hard rock bands. Johnson laughed when I suggested that if smoothing out the edges on AC/DC's sounds was his aim then Fairbairn obviously failed miserably.

'He's known for doing things like Aerosmith and Jon Von . . . whatever his bloody name is. We went up to see him in Ireland and he said, "Geez, this is great. I've been dying to do a rock and roll band, a *real* rock and roll band, and I don't want to change a thing. I want to keep it exactly the same."

'He told us he's always getting these new young bands coming to him and asking if he could make them sound like AC/DC, and he figured that after working with us he'd be able to say yes. He thought he'd be able to get all our tricks! He was such a great fellow. You can always tell when someone's enjoying himself working and not just being businesslike. He was like that, a fun type of fellow. He never sort of lost his temper or threw a tantrum. He's just a good old Canadian boy. He's too far north to be affected by Los Angeles.'

AC/DC albums never sound exactly over-produced, and *The Razors Edge* is no exception. It's simply what AC/DC do best: tough, uncompromising hard rock and roll. The band recorded it in seven weeks after extensive rehearsals at a tiny farmhouse in England where Johnson explains there was nothing to do but rehearse.

'It was like okay, let's rehearse, I'm sick of milking the cows,' he laughs.

Next stop was a studio in Northern Ireland to run through all the songs and get an idea of how they'd sound on tape. The album was finally recorded in Vancouver.

'We had a great time in Vancouver,' Johnson says. 'It's the last of the wild frontiers. It's titty boss city. Wonderful place: beef burgers and boobs . . . for lunch.'

With the success of *The Razors Edge* came pressure for extensive touring and it looked like Australia would again miss out on its best known export. Part of the reason for their infrequent visits to these shores appears to be the gear AC/DC cart around with them.

'I could never understand why we never seemed to come to Australia and it used to piss me off,' says Johnson.

'I used to love coming down there, so this time we just decided that we were definitely coming down to play. We're even going to New Zealand this time. Bugger the decibel rules down there. We'll just get out there and have a good time. The *Edge* show is a monster so we're going to have to ship the stuff down there about four months beforehand. We're having a second stage made for Europe so we can ship the American one to Australia. We've actually had to get another stage built just so that we can come down to Australia! We just wouldn't be able to get it across in time otherwise. There's too much for an aeroplane. The Japanese have got some jumbo, a 747 freighter, and I don't think they even get it all in that. There's about thirteen or fourteen trucks' worth of gear. If I can use a vernacular, there's a shitload of gear.

'But it's nice to be able to bring down to Australia what the Yanks are getting, you know? If anybody deserves it, it's the Australians. Not doing the same show you do everywhere else is cheating. It's taking money. You might as well wear a mask and carry a gun. It's just not on. You've got to do it right or just not do it at all. That might have been some of the reasoning behind not coming to Australia often enough.'

The Razors Edge tour will be the first opportunity for Australian audiences to see AC/DC's new drummer, Chris Slade, in action. Slade replaced Simon Wright, who apparently tired of waiting for AC/DC to record and tour, leaving in frustration when things didn't happen as quickly as he'd like. According to Johnson, the addition of Slade has made a huge difference to the band's sound.

'I think everybody would agree with that. The audiences are coming up raving about the drum sound and the drummer. The man's got a pedigree as long as your arm. He's played with the best. I mean he started with Tom Jones when he was fifteen!' He laughs before launching into 'It's not unusual . . .'

'I think one of the great things about Chris is that he was in Hawaii with Tom Jones and Tom was massive at the time. It was like the early seventies. Elvis was out there and he came to see Tom Jones in concert and he saw Chris playing. Elvis came up afterwards and said, "Hey man, do you want a gig with me?" And Chris said, "I can't, I'm busy at the moment." Imagine Elvis asking him to do a gig! He said that at the time he couldn't believe this guy was speaking to him. He's got a photograph of him and Elvis with their arms around each other. The man's been around and done things but he's so quiet. Funniest fellow I've ever met in my life.'

Johnson, who grew up around the Newcastle area in the UK, admits that he wasn't exactly a huge Elvis fan, being more interested in artists like Paul Butterfield and the Yardbirds. As a kid he saw many of the greats perform at Club A-Go-Go in Newcastle.

'I had to sneak in because I was underage,' he recalls. 'You had to be eighteen so me and a couple of lads from school used to sneak in under the counter. I saw Jimi Hendrix and Cream. We could hardly see them because we were just little nippers, four foot nine or something. And we had to climb on the seats to watch them, but I liked it. After Jimi Hendrix came on I was a bit like the Lord Mayor of Hiroshima: *What the fuck was that?* I couldn't understand a thing but I just knew it was good.'

Changing the subject, I remind Johnson of AC/DC's sudden boost in sales in Germany. According to *Newsweek*, after the fall of the Berlin Wall, business in West Berlin record shops went up a hundred per cent, inundated with East Germans. And what were the kids buying? AC/DC and the *Dirty Dancing* soundtrack.

'I thought they'd go straight for the Abba records. It shows that even the Commies have got a bit of sense. That was a great treat for us. We thought it was brilliant. I think they were relieved after all the stuff they'd had to listen to.'

Then there was the fact that AC/DC were indirectly responsible for bringing General Noriega to justice, American troops successfully flushing the ex-Panamanian dictator from his lair with extra loud blasts of prime AC/DC.

'Yeah, "Back in Black", "You Shook Me" and "Highway to Hell". You can imagine him thinking, what the fuck is that?'

The one unpleasant event in the AC/DC year was the death of three fans, trampled and crushed at the concert in Salt Lake City on January 18. The band were cleared of any responsibility, but it's meant that they now keep a much closer watch on concert security, ticketing and other matters relating to the safety of their audiences.

'I'll never forget that day as long as I live,' says Johnson. 'I couldn't sleep for a week. You know it's got nothing to do with you, but I was going to bed thinking, Jesus, it happened right in front of me. Then you had the kids' parents on the TV. It was a bit of a traumatic time. But the good thing was that we knew it had nothing to do with us. Nobody heard anything, it was so loud there. The great thing was when the District Attorney came to see us personally, one by one, and he shook my hand and said, "I'm so happy. The actions you took were swift and I believe that a lot more could have been killed were it not for the actions of the band." So we were completely exonerated, but once again the press had a field day, especially in my home town in Newcastle. I was really upset because my mother and father live there and the first day after it happened there were huge headlines on the front page: "THREE DIE WHILE LOCAL ROCK STAR SINGS ON". My poor mother, she's seventy years old! I phoned her up and told her not to worry about it and what they'd heard wasn't what happened, but old people, they believe the newspapers. And unfortunately in England we've got the scummiest newspapers in the whole world.'

Otherwise it's business as usual for the lads who manage to maintain a hectic touring schedule while not succumbing to the traditional excesses of their younger counterparts.

'There are a lot of ways to have a good time, you know,' replies Johnson when asked if AC/DC are ever tempted to adopt a Guns N' Roses like attitude to good times. 'Our schedule's so tight we haven't got time! Sometimes we drive straight from one gig in the night, straight to the next hotel, and we get there about seven in the morning and sleep. We're all getting a bit edgy about flying now. There are so many of the damn things coming down, so we bus it a lot. We're still going five or six gigs a week, usually six, and you're doing like two and a half hours a night and it really knocks you about. None of us are getting any younger. I work out several times a week to get ready and I take it deadly serious because it'd all fall down if I weren't fit.

'It does tell on you, though. You do start feeling the bones, and you get a cold easier.'

So is it Johnson's voice that he has the most trouble maintaining over a lengthy tour? No sir, those gravelly vocal chords hold up okay.

'It's me lungs because the set is just getting longer and longer,' he says. 'Obviously as you get more albums there are more people who want to hear more of the tracks and now the show is thirty minutes longer than the last time we toured. As you know, the band have never been one for drum solos and big feature things so I've just got to be there singing for a long time, and Angus has got to be running around. Just watching him every night . . . I've got to be fit, but mine's internal, like an internal combustion engine running out of gas, but Angus's is physical. He's actually moving physically as well as needing the lungs. But he's doing great. He never lets up, never gives up. I've seen him really ill. I've seen the lad where the doctor's come in and shook his head at what he's seen, but Angus just says, "Ah fuck it. I'm going on." We've never cancelled out.'

As well as never cancelling out, AC/DC are an example of the rare breed who never compromise. Most bands who've been going as long as they have, and it's getting on for twenty years, have become little more than pale imitations of the fiery young things they were when they started. Not AC/DC, who still rock as hard today as they did the night I first saw them, opening for Lou Reed in Adelaide in the seventies.

'I think it's mainly because of the Youngs,' says Johnson. 'Angus and Malcolm had the original idea for this band many years ago and I don't think they've budged an inch, through good and hard times. They've refused to go with lucrative offers, PR people asking us to do gigs and accept sponsorships. They've refused to do any of that where in the slightest it could lose any respect from the audience.

'And it's still not the kind of music you can play at breakfast time. I think that's the formula: if you can listen to it at breakfast it's *no fucking good*.'

And will there still be an AC/DC in ten or twenty years? Will Johnson still be screaming 'Highway to Hell', with Angus still dressed like a fourteen-year-old doing Chuck Berry duck walks across the stage? And will anyone still want to see him bend over and pull his school shorts down?

Johnson splutters with laughter. 'Fuckin' Las Vegas! As soon as Las Vegas has rock groups, I can imagine me singing "Back in Black" when I'm fifty!'

They can always get a sequined suit for you.

'If you'd asked me the same question ten years ago, I would

have said that I doubted it very much. That's a long time, ten years, but we're still going as strong as ever. I think everybody in the business looks upon us as . . . what's the word . . . they can't quite figure us out. They keep wondering what is happening here. They're back again and they're not selling out. What is going on? We've sold our soul to the devil, what's the matter with these guys? It's good for us because we feel proud of what we've done.'

And so they should.

July 1991. Original text: Stuart Coupe.

The La's

Liverpool lads on the track of the Fab Four

Noel Gallagher once asserted that Oasis's mission was to finish what the La's had started. From Liverpool, the home of British rock royalty from the Beatles to Echo and the Bunnymen, the La's were led by the gifted, and troubled, Lee Mavers. The band cut just one self-titled album helmed by the classic single 'There She Goes'. A slew of producers worked on the record, which was finally completed, under much duress, by Steve Lillywhite. Mavers, who sporadically reunites various versions of the La's, claimed he was never happy with the release and to this day is still working on the elusive follow-up.

And so the great Merseyside pop tradition continues. From the hallowed stomping grounds that formed the sounds of the Beatles, now come the La's: four lads from Liverpool with melody to burn.

Formed on the Merseyside four years ago, the La's released three singles on the Go! Discs Records label, which have since become serious collector's items on the UK underground scene. The second of these singles, 'There She Goes', is now making waves on the Australian indie front, as is the band's debut self-titled album.

Time Off asked singer, guitarist, songwriter and founding member (man, that's some title), Lee Mavers, about the formation of the band back in '86.

'The band that I've got at the moment has been together for about two years,' Lee explains from his Liverpool flat where he sits wrapped in a towel, my call having interrupted his shower (I did offer to call back, by the way). 'Before that we had a couple of change-arounds, the drummer and the guitarist. But me and John [the bass player] met in 1986 and we used to have a smoke and that in this club in town called Kirklands. We used to meet there every day and have lunch and just go and jam in the afternoon, like. There was a great buzz goin' on. Do you know what I mean?'

As Lee explains, the current line-up had solidified by '88 and the La's began constantly gigging around Liverpool and London. In one single fortnight, the band performed a staggering *seventeen* shows. Early last year, the twelve-song debut LP hit the streets and the band became more selective about their live appearances, preferring to play larger venues. According to Lee, however, he and the other members are not at all pleased with the album.

'We don't like the record really. It's just not a good indication of our music. What happened was we went into the studio, like, and tried to get the sound that we wanted and had to pull out after two months of slaving in there. When we pulled out I think our financial situation with the record company prompted them to put the record out and start recouping some of the debt. Do you know what I mean?'

Well, yes I do, actually.

'It was a fair bit of a compromise, like.' Lee continues. 'It's like the un-ideal situation because that music is now down in history. We'd have preferred it to go down in a much greater way.'

As well as his great desire for me to understand what he means, Lee is very concerned about finding a suitable producer for his band's soon-to-be-recorded second album.

'We've done a lot of looking around and tried out a lot of guys, like, but haven't settled on anybody. We've just been working with a guy called Bob Pridden, who used to work with Pete Townshend and the Who. He was Pete's guitar engineer. I reckon, judging by the work we've done with him over the past couple of days, he'll be able to get a sound for us in a studio, when we come back from America in the Autumn.'

Is that America you say?

'Yeah, we're going to America for a few weeks, like, then coming back home for a couple of gigs. We'll get down to Australia when we tour to promote the second album, but that won't be until probably the middle of next year.'

Well, until then, check out the melodies, the harmonies and the clean-cut guitars of the La's.

July 1991. Original text: Brent Hampstead.

Massive Attack

Australia gets the Mushroom treatment

Massive Attack were at the core of the early nineties Bristol sound. Starting life as part of the Wild Bunch collective, their debut album, 1991's *Blue Lines*, is an era-defining piece of work. The band brought trip-hop into the mainstream and launched the careers of many. Mushroom, aka Andy Vowles, has now left the fold, but at the time of this interview he was in the thick of it, describing his love of the WM-DD100 'Boodo Khan' Walkman, living in a creative bubble and wondering aloud if a kangaroo's tail can kill you.

Simple music for thinking minds is the Massive Attack formula. Their multi-layered sounds and stream-of-consciousness word-play inspire a listening pleasure that's hard to define. Together, DJs Mushroom and Daddy G and vocalists 3D and Shara Nelson (plus a few distinguished guests) have created music that should make history. For once, you can believe the hype, because their debut album, *Blue Lines*, really is *that* good.

And I'm sure Mushroom would agree with me – if I could get him on to the subject for long enough. Settled back in his Bristol flat, he just wants to have a good old chinwag with some Aussies. Questions about the business of hit records, remixes and the Bristol sound elicit replies that point to a distinct disregard for the politics of making music. But then, Mushroom isn't your average band spokesperson and Massive Attack aren't your average band.

'Who's paying for this call?' he asks me in his amiable west-country accent.

'Virgin Australia,' is my reply.

'Well, Richard Branson can afford it so let's talk about Australia, man. It's not often I get to chat with people twelve thousand miles away!'

Get the picture?

Although *Blue Lines* is the first album under the name Massive Attack, Mushroom, Daddy G, and 3D have a long history together as the Wild Bunch: a loose Bristol-based collective that included DJs, rappers and any other would-bes around an original nucleus of Nellee Hooper and Milo Johnson. Through late night parties in disused car showrooms, warehouses, and any other inviting open spaces, the collective's reputation for fearsome grooves grew.

When Nellee wandered off to mix it up with Soul II Soul and Milo left for Japan, it was the future members of Massive Attack who were left to carry on the legacy. If there's one thing they have retained from the Wild Bunch, it's a sense of individuality that consistently crops up not just in their music but in their visuals and videos as well.

'Much to the dismay of the suits in the corridors of Virgin, Massive Attack makes music we personally want to hear and that's really it. To a large degree we don't really care what anyone else wants to hear,' says Mushroom, matter-of-factly. 'In the Wild Bunch days, we all came from so many different backgrounds. Some of us were punks and some of us were into jazz, soul and reggae. We used to hold parties and we'd play all the music that we individually wanted to hear so you'd have like six DJs coming on the set just playing what they themselves wanted to hear. It was all about being natural.'

It's hard to pigeonhole Massive Attack and that's the way Mushroom likes it.

'We're not a club act that spews out twelve-inches for the hell of it. In fact, we want to pull ourselves out from that dance category. We don't want any label, we just want to be ourselves.'

Overlaying everything from old Studio One sounds with a forty-piece orchestra and mixing in some hop with 3D's soothing overlapping raps, Massive Attack make the current wave of post-rave techno sound like the soulless shit that it is. But the icing is their controversial lyrics that wander through each track, waxing lyrical about Thatcher, Studio One or their prized Sony 'Boodo Khan' Walkmans (which get a mention in more than one track).

'With our lyrics, we've never said we're the greatest writers. We've just talked about the things we're interested in like Boodo Khan Walkmans and Pink Floyd albums. Sony came out with this incredible Walkman, which is the ultimate bass Walkman – they even give you this cushion to sit on when you listen to it – and it's a prize thing in our life, so we bring it up in a song like we do in conversation. We're not pushing anything on people; we're just talking about what's important in our lives.

'You know, I don't watch television 'cause I refuse to pay my licence. I don't have a radio and I don't read magazines. I'm not really happy going out these days because I don't hear the music I want to hear and all I see is just a bunch of pop-crazed zombies. I'd rather sit in my front room and listen through headphones. When our album was at number thirteen in the British charts, someone had to keep reminding me because I was more interested in getting the seats of my car cleaned.'

Before Massive Attack came to such car-cleaning prominence, Mushroom had already made a name for his remixing work with the likes of Neneh Cherry, Lisa Stanfield and Boy George. But when I bring up the subject of Nellee Hooper's remixes of Massive Attack, Mushroom doesn't mince his words.

'Nellee did the job and he did it well, but I've got this phobia about remixes. It's like building a wall and then someone coming along and knocking it down and rebuilding it because the public won't accept yours. So it makes me wonder why we are doing it in the first place if people won't accept our individual art. It's just an example of how money and politics always seem to get in the way.'

Apart from his apparent interest in Australian flora and fauna, Mushroom's penchant is sound. It's something that shines through time and again on *Blue Lines*: an incredible layering of weird but complementary sounds emerges with each listen.

'I'm really into sounds of the world and the concept of sound amazes me. I was in the bath the other day and I was listening to my heart beating so I taped it. I know that sounds weird, but I think it's an interesting thing. Just recently, I've been chatting to this guy that used to operate sonar for the navy and he was telling me about the science behind it. To me that's absolutely fascinating.'

It's getting late and Mushroom has decided he's had enough of talking about music. Besides, he has some pressing geography questions and he's not putting down the phone until he gets some straight answers.

'I know people that have come out from Australia and they tell me these atrocious spider stories. They lifted up a stone and there was a funnel-web and it came up and attacked them. I've heard stories that you can't even tread on a spider cause they're so big. I don't know how you lot can accept venomous spiders living right in your own back gardens!'

It's not something you think about all that often.

'What about those red kangaroos? Man! Is it true they can kill you with one swipe of their tail? And I've been told that people try and keep them as pets! You know, I'd really like to come to Australia and just hang out in the countryside, but there's no way I could handle crocodiles trying to eat me or huge kangaroos jumping all over me.'

Don't worry, Mushroom. We'll keep our kangaroos on a leash while you're here.

July 1991. Original text: Emma Marlin.

Violent Femmes

Fine Femmes return to form

With the release of their eponymous debut in 1982, the Violent Femmes sent shockwaves through alternative radio that eventually reverberated through to the mainstream. At the time, the Milwaukee trio's album sounded like a roughly hewn demo. Front man Gordon Gano's pathos rang through the likes of 'Blister in the Sun', 'Gone Daddy Gone', 'Kiss Off' and 'Add It Up'. Adopted by legions of fans, there was nothing more cathartic than singing a Femmes chorus at the top of your lungs during one of their many visits to Australia. 1991's *Why Do Birds Sing?* was the last album for the original line-up of Gano, bassist Brian Ritchie and drummer Victor DeLorenzo. On a comeback of sorts, the band played Brisbane's Festival Hall with Nirvana when they toured the album in 1992.

If Gordon Gano never writes another song, he'll always be remembered for 'Blister in the Sun'. From the debut Violent Femmes album, the song has achieved anthem status. It's hardly Gano's most accomplished piece, but it played a major part in turning FM music listeners on to what the indie scene was all about.

For close to a decade the Femmes' first album – easily one of the best debuts of all time – has become a staple of every cool (even marginally so) record collection.

Fortunately, Gano didn't close shop after 'Blister in the Sun'. The Femmes, despite a two-year split in the late eighties, kept going. *Time Off* caught up with the front man – otherwise known as the 'best thing to come out of Milwaukee since the Harley

Davidson' – to discuss the release of the Femmes' most talked about record in years.

Why Do Birds Sing?, recorded in only six weeks, is a fine return to form. Despite the Femmes' formidable track record, the band still have record company problems. Tired of giving stock answers all night, Gano admits that the trio was under a certain amount of pressure to deliver the 'right' album. The showdown occurred when the record executives insisted the band use outside producer Michael Beinhorn (Red Hot Chili Peppers).

'That was prompted by . . . ' begins Gano, before changing tack, ' . . . no, I'll tell you the truth. I've done too many interviews now; I've got to tell it like it is. We wanted to work with the record company. But we were also told if we didn't let them bring in an outside producer they wouldn't do anything for our record. That's the word we were hearing back. We have to fight the perception of us as these three weirdos who make this weird music to which the industry shrugs its shoulders and thinks, "Oh, it's a little miracle they actually make some money."'

True to form, the new album is full of Gano angst. At times, his lyrics are every bit as compelling as John Lennon's primal therapy exorcism on *Plastic Ono Band*. The songs on *Why Do Birds Sing?* were culled from a long period.

'There's a whole mixture on the album. Some songs on the record are very recent. Then there are three songs ("Girl Trouble", "Flamingo Baby" and "Life is a Scream") that I wrote probably when I was sixteen. We played them in our live shows before we recorded our first album. We just never got around to putting them on record.'

One of the highlights on the disc is a cover of Culture Club's 'Do You Really Want to Hurt Me?'

'We went into the record thinking we wanted to do a cover tune and we asked people to make suggestions. That song was the most unthinkable. I couldn't even imagine it. We tried it a little and gave up after a while. But by then, people heard we were working on it. The idea of us doing it really struck everyone's fancy, so we gave it another go. We altered the arrangement and rewrote a lot of the song. It came together in a way that we like quite a bit.'

Like the Femmes' previous albums, *Hallowed Ground*, *The Blind Leading the Naked* and *3*, *Why Do Birds Sing?* is stamped with Gano's desperate vocal delivery and purging lyrics. Gano admits that his songs are often intensely personal and always have been.

'It's kind of a form of self-therapy. I said that one time and a friend of mine who works in therapeutic ways with battered children corrected me. She said that writing isn't all there is to it: you don't write a song and you're cured, but it has certainly been a great outlet for me. It helped a lot in the past and it still does. I can be very upset about something, I feel like everything's shutting down and I can't focus, so I just have to write a song. It's a release and I feel better because of it.

'I'm not writing songs now because I'll have my option picked up and I'll have the chance to work in a studio for another eight months. I just write songs because I have to. It's a part of me.'

Gano doesn't believe the creative process will flounder, even in the unlikely event that he becomes completely happy.

'I don't wake up in the middle of the night in a cold sweat and think, "Oh no, I'm becoming too happy." I don't have that happening. All the same, there are a lot of questions about art and the process of creating – I mull them about in my head. I guess I don't have any final statement on the subject. A lot of great work is produced under a sense of duress.'

With two 'comeback albums' and a retrospective LP under his band's belt, Gano has never felt happier about being a Violent Femme.

'I feel like the band's going to go on for a very long time,' he says. 'It's feeling very good. Having gone through the experience of a break-up, we're much less likely to do it again. I think we gained a lot by it. In my life, it was a little miracle that we got back together. It's not a day-to-day, touch-and-go thing. It's never felt stronger.'

August 1991. Original text: Sean Sennett.

The Cult

On the wagon, but still volatile

Ian Astbury has led quite a life both inside and outside the Cult. When the band were on an extended hiatus, he opted for the Jim Morrison spot with the re-formed Doors. Out front of Ray Manzarek and Robbie Krieger, Astbury did an admirable job, though his heart seems to have always been with the Cult – whose origins can be traced back to 1981 when they started life as the Southern Death Cult in Bradford, Yorkshire. Over the years, the Cult have endured multiple break-ups and reunions. When *Ceremony* arrived in 1991, the band were on a creative high following the success of the albums *Electric* and *Sonic Temple*. Despite some chart action, grunge was getting ready to take over the world and the Cult were slightly out of step with the changing times.

Let's face it: the past few years have not been kind to Ian Astbury. He claims his sole reason to live was to drink and that he didn't care about himself or those around him. His doctor confronted Astbury with the warning that he would have little more than three years left to live if he remained on the same track. He now uses the term 'mental exhaustion' to describe his state of mind. Meanwhile, his group of merry men, the Cult, has not been without a few . . . um . . . little difficulties either. Ian doesn't remember 'much' of the *Sonic Temple* tour or the album of the same name.

'It was our most successful record, but it's the album I was least involved with. I just wrote the lyrics and pretty much kept out of the way. I was very unhappy with the sound of it,' he says, laying much of the blame at the feet (or more precisely the fingers) of producer Bob Rock, but more of that later.

Astbury, twenty-nine, is speaking from his Los Angeles home. He is reflecting on what can only be termed a major life crisis – one he declares is truly behind him. In his soft northern English burr he continues: 'I gave in for a long period of time. I was a physical mess: overweight, grey skin, hair falling out. For years, since I was eighteen or nineteen, I've been under so much pressure. In fact, at the end of the *Sonic Temple* tour we were all burned out, we had been working without a break for so long.'

Each member of the Cult dealt with the pressure in his own way.

'Jamie went off to start a family and Matt turned around and said he's been offered a gig with the biggest rock group in the world, Guns N' Roses.'

It has to be said, Ian sounds none too impressed with this.

'He went for about a million dollars, and because he said he had more in common with them than us so that was that.'

It was some time after the *Sonic Temple* tour hit Australia in . . . (no, Ian doesn't remember, so anybody who does is one ahead of him already) . . . that the quack sat him down and warned him that he was within three years of the big D if he didn't pack in all this . . . um . . . revelry – words that had a literally sobering effect.

'I've been on the wagon for twenty-one months now,' he says softly. 'Do I miss a drink? Um, occasionally, but there are more important things in my life now.'

Such as?

'Writing and creating music.'

The new LP, *Ceremony*, is a Cult album alright: native American imagery tied to earthy guitars and rhythms.

'The whole spirit of the album is about ritual space and the need to question spiritual values and the need to question things generally.'

The kind of stuff you expect from the Cult, really; however, in a more unpredictable move, they decided to use crumbled old

AOR producer Richie Zito. Why Zito? I mean, for heaven's sake, he produces Heart.

'I know, I know,' laughs Ian. 'When our manager suggested him to us we just looked at him and laughed, saying no way. We've worked with people like Heart and Cheap Trick and we really don't like those records 'cause they suck!'

Despite their misgivings, the band agreed to meet Zito and discovered that he was a 'sweet natured sort of guy' who was quite happy to be a technician, rather than impose any particular 'sound' on the album.

'Billy and I realised it would be alright. Anyway, we decided if it sounded even remotely like a Heart record we'd throw it out and start over again.'

The band consciously decided not to use Bob Rock, producer of *Sonic Temple*.

'We went to Bob Rock and nailed him on everything we thought was wrong with *Sonic Temple*: the guitars too middle of the road, the stinky arrangements. He was cool. He knew what we were saying. We talked about how we wanted rhythm and cellos, but in the end we decided too much had been said and done between us and went our separate ways.

'It's funny though, how he went away and put cellos on Metallica. It's also funny how they've become a household name in America. Just shows you how many sexually frustrated boys there are in the world.'

Pardon?

'That's who Metallica sell to. Their album is like a gathering space for little boys. It's alright for them, I suppose, but I'm not really inspired or intrigued by songs about the sandman. I don't think thirty-year-old geezers should be writing about comic book characters.'

And, in case this is beginning to sound like a tirade, Ian is quick to point out that he likes Metallica and that they are good acquaintances, but their latest record is 'just not the kind of thing I get off on'.

What does get Astbury off, though, comes as a surprise.

'Seal. He's a star. His album is a phenomenal record; most contemporary rock is about as deep as a two-foot water hole, but Seal's got soul.'

As it turns out, so has Lenny Kravitz.

'When his first album came out, I wrote to *Rolling Stone* and told them how brilliant he is. He's unbelievable.'

So, despite the trauma of the few years, Ian Astbury today seems a happy man.

'I *am* happy now. I've got a really good personal life. I've decided that trying to kill myself every day is not a worthwhile venture. We're still very volatile and I think that element will always be there – it's just that I don't tend to be so destructive in my day-to-day life. And the effect of that is I have more time for creativity. You won't find me walking round with a fucking pipe and slippers, though! It's just a case of pacing yourself.

'And I guess we've come back. A lot of musicians say they please themselves, when they're really trying to make records that sell. A lot of them talk bollocks. After all we'd been through, when we got to down planning *Ceremony*, Billy and I said to each other, "Why are we in this?" And we remembered. We do this because we love music and that's that, end of story.'

End of story indeed.

November 1991. Original text: Lisa Anthony.

Nirvana

The dangers of drum diving

On 27 January 1992, Nirvana played Brisbane's Festival Hall, a day after a performance at Fisherman's Wharf on the Gold Coast and just sixteen days after *Nevermind* hit number one in the US charts. The timing was nothing short of a miraculous fluke for their Australian fans. The band were initially booked as the support act for the Violent Femmes, but history has recast the show as a double bill.

Of course, now the number of people who claim to have been at that show could fill a football stadium twice over. At the time, though, there was little indication – number one status notwithstanding – of the Zeitgeist shift in popular music about to take place and Nirvana's spot at the centre of that shift. One of the most remarkable things about Murray Engleheart's short interview with Dave Grohl is its ordinariness. Placed alongside an advertisement for cockroach races at the Story Bridge Hotel, an interview with Nirvana was given as much gravitas as the conversations with the Dreamkillers or Big Audio Dynamite. Actually, Big Audio Dynamite was far more feted than the band who would redefine music for the next ten years.

Nirvana drummer Dave Grohl begins in a matter-of-fact tone.

'I remember one night when we played in Chicago on the last tour. I'd had the same drum set for four years and it started getting really, really fucked up. And it got to the point where it didn't sound good anymore. I kept on telling the tour manager I need a new drum kit really badly. And the tour manager would say, how long can you hold out? And I said, well I can wait until the end of the tour, but I just want something to sound good.

'Finally, my bag got stolen in Detroit and I was really pissed off. So the next day I said, okay this is it, this is the last night I'll play on this drum kit, I'm not going to take it anymore. And Kurt and I sat there for ten minutes in front of a thousand people just destroying the drum kit and handing it to them. So everybody walked out of there with a little souvenir.'

It wasn't the first such disruption to a Nirvana gig. During the band's performance at the Reading Festival in the UK, Kurt was moved to dive into the drum kit and sprained his arm. The problem was, the band had several more weeks of engagements to fulfil.

But although things sometimes don't work out for Nirvana, the band once blindly branded as some sort of kneejerk consequence of Mudhoney are now – as their first album, *Bleach*, indicated to those with real ears – very much on their own raw, ragged and brutally emotive turf.

And what's more, now this bunch of scruffs and their stunning *Nevermind* album have grabbed the upper reaches of the American charts.

Now that's an achievement for rock and roll.

Nevermind includes material written before *Bleach* was recorded and has firmed up a territory specifically and totally for Nirvana. And it's attracting an increasing number of major league fans. The band were offered support slots with, among others, Ozzy Osbourne and Skid Row.

'It's kind of amusing that all these bands want us to open for them, but there's absolutely no way we'd ever do it. People tell us we're number nine on the Billboard charts in America and we don't jump up around and laugh or jump for joy; we just sort of shrug it off. When someone says a band like Rush want us to tour with them, we burst out laughing!

'But actually, you know what? Someone asked us if we would open for Guns N' Roses, so I think we're going to play one show in New Zealand at some festival or something. That kind of thing is okay. We just wanted to make sure that we never play with some massive travelling cock-rock show all over America. That would just ruin the whole touring experience. So playing a single show with Guns N' Roses in New Zealand in front of forty thousand people, that might be kind of fun.'

That event now seems to be off as Guns N' Roses won't be in this part of the world as planned. But the show probably wouldn't have been much of a surprise. Axl went backstage to see Nirvana in Los Angeles and expressed an interest in 'hanging out' with them.

Dave didn't see the second *Clash of the Titans* tour with Slayer, Anthrax, Megadeth and fellow local lads Alice in Chains. I mention, with Alice in Chains' genre jumping in mind, that maybe if there was a third *Clash* tour, Nirvana could join the caravan. Dave is not comfortable with the notion. They want to avoid the heavy metal market as much as possible.

'We'd rather be just Nirvana than Nirvana-the-Heavy-Metal-Band. We did a thing for MTV. There's a show called Headbangers Ball and we were sort of hesitant. We weren't sure if we wanted to do it. Kurt and Krist [Novoselic, bass] went anyway to do an interview on the show and it turned out okay.'

I mention to Dave that the night we spoke, AC/DC were doing the last of their Sydney shows and he bubbles with enthusiasm.

'When I was in the fifth grade, I guess I was ten years old, my best friend and I went to see that movie *Let There Be Rock*. And I had never been to a rock concert or seen a rock movie and that movie changed my life, man. They had a PA system in the theatre that was the same size as the PA system in the local Coliseum.

'It was the first time I'd ever had the feeling of getting up and playing air guitar and killing my teacher, smashing the chairs in the movie theatre, whatever. Total adrenaline. It was so loud it was just like *RRRRRRR!*'

Going *RRRRRRR!* is a mode of operation very dear to the heart of Nirvana. It's what their ears do after a show. 'The only time you think about going deaf is when you try and go to sleep at night and you can't go to sleep because your ears are ringing so loud. That's when you start thinking about the singer of Soul Asylum having to put a fibreglass thing around the drum set so that he won't hear the cymbals or something like that.

'My problem is a lot of the time I don't hit my ride cymbal like a ping. I just like to crash and wash on the side of it. So my right ear sometimes will just totally go out and I'll be deaf for a minute.'

Cymbals create a kind of white noise if you hit them hard enough.

'Yeah, but it's a beautiful sound, though.'

January 1992. Original text: Murray Engleheart.

Bob Dylan

He's a weird cat, Bob is

Bob Dylan was in the foothills of what was called the *Never-Ending Tour* when he spoke to Stuart Coupe. A Dylan expert, Coupe was given the tip to play it straight when speaking to Bob. Dylan prefers chatting to newsmen rather than fans. Mentioning a bootleg tape of Dylan covering Townes Van Zandt's 'Pancho and Lefty' almost blew his cover, but Coupe made it through to capture Dylan's thoughts on touring and recording. This piece, when it appeared in 1992, was a cover story for *Time Off*, and it literally disappeared off the streets faster than any other issue in memory.

At the age of fifty, he is arguably the most significant rock musician of the last thirty years. With twenty-one certified gold albums, the writer of some of the best known songs of the last century is, by any assessment, phenomenally wealthy. He has no need to be on the road.

So why has Bob Dylan spent the last four years subjecting himself to the most punishing touring schedule of his entire career? Why, in most cases, does he insist on playing multiple nights at small venues instead of playing to the same number of people in one night at a large theatre? For the latter we should be thankful, while the former raises interesting questions about Dylan's motivations.

Since June 1988, Dylan has played an average 125 concerts per year on what even he now refers to as the *Never-Ending Tour*. Along with constant touring throughout North America, he's traversed the planet, playing in many countries for the first time in his career. There have been concerts in locations as diverse as Iceland, Mexico, Brazil, Argentina, Uruguay, Greece, Turkey, Hungary and Yugoslavia.

And finally the *Never-Ending Tour* has found its way to Australia. It's Dylan's fourth visit to this country. In 1966, he toured at the peak of his encounter with electric rock and roll, in 1978 he returned with a Las Vegas–style cabaret routine notable for little besides its blandness and Dylan's fixation with facial make-up, and in 1986, he joined forces with Tom Petty and the Heartbreakers for an equally dismal series of concerts.

This time, he arrives with a stripped-down outfit, dividing the concert between electric band performances and acoustic renditions. If overseas set lists are any indication, expect a greatest hits–style show featuring as many of his famous songs as any fan could reasonably expect to hear in two hours, plus a smattering of material from recent albums like the critically acclaimed *Oh Mercy* and the far less enthusiastically received *Under the Red Sky*. Yes, he'll probably play 'Like a Rolling Stone', 'Mr Tambourine Man', and 'Blowin' in the Wind' and, if the tapes I've heard circulating among Dylanophiles are any indication, he's still a hit and miss proposition, but when he's on, the performances are as fiery and passionate as anything he's done on stage in many a year.

'My old songs are always interesting to me,' replies a slightly defensive Dylan on the telephone from Los Angeles just prior to his departure for Australia. I'd just suggested to him that playing so many of his older songs might get just a little boring for him.

This is my second encounter with Dylan. In 1986, I 'interviewed' him after a concert in Auckland. The conversation lasted a good seven and a half minutes and it was obvious that Dylan had absolutely no interest in talking to the media. He sidestepped any specific questions in much the same way as he toyed with journalists in the mid-sixties. His only straight answer was to a question about the legendary American country singer Hank Williams, who Dylan had said in a previous interview he would have liked to meet (Williams died in the early 1950s).

'What would you ask him if he was sitting here now?' I asked.

Dylan leaned across the table and said, 'I'd wanna know where he got his drugs from!'

Dylan's aversion to being interviewed is part of rock legend. Before this encounter, I'm told not to ask any questions about the old days, not to bring up Joan Baez or to ask him what the fourteenth line of 'Desolation Row' *really* means. It's better, comes the instruction, to keep my questions to the last year and not to come across like a Dylan expert or fan. Dylan likes 'straight media'.

This time, the man's in fine form. He laughs every so often and at least attempts to deal with each question. But still, Dylan is not a great conversationalist: every answer is punctuated by mutterings, sniffling, and pauses that seem to go on forever. An interview with Dylan is rarely anything but a series of frustrating attempts to get coherent answers. Dylan is at least relatively expansive on the subject of the *Never-Ending Tour*, which he says wasn't started with the intention that it would continue for so many years.

'No, this is just my pattern over the last three or four years: to play at least a hundred times a year, maybe a little bit more, maybe a little bit less. It just works out better for me because it's not necessary to be looking for a band all the time. That's the advantage of just going out to play. It you're only going out once in a while, then, you know, you have a problem trying to find a band and trying to find people who aren't playing with somebody else at that time, and it's . . . in the long run, it's better to just go out and do the shows and either it's happening or it's not.'

It's a reasonable leap of faith to take that on face value, to accept that someone of Dylan's stature has played around five hundred shows in the last four years merely because he's worried his band members might go off and play with someone else. Maybe he's taking the travelling troubadour caper to extremes. Maybe he genuinely needs the adoration. Certainly there are other things he could be doing.

Of all the new countries Dylan has visited during the *Never-Ending Tour*, it's Argentina and Brazil that he's the most expansive about.

'It's a different scene. You never know really . . . it's kind of like makeshift sound almost. You're never really sure about the facilities you're playing in and what can be heard because everything looks so funky but, ah . . . ah . . . ah . . . the people were very responsive and it was relaxing being there.'

One of the most significant experiences for Dylan over the tour was visiting the site of the concentration camp at Dachau.

'No one had ever taken me there before, and so, yeah, last time we were in Germany, someone took me to one of them concentration camps. It's a pretty spooky place.'

A moving experience?

'Well, you can't help but be moved by seeing all the regalia they have in there. It looked pretty much like whatever they were supposed to look like. Monuments you know, monuments of death. That's what they were.'

The last year has seen the usual accolades heaped on Dylan. *Life* magazine listed him as one of the hundred most important Americans of the twentieth century. The National Academy of Recording Arts and Sciences awarded him the Lifetime Achievement Award at the Grammys, and, most significantly for Dylan, the French Government recognised his contributions with their highest cultural honour, *Commandeur de L'Ordre des Arts et des Lettres*, which has only been awarded to thirty-five individuals since the Revolution (including Chevalier, Chaplin and very few Americans). The Minister of Culture and Communications decorated Dylan during the course of a five-night engagement at Le Grand Rex in Paris. This was obviously one award that Dylan took extremely seriously.

'Oh yeah,' he says, 'that was a heavy thing, being given an award by the French Government, especially in the area of creativity, you know, because of the French influence in my own stuff.'

Questioned why he plays smaller venues in preference to larger auditoriums, he's typically offhanded.

'The sound is easier to control and it's not so much of a circus,' he says.

So does Dylan still enjoy the grind of touring? Doesn't there come a point when he'd prefer to get back home for an extended period?

'There comes a point for everything, but . . . ah, you know . . . playing music's a full-time job, you know,' he mutters. 'It's hard to shut if off and turn it off and on like a faucet.'

Possibly that's the (unlikely) key to it all: the music remains in his blood and he feels as though he doesn't have a choice. It doesn't, however, explain Dylan's extended period away from touring: breaks, punctuated by occasional performances, that have lasted as long as seven years. In his excellent biography of Dylan, *Behind the Shades*, Clinton Heylin suggests this is one of only three periods in his career when Dylan has combined frequent studio activity with prodigious performance. All tours have coincided with periods of turmoil in Dylan's personal life, almost as if the road becomes an easy escape from the issues he must face head-on in real life, away from the road. If that's the case with the *Never-Ending Tour*, Dylan certainly isn't saying anything. Questions about his personal life are strictly off limits. A strong air of paranoia surrounds most of his activities. In a 1990 interview, he explained his dislike of being photographed: 'It rubs me the wrong way, a camera. It doesn't matter who it is, someone in my own family could be pointing a camera around. It's a frightening feeling. Cameras make ghosts out of people.'

At recent concerts, Dylan has refused to allow photographers in the theatres, and made things even more difficult by shrouding himself in darkness for most of the concert. It has been reported that these days Dylan is rarely seen by members of his band or crew. He travels in his own bus, away from the musicians, and often stays at different hotels. An appearance at sound check is rare and he rarely turns up for rehearsals. Agreeing to sign an autograph for a fan is extremely unusual. Dylan also doesn't like his concerts being recorded and the tapes circulated. During the *Never-Ending Tour*, he's been known to throw in covers of songs as diverse as Bruce Springsteen's 'Dancing in the Dark', and Townes Van Zandt's 'Pancho and Lefty'.

'Where did you hear that, if you don't mind me asking?' says a suddenly serious Dylan. Told that I haven't actually heard the tapes, but have read they're occasional inclusions, he audibly relaxes.

While the Dylan industry rolls on around him with a regular stream of biographies and critical studies appearing on the market, Dylan at least feigns disinterest.

'Not really,' he replies when asked if he bothers to look at any of the books to find out what people are saying about him and his work. 'No. It seems like they come out pretty regular now. It's . . . it's . . . ah . . . it's . . . ah . . . they really don't . . . it doesn't knock me out to read a book about myself, you know?'

There are other books to read?

'Yeah, yeah, exactly.'

So what has Dylan been reading of late?

'My, ah, my latest book . . . it's been out for a long time, but my latest thing I'm just reading is . . . back into reading the William Blake poems again,' Dylan says. 'It seems like when you're young and you read 'em, they don't have the effect on you that they do when you get older. It was years ago when it was time just to read all those guys, but lately it's been necessary for me to find some time to go back and re-read someone like Blake, Shelley, Byron, some of those people.'

Aside from his reading, Dylan spends much of his time on the road painting and drawing. He explains that Random House has a book of his drawings coming out later this year, the majority of it being his output from the last three years. And, in keeping with his current workaholic state, Dylan is also preparing to record another album. He says that half the songs are written, they're more acoustically based than recent albums, and he expects to record in Chicago soon after the Australian tour.

Does Dylan find that the songs come easier as he gets older or is it more difficult to find new things that he wants to say? Certainly songs like 'Wiggle Wiggle' from his last album weren't exactly highpoints of his songwriting career.

'Well, they're coming natural, if they come at all,' he says, laughing loudly. 'So . . . um . . . when it's not coming . . . ah . . . ah . . . there's really no inclination on my part to make it happen.'

Dylan's apparent jovial mood suggests that maybe it's time to throw in the inevitable question about Gypsy Fire, the woman who's been consistently in the media over recent years because of her (successful) action against the *Truth* newspaper over allegations that she was Dylan's sex slave during the 1986 tour.

'Oh yeah, is she still around?' Dylan chuckles.

After being told that Fire is planning to write a book about their time together and the court case, Dylan sighs.

'Oooooh, poor girl, you know.'

Then, out of the blue, Dylan says, 'Hey listen, can you say hi to that guy Brett Whiteley? Is he still around there painting? He gave me some drawings the last time I was there and they still look good to me.'

A couple of hours later, I call Whiteley to pass on the message.

'He's a weird cat, Bob is,' Whiteley says.

Couldn't have put it better myself.

April 1992. Original text: Stuart Coupe.

Keith Richards

A bit of Peter Pan, a bit of Captain Hook

When the Rolling Stones were on hiatus, Keith Richards took the opportunity to cut a solo album, *Talk Is Cheap*. Bootleg tapes began to circulate of Richards on the road with his pals the X-Pensive Winos, so the guitarist decided to release his own recordings from a December 1988 Hollywood Palladium show. It was here Richards showcased new material as well as dragging out such Stones nuggets as 'Connection' and 'Happy'. Murray Engleheart compares Richards to a rock and roll Peter Pan; Keith suggests he's more like Captain Hook, which, given his big screen debut nearly two decades later, was rather apt.

Meet Keith Richards, riff master: the man who reportedly thinks nothing of boring the hell out of his companions while he spends several hours getting a particular riff just so; the original rock and roll gypsy warrior; the world's greatest rhythm guitarist; the man with the Brando aura; the man who drove me to get a silver skull ring that hasn't left my hand since 1982, much to my wife's horror.

Richards could reasonably be called the Rolling Stones personified. He gave the rock and roll blues baby its swagger. Keith Richards is to rock and roll what Muddy Waters is to blues. Little wonder he is an AC/DC fan.

'*Powerage* is one of my favourite rock and roll records,' he says. 'That's one of their early ones,' he adds, unnecessarily.

Richards's guitar tech of many years, Allan Rogan, is now in Angus Young's employ. Brian Johnson told me last year that it was

Rogan who introduced Keith to the sound of the eternal schoolboy and company. Brian also said that he and his wife saw the Stones on the *Steel Wheels* tour, one of the few shows in his life that the singer saw in its entirety.

Keith chuckles at Brian's confession.

'Great! I'm glad I captured his attention span.'

While he plays every chance he gets – whether ripping up a version of Hendrix's 'Purple Haze' with Johnny Cash or contributing to John Lee Hooker's *Mr Lucky* album – Keith Richards is hardly a frequent interviewee.

Today, he has made an exception to mark the release of a gloriously spirited live set by his second passion, the X-Pensive Winos, recorded at the Hollywood Palladium. My questions had to be faxed to management in the first instance. They were obviously okay. When we spoke, Keith had just returned from a few weeks sunning in the Caribbean and was well satisfied with the live recording.

'It's what it was. I taped it really just for the Winos to sort of get a look at ourselves, what we were doing. And then I kind of forgot about it while I was doing the *Steel Wheels* thing. It came up again because of all these Winos' bootlegs that started to come around and the guys were saying, hell, we've got better stuff than those bootlegs in the can. So we took it out and dusted it off and looked at it and said, well, why not, let's put it out. So it really kind of came about like that.'

What do you see as the difference between the Winos and your New Barbarians project of years back?

'Well, with the Winos there's not so much pressure on. It's not such a big deal, you know? In a way, it's kind of reminiscent of earlier days with the Stones when you kind of made up your mind what to do and the next day you did it. Now with the Stones you're talking about a year or two in front every time, which is kind of difficult for musicians!' he laughs.

The Palladium live set includes such Stones nuggets as Keith's own signature, 'Happy', as well as 'Time Is on My Side' and

'Connection'. I wondered if there was any Stones material he shied away from.

'Um, well nearly all of it except stuff I knew the Stones had already done a cover version of or ones I particularly sang on. I try to leave it at that. It's kind of difficult. I mean, if I start playing Stones stuff on stage and turn around and the Winos are there, I'd get a shock,' he laughs. 'I got so used to the faces I would see there. But apart from that I suppose really what I do with the Winos is not really that different to what I do with the Stones except that singing and playing at the same time, that makes a difference in the way that you play because you're kind of doing your thing so you fill in a bit more with the guitar. It changes your style a bit. It makes me a bit more aware when I'm playing with the Stones. I'm sort of, kind of more appreciative now of what Mick does. A little bit more dynamic. One helps the other, hopefully, you know?'

So you can never see the day when you'll just sing?

'Nah,' he breathes with a tone of what seemed at least partial disappointment. 'I wouldn't know what to do with my hands.'

I've always seen you as something of a Peter Pan rock and roll figure and at the same time an elder statesman.

'A bit of Peter Pan, a bit of Captain Hook?' he chuckles.

Are the Winos the Peter Pan element?

'Um, I don't know really. I never really think about it in those terms, but it does make a difference playing with another bunch of guys that really enjoy playing together. And they are a lot younger than I am and they don't give me much time to get a breather, you know?' he laughs. 'They're dedicated guys. C'mon Keith, do it again! Hey, I'm one of the Stones, man. I'm going to take a break. No, you're not!' he cackles. 'You're one of the Winos now.'

The Winos have a strong snare drum sound very much like Charlie Watts. Is that a sound you feel you need behind you?

'I'm a lucky man. I'm kind of spoilt with drummers. Since Charlie virtually introduced me to Steve [Jordan] and Steve has been listening to Charlie for years and years, it's very easy for me to play with either of them. They both understand what I need. A great drummer is the hardest thing to find.'

What comes first for you: the rebel or the rock and roll?

'Er . . . the music first. I mean, how you present it is another thing, but it's always the music first, that's what's interesting, that's what keeps it all going.'

Are the rebel and the rock and roll divisible?

'Probably not anymore,' he laughs. 'But like I say, to me that's just what happens. I get up there and play the music and that's the way it is and the other bit just gets attached as you go along.'

What's the strangest thing you've ever heard about yourself?

'Oh, I don't know, probably the blood change.' He roars with laughter. 'Really, I'm too squeamish. Yeah, but that one, I have to live with that one.'

Do you make any attempt to play up or play down your image?

'No, I'm sort or stuck with it. I mean, who in their right mind would do those things just to get in the papers?' And everyone's favourite rock and roll uncle explodes into laughter once again.

April 1992. Original text: Murray Engleheart.

Tori Amos

Not the girl next door

In the early 1990s, Tori Amos became the poster girl for a new generation. Tori carved her own path with eighty-eight keys, lyrical intensity, a now trademark confessional honesty, and a devotion to crafting fine albums. *Little Earthquakes* was an early benchmark for Amos. On her first promotional trip to Australia, she spent a week doing the media rounds discussing her new work. Her final interview took place as she was heading to the airport to leave the country. Richard Kwong was on the other end of the line.

I had a hepcat chat recently with the twenty-eight-year-old North Carolina preacher's daughter Tori Amos now based in a more vibin' London and just as distant mentally from her stifling hicks-ville upbringing.

And yet this journo found it a little disturbing that here was this promoter's dream – a gorgeous, fire-maned creature bursting with angst-ridden poetics – and yet nearly all the press I've laid eyes on blathers on about pretence and insincerity. It's almost a 'look out for another Milli Vanilli' vibe. I sure as hell hope this *ain't* the vibe 'cause her tale's ragged enough as it is. Like, give the chick a break!

But it's hell easy to chop this pretty poppy down if ya *want* to. Here's a hillbilly-LA-blended-Yank tryin' to be cred with a piano, angelic imagery and fetchingly fragile verse.

She sets herself up again by having the gall to move to London one and a half years ago, break there, *then* show the homeboys just what they've been-a-missin'. Atop all this, she ain't yer average babe next door. With respect to babes next door all over the world, well, she's a damn sight more intriguing. But, hell, I always fall for intrigue.

Hmmm, what else do ya need, viewers? Um, she *does* have a heavy Bush, K aura about her, has played piano since childhood: a time she also battled creative and character-crumbling claustrophobia.

At twenty-two she moved to Los Angeles, rocked out with axe-grinders Y Kant Tori Read, then released her first LP, bereft of the peaceful Tori afront the current LP, *Little Earthquakes*. The former Tori was more your typical Californian wet-dream rock chick, whip in hand.

But, ch-ch-ch-changes. Yep, from LA bimbo to alleged 'misery guts' (as one Brit wrote). Ms Amos, methinks you needed more than a mere seven days' PR here in Oz to counter all this crap.

Surely the last interview of her recent stay, like from a car phone and *this* far away from a Sydney plane bound for South Korea, Tori intrigued *moi* like a nervous kid in a brand new school . . .

Was your move to London a total escape or more simply a career-related relocation?

'When you leave a place, you have to want to change. You know what I mean? The head of Atlantic [US] said "I don't think the record'll be alive here more than one week," but the English side of the label really responded [up to top twenty]. In America things are so formatted and if you don't fit in, no one knows what to do with you.'

Is that how you felt generally and perhaps personally?

'I was just sick of the vibe. I needed to think. I lived in Los Angeles for seven years and needed to get out. It was really oppressive.'

Do you feel freer in England?

'Well, you know, going there, I've had some distance now from everything I've ever known. That's gonna change anybody. I have a much better sense of humour. I had this real desire to go to England so it all worked out that I got to go there and this country understood my music, which was like a window for the rest of the world.'

For me, the title *Little Earthquakes* evokes thoughts of smaller life upheavals that ultimately engender an enormous tremor. Do you think that's applicable or just tell me to shut up if I'm prying!

'When I wrote this record I had to go through, um, get-spread-out-on-the-kitchen-floor-time.'

Huh?

'When you start looking at yourself, it's hard to swallow at first, 'cause you've spent your whole life building up this idea of how you want to see yourself and then what you really are.'

I put to Tori what I believe is an unintentionally negative press assessment of her: 'oddball'.

'All I can do is give you a bit of a smiling sneer. 'Cause I mean *really* Richard, most people aren't talking about what's really going on. It's what they're *not* saying where I get the picture. When I'm talking to somebody, I have my own little subtext running, but I lay a lot on the table because I'm a bit bored with the other thing, right? Some people find that a bit odd. They don't really know what to make of it.'

Well, you certainly *do* lay things on the table, personally.

'But I'm not going to give names and numbers, though [in songs]. I mean, you've got to keep a little mystery, don't you think? I think there are so many articles written about people and people choose certain things because they only have a certain amount of space, right? But, um, I guess we'd have to talk for quite a long time to get to where it all comes from.'

Please!

'I played music 'cause I loved it. I stopped when I was about seven because I started listening to everybody outside who didn't really know what was right for me and this isn't just my parents. But when you're a kid and you're talented at something, everybody tries to mould you. So I thought *everybody's* thoughts so I became crazy. Not "crazy" as in, you know, uh, spitting at people on the street saying every dirty word in the book, but I just became a follower.'

When did that stop?

'It stopped with that first record. It was the final event where I decided I have no self-respect and I have to find out my true feelings about things.'

Woah, Tori! Heavy . . .

But things *have* changed – and not only with the release of *Little Earthquakes*. Check out the fab new *Winter* EP, which includes eased-up pianoforte versions of – wait for 'em – the Stones' 'Angie', Zep's wooser 'Thank You' and, yip yah, that 'Teen Spirit' thing. Can you believe this girl? What a nerve – or maybe she's just unafraid.

Still silent all these years? No way, eh Tori?

June 1992. Original text: Richard Kwong.

Nick Cave

The literary world of Nick Cave

Musicians who break out into other arts are either hailed as Renaissance Men (or Women) or, more frequently, derided as dilettantes. But this early nineties interview with Nick Cave sidesteps almost any mention of the musician in favour of Cave's literary side. There is a sense of shifting ground, a growing acceptance that musicians are free to experiment outside the parameters their fame has set. A music street magazine delves into the dark world of crime fiction? Why not? *Time Off* ran the interview over successive weeks. Cave himself has, with film and more literary titles to his name, never looked back.

'I have no problems reading a good, nasty crime novel,' laughs Nick Cave, rock and roll's resident black comic.

It's Friday night in the Brazilian city of São Paulo, and Cave, while not relishing the idea of spending the evening sitting at home doing interviews with the Australian media to publicise his December tour of this country, happily chats away about crime and violence of a fictional kind.

'For some people, Friday night means they go out and get pissed and have a good time, but I have to sit here and do interviews,' he says somewhat ruefully before warming to the idea of not having to answer the obligatory Ten Standard Questions.

Cave has a reputation for not being the easiest of interview subjects, especially when confronted by the usual array of queries about new records, tours and the current state of rock and roll. There are, however, no problems tonight.

'Hello, Stuart! I haven't talked to you for a long while. We were young kids once, weren't we?' He laughs. The jovial manner is, I suspect, because he's been forewarned that I come not to discuss music, but for our mutual passion for crime fiction.

In a past interview I'd noted that Cave waxed lyrical about his admiration for American crime writer James Ellroy, who deals with violence and psychopathic individuals in a way that's not dissimilar from many of Cave's lyrics.

'I'm a big James Ellroy fan,' he says. 'Particularly the last three books. *Silent Terror*, I love that book. I read *Brown's Requiem* first which I didn't like all that much, then I read *Silent Terror*, which I thought was absolutely brilliant.'

Silent Terror (also published in some countries as *Killer on the Road*) is possibly the darkest and most hauntingly realistic serial killer novel ever written. The back cover blurb from one edition is pure Cave territory: 'There's a man on the loose in America: a man who kills for the sheer pleasure of spilling blood, a man who rearranges the mutilated bodies of his victims in positions that, to him, have the purity of art. His appetite is insatiable and the sexual release can only come from the sight, the scent and the taste of fresh blood spurting from gaping wounds. He kills without words and his next victim could be anyone, any time, any place, anywhere.'

From *Silent Terror*, Cave moved onto Ellroy's series of novels about Los Angeles in the 1950s: *The Black Dahlia*, *The Big Nowhere* and *LA Confidential*, though he is yet to read the recently published *White Jazz*. Taken together, they form the most astonishing, powerful and challenging collection of crime fiction published in at least thirty years.

'*The Black Dahlia*, *The Big Nowhere* and *LA Confidential*, those three books are just unbelievable,' he says. 'It's amazing that anyone can write such works of genius after so many books.'

So what intrigues Cave about Ellroy?

'He's just so violent. That's why I like him, basically. He's just so violent and I also like what often happens to his central characters, the way they sometimes die off halfway through the story or whatever. Suddenly they're dead or they commit suicide or whatever. It's really shocking. You read it and you just go, "Fuck!" That doesn't happen so much in a lot of the literature you read. You kind of wade through a book and the character carries on to the end and the story rounds off in a nice way.

'With Ellroy's books your mouth just drops open. Things happen that you never really expect, like the hero turns out to be homosexual. Ellroy just has this way of writing about things where you're continually shocked. That just doesn't happen with your average book. Three crime writers do that to me: Ellroy, Jim Thompson and Derek Raymond.'

In the mean'n'nasty'n'dark stakes, Derek Raymond is the English equivalent of James Ellroy. Raymond is the author of *I Was Dora Suarez*, which contains an astonishing articulation of Raymond's world view, one that might well connect with Cave's: 'To work in A14 is to see everything that no one sees: the violence, misery and despair, the immeasurable distance in the mind of a human being that knows nothing but suffering between its dreams and death.'

Says Cave: 'Violence in literature can be written beautifully, especially if there's a certain pathos to it, a certain sadness that isn't glamorised or cheapened. For me there's no better literature than that. I love it in films too.

'Derek Raymond is the perfect example: the way he can incorporate the sadness of existence with horrible sordid violence. *I Was Dora Suarez* is brilliant, though I actually prefer his first book, *He Died With His Eyes Open*. It's almost identical to *Suarez* except it's a bum he discovers, this drunk under a bush who's had his head completely destroyed. Just some bum and it's the same story: no one wants to know about it and the cop goes after it. There's a bunch of diaries the guy's left behind so the cop becomes obsessed with this character in the same way he later becomes obsessed with Dora Suarez, only, with the bum, it's kind of sadder and more horrible. More helpless.

'Then there's big Jim Thompson who's been significantly rediscovered over the last few years. Virtually all his books have been reissued and there are film adaptations being made.'

Interestingly, the first biography of Thompson begins with the lyrics to 'Prayers of Fire' from Cave's Birthday Party days.

Cave likes the first-person Thompson books and is particularly fond of *The Killer Inside Me*, *A Hell of a Woman*, *Savage Night* and *Pop. 1280*.

'Those four are brilliant, works of genius. The rest are good, nasty crime books.'

Dylan talks about how he returns to Byron, Shelley and Blake and how he finds new things in those writers as he gets older. Does Nick Cave return to certain books over time?

'My theory is that we artists are really impressed by the work of other artists in our youth and I think many of those you lose after a while. But other works, important films and books, ingrain themselves into you and become a part of you so you never lose them. It's like those books live in your system forever and everything else is kind of a disappointment. It's very much how you relate to these things when you discover them; a discovery is always exciting. The older you get the less exciting everything becomes, I guess.

'I don't believe I'll ever discover anything like when I first read *Lolita* by Nabokov, for example, or the Jim Thompson books or whatever. With those books, it was a complete journey into something that would alter my life. I just don't believe it can happen anymore. I've discovered Derek Raymond over the last year and I love those books, but the same thrill of discovery isn't there. I guess that's possibly what Dylan is saying.'

Given Cave's obsession with violence, both in his music and in the books he admires, has he had any direct experience with the criminal mind? There's a theory that the violent criminal is essentially a very dull human being.

'That's Derek Raymond's view, right. I went and saw him recently in London. He read from his new book that he's writing at the moment. It's very much about the killer or the psychopath as a boring, hideously monotonous individual. But that's literature. Literature is literature. People often write about things they don't really know about and speculate. But, to answer your question, no. I don't think I've known a true psychopath.'

Cave himself is the author of two books: *King Ink*, a collection of lyrics, poems and fragments, and the extremely well received novel *And the Ass Saw the Angel* first published in 1989.

After his Australian tour, expect Cave to begin working on a new book.

'I've got a place in London at the moment, which I'm going to shift into in March. It actually has an office separate from the house so I have no excuse not to write a book now,' he says. 'I've had a lot of excuses not to venture into writing over the last couple of years, but I'm going to try and do it next year.

'The last one took five years to write and in doing it I was basically teaching myself as well as having this little over-enthusiastic love affair with the English language, which possibly shows in the book. But I think, mercifully, I've lost that and the next book I write will be a bit simpler.'

Is the process of writing a song dramatically different to creating a novel?

'A song is a song: three verses long. A book is two hundred pages or, in the case of my books, four hundred. But then in some ways it's easier to write a book once you get going. It's one idea you're pursuing and, with my one book, once the ball got rolling I couldn't really stop. It all seemed immediately apparent when I was writing it. But in a song, you have to think of an idea and find a way into the music, which is very difficult. It's quite a frightening situation, in a way, because these are not the kind of ideas you have every day.'

November 1992. Original text: Stuart Coupe.

Powderfinger

Operation Powderfinger

It's hard to imagine a time when Powderfinger were just another local band.

In September 1992, an article titled 'The All New All(most) Original Powderfinger' announced that Powderfinger were bravely leaving behind their Led Zeppelin covers and becoming an originals outfit. It marks the official commencement of what would become the most successful Australian band of the decade (right above an advertisement for a gig featuring members of what would soon become Regurgitator). The following February, Simon McKenzie spoke to a rather hirsute Ian Haug and Bernard Fanning. Yet to score a major label deal and with an independently released (and now long lost) EP in local stores, Powderfinger were indeed just another local band with hopes of cracking the big time.

The rest, as they say, is history, but take comfort from the likelihood that Bernard Fanning remembers the sixty CDs that somebody stole from him back around 1993. To the culprit (and we know you're out there), may your foul deeds have brought you only shame and misery.

In the three years or so since Powderfinger first began, they've risen to the forefront of the ranks of Brisbane bands. They've got a large and strong local following that means at least eighty per cent of the crowd is right behind them every time they play – and the crowd is usually pretty damn sizeable. There's plenty of natural talent and originality between the five of them, but Powderfinger are thoroughly aware of the fact that you make your own luck in this industry.

While a lot of luck comes from outside a band (record company people just happening to see them on a *really* good night, things like that), you can shorten the odds a lot with practice, perseverance and planning. You need to have a plan. And now that Powderfinger have built a very solid base here in Brisbane, it's time for *their* plan's second phase.

Powderfinger have been to Sydney twice and played smaller shows, but they're starting to make an impression. In a couple of weeks, they'll be doing Sydney again and Melbourne for the first time. They have a handful of interested industry people who'll be there to see what they're like. They'll be lucky to break even financially, but it'll be worth it in terms of exposure to record companies and creating a fan base in the Great South. And when they again head south – probably April – they should break even or possibly make some money. They're under no illusions and they're going about it the right way – to say nothing of the fact that they've got the songs and the sound to be great, no matter what.

'It's a real image thing in Sydney, like, you have to hang out and be cool before you can start a band,' says Powderfinger singer/lyricist, Bernie Fanning. 'A band have to have credibility in Sydney before people can get into them. But it was a lot better the last time there, because a lot of people who saw us the first time came back.'

The band's name comes from the Neil Young song and they cut their teeth in Brisbane pubs doing Zeppelin and Doors covers. But, while they speak of Jimi Hendrix and John Lennon with a certain tone of reverence, they're far from being sixties retrograde guitar heroes. Their sound bears these influences out, but it's still young, brash and modern. And with Fanning's distinctive, raw vocals and the band's impressive songwriting skill, they have a wonderfully unique and even refreshing sonic identity.

'You can listen to anything,' says Fanning. 'You can listen to C&C Music Factory and learn something – I mean you might, you never know. Everyone has different ideas so you might as well absorb as many as you can.

'I listen to a lot of Soundgarden,' he adds.

'Not at the moment!' says guitarist Ian Haug.

'Yeah, I got my discs stolen from the house last Friday while we were at the gig. Sixty discs, that's all the fuckers took! The cops seem to think it might have been someone we know. It's a real bummer, because now I've got nothing to learn from.'

Their self-financed, self-titled debut CD sold about four hundred copies in Brisbane shops and was sent to all the record companies, so it has proved a worthwhile venture. Now they're looking for a deal that will give them some more money and better recording facilities to play with. In the time since that first disc, their sound has become a lot heavier, but they're quick to put to rest any Seattle comparisons.

'We're not going to do the guitar sitting on the ground feeding back or anything,' says Haug. 'Everybody's doing that, so there's no point in us doing it as well. It'd just become really messy. I don't know that volume really matters that much anyway. So many people are into the grunge thing and we like it, but we don't want to sound like it.'

'We've always been a lot heavier live,' Fanning explains. 'That just wasn't perfected on the disc. And it's been nearly a year since we recorded; we've written so much stuff since then and the sound has just become heavier. Not by choice, just by accident. Probably because of the music we listen to, but we've still got the same ideals and the same ideas of how we want to sound.'

Powderfinger are young and original and they're good enough that they don't have to try hard to sound unique. They just are. They're gearing up to break ground down south and they're all focused and dedicated to taking it as far as they can go. They haven't got any plans to leave Brisbane permanently yet and thankfully the industry might just be getting to the stage where they don't have to to become *really* successful. Because my money says they will.

February 1993. Original text: Simon McKenzie.

The Lemonheads

Have a good time and don't talk about it too much

The Lemonheads have always been a revolving door for musicians, unless you're Evan Dando. Formed in 1986, the Bostonians hit commercial paydirt with *It's a Shame about Ray* in 1992. Dando has had a long affinity with Australia. Much of that album was co-written by Smudge's Tom Morgan, while Nic Dalton, the man behind indie label Half A Cow and a million Sydney bands, also contributed to the tunes and played bass in the group. Drugs took a toll and Dando was in danger of surrendering his 'slacker sex kitten' credit points. After a hiatus of six years, Dando reconvened the Lemonheads. *It's a Shame about Ray* continues to be celebrated and was re-released in 2008 with bonus tracks and an accompanying DVD.

The Lemonheads are – and always have been – a three-piece band, it's just that the only person who's always been there is Evan Dando. As the singer/songwriter/guitarist, Dando has freehold title on the name, but the Lemonheads are more than just Evan Dando and Friends. Mention ex-Plunderer Nic Dalton – now the Lemonheads' bassist among many other things – and Dando becomes enthusiastic to the point of glee.

'Awesome. It's like totally made the band gel,' Dando declares. 'I think it's like the thing the band needed. You know, he presses his guitar pedals with the butt of his bass, you know he goes pkkkw! He's quite a showman.'

Dalton met Dando when the Lemonheads first came to Australia and the two promptly painted towns from Sydney to Los

Angeles not just red, but dayglo, forming a fast friendship and a musical collaboration made in whatever equivalent of heaven they ascribe to.

Dalton is the co-founder of Sydney's prodigious Half A Cow record label, whose output and band roster is comparable in coolness only to New Zealand's legendary Flying Nun. Then there's Dalton, Dando and Smudge's Tom Morgan, who form Godstar: a half-whimsical, half-serious collaboration that produces some extremely wonderful music. With a successful record company and at least two bands in as many countries, it seems as though Dalton is something of a workaholic.

'Yeah, he is. He wishes he could clone himself, like y'know, a couple of times over,' says Dando of his cohort. 'He has such a deep love of music, it really comes through and he really enjoys playing, that's the best thing. And he's so knowledgeable about music, he's a tried and true music nerd.'

With the obscure but delightful range of cover versions amongst the Lemonheads' repertoire, could the same be said of Dando?

'I guess so, yeah, 'cause I call him a music nerd and he says, well, *you're* a music nerd too. So I guess we're both tarred with the same brush.'

Evan Dando spent a lot of time in Australia following that fateful first tour – even returning for a series of solo acoustic shows. Then there's the Dalton connection and the friends he has here: a bunch of whom called all strangers 'Ray'. When Dando saw a post-accident story about the death of a young man in Melbourne, which ended with the quote, *It's a shame about Ray*, the name for the next Lemonheads album was as good as written in stone. But what is it about Australia that Dando finds so likeable?

'People don't, like, make a big deal out of everything here,' he says. 'In America, I notice everyone kind of talks about everything too much. Here it seems there's an unspoken understanding that it's good to have a good time and don't talk about it too much. I like that. And I just have a lot of friends here.'

It might sound strange, asking a guy from Boston, but is Dando anti-American at all?

'Well, I'm not anti-American. I just don't like being there, y'know? There are some great towns – like Austin, Texas, is a great town – there are a couple in America. But on the whole, it's like been taken over by big corporations and stuff and the quality of everything has gone down steadily with that kind of action. It's not as localised as it used to be, say, in the fifties or something, there were still a lot of . . . kind of Ma-and-Pa concerns. Now with . . . what is it . . . the *worship* of money, you know, it's a little bit of a downer after a while.'

So what inspires you to write songs?

'Sometimes it's some kind of therapy for me and then it's also just fun, to make something,' he says. 'It's the only thing I can really make. You know, I've never learned how to make, like, macramé or anything. I can't draw well or anything so I write songs. It's a really satisfying thing to *make* something.'

Do you write much prose?

'I did it in High School a lot, I wrote a lot of short stories, but now I just write songs. Someday I'd like to get back to that, but I figure I'm a little green yet to really write. So I'll wait until I'm older.'

So how do you see yourself getting older?

'I really don't know. I've never been one to map things out in advance so we'll see how this whole thing pans out and go with it.'

March 1993. Original text: Simon McKenzie.

INXS

Live and Kick-ing

For a brief shining moment it felt like INXS were the hottest band in the world. They played Wembley under their own steam and the Rolling Stones requested them as an opening act when they regrouped for the *Steel Wheels* tour. Buoyed by their collective musical strength, as well as the songwriting skill of Andrew Farris and the charisma of front man and co-writer Michael Hutchence, INXS, with the release of *Kick*, became a global commodity. They appeared to falter commercially with *X*, but go back and listen to the subsequent albums *Welcome to Wherever You Are*; *Full Moon, Dirty Hearts*; and *Elegantly Wasted* and you'll find that INXS still had a lot to offer; it's just that grunge had taken over the world and they were sonically out of step. In the live arena, with Hutchence out front, the band were rarely short of incendiary.

Michael Hutchence kicks his sandals off, sticks his feet up on the table and leans back in his chair. The sun's warm, the pool at the Esplanade Hotel in Fremantle glistens. It's all so laid back and easy. And so is Hutchence, remarkably so, since enduring his first round of interviews in several years.

We are talking about INXS's return to the pubs and clubs of Australia: an attempt to reclaim their roots and get back to the people. On the evidence of the first two shows – a passionate and sexy first night and a metallic knockout second night – it's a move long overdue: never have INXS been so raw, so powerful, so edgy, such a rock and roll animal.

'We're like kids at the moment,' says Hutchence. 'It's hard to understand how different this is for us and how much it means doing these kind of shows. I'm going to be kind of upset going back to the bigger venues and the arenas. We did this to give ourselves a bit of a charge and it has certainly done that. We've gone the whole way with it, even down to starting in Perth where we first started. The only reason any band lose perspective is when they get shackled to success and the products of it. You end up doing arenas, bigger places. There's the merchandise and the t-shirts and the record company always wants the album now, now, now. Eventually, you have to realise you have a choice. You can do something else.

'This kind of tour isn't something we would have done a few years ago. We were running from this then, we'd just escaped seven years of pubs. But, even while we were running away from it, we recognised the pub scene as the great Australian tradition, I'm always talking about it to people overseas. But it is just a cartoon in their minds. They don't really understand how bands develop through this circuit.'

On introducing a new song, 'Cut the Roses', the previous night, Hutchence yelled, 'This is a song about fucking fascist arseholes!' Quite the attitude, not something often associated with INXS, at least not until now.

The band have spent two months cutting a new album on the Italian island Capri and the new songs, several of which are contained in the current set, are tough-edged, meaty funk-and-rock bastards that kick some arse musically. The signs were there on their last effort, *Welcome to Wherever You Are*: the sound was tougher and the tracks brought a spontaneity missing from earlier opuses such as *Kick*. Listen out for the song 'Full Moon' during the shows: it's the sexiest, most perfect fusion of gentle keyboards and dirty guitar, a ballad-yet-rocking song to rival 'Never Tear Us Apart' and while it might be about relationships it's no 'boy meets girl under a full moon'.

'There's only one straight love song on the whole album,' Hutchence says. 'The rest of the songs all have a real cutting edge. There's a lot I wanted to say: life, death and all that. That's what they are about. "Roses" is about all those fascists running around out there. But even if I was doing a song about a relationship I found a new angle to expand on anything I'd done before. I guess with songwriting, I have different mountains to climb to get to the song now. There's a lot more blood spilled these days. You don't want to be a pastiche. It is one way to be successful in pop, but we aren't interested in that. We want to keep exploring new ways to do funk and rock. That drive is still there for us. We've done a lot of albums, but it still seems valid for us to be in a studio making records. We aren't embarrassing ourselves.'

The conversation shapes and drifts over the next twenty minutes.

'I do think Australians should realise we aren't as naïve as we think we are. The whole republican thing is a very good idea. Australia seems to uneasily float somewhere between the United States and the United Kingdom, although the latter link is dying away now. So, naturally, Australia is turning towards the United States as a role model. And that is the last thing this country wants to become. Christ, look at them! Australians need their own identity not a borrowed or adopted one. That's why becoming a republic is a good idea. It should make Australians focus on Australia.'

He bums a cigarette, talks loosely about the indie scene – how there's a real need for a middle ground to develop in Australian music from which young bands can launch themselves, puts the boot into Barnsey even while recognising his achievements, and stresses the need for a strong independent base for Australian music outside major labels.

All too quickly, the time is up. He stretches, smiles, takes in the surroundings and orders another iced tea. American and European tours loom in the not-too-distant future, but right now the world is young and exciting again and INXS have slipped into fifth gear, foot to the floorboard, cutting a swathe through the night to the heart of rock and roll. It's a damn fine thing and about time too.

April 1993. Original text: Mike Gee.

Radiohead

So fucking special

When they toured in early 1994, Australia caught a glimpse of Radiohead undergoing the first of many transitions. The initially heartening success of 'Creep' had become a nightmarish millstone for the band to drag around the world for nearly two years. It's interesting to note how deftly Thom Yorke places the song to one side here, eager to move on to talking about the album that would become The Bends*, before it pops back up again towards the end. In many ways, this period marks the beginning of Radiohead's career proper, although few at the time would have dared imagine where that career would lead.*

As an aside, for a band famous for taking years to complete songs, what do you think the chances are that 'Dead Bank Clerk' will turn up on their next album?

The omens are good. On my way to interview Radiohead's front man, Thom Yorke, I wind down the window and turn on the radio. 'So fucking special . . . ' sings Thom, the instant I flick the switch. The announcers on our friendly neighbourhood cultural imperialist lament (as you would expect them to, I guess) that it's a sad reflection on their listeners that the year's three favourite songs are called 'Creep', 'Asshole', and 'Detachable Penis'.

What a way to start an interview!

Dutifully, I paraphrase the radio voice's comment, and Thom chuckles. He's an ardent admirer of Denis Leary (whose stand-up comedy is *The Thing* in Britain right now), but he hasn't heard the inimitable 'Asshole' number.

'When I wrote "Creep", I didn't realise creep was such a heavy word,' Thom explains. 'Especially in America, "creep" is a very abusive term. In Britain, "creep" is almost a joke, you know. "You're a creep" is like you're from a horror film or something. It's not like arsehole or anything like that. It's great being linked to Denis Leary, though; he's wonderful. Definitely a nineties comedian is our Denis.'

I am surprised 'Asshole' isn't as well known in Britain as it is here, especially given the fact Leary is virtually a household name there.

'I'm not with Radio One,' says Thom, in much the tone of voice your average 4ZZZ community-radio announcer would say the words 'Take 40 Australia'.

Radiohead have been fighting a pitched battle against British music press and radio since their inception and they've almost given up in disgust. Though they hail from Oxford, they remain less than huge in their homeland, while, in America, they're household all-sorts-of-things. Household. In America, they outsell Suede fifteen-to-one. For once, the Americans have got it right.

American success has meant a long and winding tour road for Radiohead, who have been 'on the go all year basically'. They've played the length and breadth of the United States and set out across Europe to return home for some shows near the end of the year.

'When we're touring, we don't really get to see anywhere,' says Thom. 'I mean the last American tour, literally, we drove fifty miles away from the Grand Canyon and we didn't have time to stop and have a look because we were late for the next gig. We couldn't believe we did that! But then, it was like that the whole tour.'

In Switzerland for Radiohead's European tour, Yorke has a little more time to take in the sights, but it's still a bit of a blur, really.

'Cologne was beautiful . . . Oh God, my mind's just turned to jelly. Where have I been?' he mutters. 'Touring does strange things to people, definitely.'

I wonder if it's any different for bands like U2, who play once a week and spend the rest of the time lounging about close to pools and cocktails.

'Now *that* is the way to do it!' exclaims Thom. 'We've got something loosely called a World Tour shaped up for the next album, which is quite amusing,' he chuckles wryly. 'The problem with a lot of British bands is they make it in Britain and think that's it. They don't really care if the rest of the world never catches up, because Britain's Britain. And I think that's a really fucking arrogant attitude. One of the reasons, in fact – it's boring I know – but one of the reasons we signed to EMI was because we knew that that way we could get our record released worldwide, which to us is really important. Not simply because the cash is great, but . . . this was really funny: there was this clause in the contract, the territory for our recordings is apparently "The World and the Known Universe". Literally, that's what it says. You know, it's going to be a hit on Mars.'

Thom Yorke is not a fame seeker. He doesn't court stardom so much as he laughs at it. And the trappings of Radiohead's success have given him much to laugh at.

The more astute among you would have noticed Thom mention the Next Album. Well, not only is it the Next Album, it's the Second Album, a hurdle many bands are unable to clear successfully, largely a result of the pressure to follow up on the success of your last record. The standard brief in short: further define the band's strengths, grow up a bit, and just make a better record. Make it different to the first one, but not too much, just different enough. To this, Radiohead say bugger off. They don't see their new album as an attempt to follow up their debut, *Pablo Honey*. They see it as merely recording some more songs.

'Jonny and I have been working on the new stuff for the new album – working a lot closer than we did on the first album, which has really helped me,' Thom says. 'It's a lot less frantic, which probably certain members of our audience will hate, but tough shit! It's a bit less thrashy. It's a more frightening album, a more desolate album than the first one. And a more focused one, I think. Jonny and I have really got into the songwriting, pushing it as far as we possibly can. He knows a lot more chords than I do, so that's helped! One of my favourite songs – I'm not sure whether it will get on the album, though – is a song called "Dead Bank Clerk", which is just about an argument I had in my bank. I yelled at them: "Look! I'm a bloody popstar now! Give me back my bloody credit card!" But they wouldn't. So I went back and wrote "Dead Bank Clerk".'

Thom sees songwriting as a skill in itself, something that can be improved.

'It's definitely something that can be improved on, but the actual first impetus for a song – the thing that makes you write it in the first place – is something you can't learn or teach yourself. You just have to be open to it happening and there has to be a reason to do it. I'm at the stage now where . . . there's a visual artist I'm really into called Alan Davie. I read this biography of him where he talks about how he'd go for a year without doing any painting or he would be working, but nothing would make sense. He just got used to it and just got used to the idea that if nothing's going to happen, nothing's going to happen. Then he'd suddenly come up with the most amazing painting at the end of it, almost despite himself. I've gotten used to all the distractions – the fact we are signed to this huge record label and blah blah blah – but what really keeps us going is that initial kick we still get. It's usually just one simple idea. It's like Neil Young, the reason Neil Young is still good is that he still gets that initial kick. You'll hear it in his work. So long as you don't lose that.'

It's obvious when a song is calculated, almost made with instructions like Lego.

'I find it really strange that people do that. I don't understand how it could get past anybody if you're doing that, writing songs by numbers like that. It doesn't make sense. I don't even understand the mental framework behind it, but maybe that's because I'm able to do it the other way.

'I think a lot of songs get born out of wanting to rewrite things around you, how you want to see them. The reason people write poetry and books is that they want to rewrite the world as they see it, to create a slightly more comfortable world. Some people say that it's like getting revenge on reality, getting revenge on things around you that you don't like by completely rewriting them. I like that idea. I think "Creep" is a revenge song.'

Does the inspiration for a song often come from negative emotions?

'Negative emotions just tend to be the strongest. Also, I think it's very difficult to write songs that are genuinely uplifting. I know certain people can do it, I suppose Evan Dando is a guy who can do it, but then he's permanently stoned. I think it's probably just that the emotions that are really sharp and painful are the ones I tend to use, the down ones.'

December 1993. Original text: Simon McKenzie.

Smashing Pumpkins

Shining bright

Billy Corgan runs the Smashing Pumpkins as something of a benign dictatorship. Think of him as 'Il Pumpkino' if you like, first Pumpkin among equals. His obsessive control and slightly paranoid tendencies frequently place him in conflict not only with his changing line-up of band mates, but also with the rest of the music industry generally, as he amply demonstrates in this 1994 interview with Murray Engleheart. It's a frustrating situation for a musician and songwriter who has created an impressive catalogue of searing sonic adventures and moments of beautiful intimacy in roughly equal number.

According to the legend that has rapidly surrounded the Smashing Pumpkins, vocalist and guitarist Billy Corgan was kicked out of a succession of bands because he made the other members feel uncomfortable. What those fools didn't realise was that they could have made the man's intensities one of his talents.

'Most people are stupid,' Billy laughs with a hint of venom after expressing mild disbelief at the tale. 'I don't think about what could have been because it's too late. It's only down to what is. I know who my band are, we know each other, and we know the kind of power we can generate as four people. Without sounding cocky about it, we can always be powerful together. We trust that relationship.'

Trust is not something that comes easily to Corgan, which may explain why, by his reckoning, this is only about his fifteenth interview since the stunning *Siamese Dream* album was released. He felt each new discussion with a journalist amounted to little more than a rehash of the last, like discussing his somewhat detached childhood.

'A lot seems to be made of that these days,' he sighs. 'I think it's getting to the point of entertainment. It becomes too easy: he has brown hair, he's six foot three, he had a troubled childhood. It becomes part of the entertainment pastiche and I think in the end it almost begins to trivialise any problems I might have had. People begin to perceive that it's something I'm always putting out there, trying to push on everyone and it begins to kind of create a negative dissonance towards me, which I don't really like.'

Subject closed. And before you ask, yes, putting *Siamese Dream* together was apparently hellish, with reports of one band member absconding to rehab because of the trauma. Like Corgan's childhood, the story has become part of the band's mythology and Billy is quick to ensure that that myth doesn't overshadow what the Pumpkins do creatively.

A week before we spoke the band finished a five-month US tour, which culminated in a pre-Christmas acoustic show in Los Angeles with Primus, Belly, Porno for Pyros and Rage Against the Machine. Billy recalls the highlight of the tour as 'living and breathing'. None of his heroes attended any of the shows 'unless you count the people throwing things at us heroes'.

Despair? Depression? I'm not sure. Somehow, I doubt it. Performing can be heaven or hell for Billy Corgan.

'It's such a roulette wheel. It really depends on how the band feel, how comfortable the band are, and the audience's basic reaction towards the band. What happens in the first ten minutes of a show can really determine whether the show will be good or great or bad. There's no formula for it. Sometimes you can walk on stage feeling completely awful and go on to do the greatest show you've ever played. Sometimes I walk on stage in such a good mood and the first five minutes somebody hits me in the face with a shoe. After that I couldn't care less about playing because then it's more about dignity and my life than it is about being an entertainer.'

I wonder, in what seems to be an insecure and volatile environment, with which member of the band Billy feels he has the greatest affinity.

'It tends to rotate,' he laughs slightly uncomfortably.

You are clearly very separate individuals.

'Very, very different people,' he agrees. 'Most bands I've met, the members tend to be very much alike; they're like a little pack of rats. We're so completely different from each other, which in the end is our greatest strength. But it does cause a lot of problems. It's very rare that we argue about songs. More often, we argue about someone not working on a song or somebody not giving enough effort, when three of us, say, tell the fourth person he or she is not trying hard enough. It tends to go in cycles. We all go through our little moods and spaces and sometimes somebody goes two or three months where you can just tell they're not really interested in being in the band, but it pays their bills and that's what they have to do. I go through those phases too, but I try to line it up with when we're not working,' he laughs.

When Billy says that five years in the Pumpkins have been pretty intense, I don't doubt him for a second. Such difficult periods seem like a massive black hole with only some of the most uplifting music of the last five years as redemption.

'It was pretty hard before we ever had a record out because it was completely based on faith. There was only the band and a couple of our friends and that was our universe. Yet, in the back of your head, you believe that one day we'll be this big act or whatever. But it's all faith; there's nothing you can point to. Then the other hard part was really between the first and the second album because everything we had steered towards becoming on the first album was no longer valid. We had grown beyond that band and beyond that dream.

'I would liken it to an infatuation: you pour all your energy into winning them over, so, when it actually happens, you don't really know how to get beyond that. We put a lot of our energy into impressing people and making what you would call an immediate kind of impact, but I don't think we had that much lasting impact. So it took a while for us to shift gears and that caused a lot of problems within the band.'

One of the greatest problems for any artist is laying down a piece of work that becomes a near religious experience and then having to contend with their self-made divinity. Creating expectations in your audience can quickly become a millstone around your neck, especially if you can't follow through. Corgan is unconcerned about the level of hope the Pumpkins fuelled in their fans.

'I think it's hard to live down, but I don't think you can ever create too great an expectation. I think that's a necessary component of making records that are timely. You know, when you're hungry, food tastes better and I think if you create a hunger in people to hear more and to want more from your band, then they'll savour what you offer them. It just won't be something they just toss aside.'

But isn't being set up as a Godhead figure going to pressurise further what the band do?

'Oh I'm sure it does, but I have a nothing-to-lose kind of optimism about the whole thing anyway. Really, what's to lose? I don't want to spend my twenties and thirties being some sub-popular footnote of a band that people are going to discover twenty years from now. If we're going to do this, I'd rather do it full on and burn as bright as we can for as long as we can than spend the rest of our lives regretting what happened.'

In the centre of that brilliant blue flame there would have been some sort of intangible code by which Billy's thoughts and actions were directed.

'It's always hard to talk about this stuff without sounding like a guru, like I'm sitting here talking to you in the lotus position,' Corgan says of his spirituality. 'Ever since I was a little kid, I felt that there's got to be more to me than just going to work and buying cookies and things like that. I guess in an unseen way, I've always guided my life in pursuit of more lofty spiritual ideals.

I can't necessarily explain it and it does have a lot to do with what I do and why I do it a certain way.'

The Smashing Pumpkins: one hell of an argument for faith of some description.

January 1994. Original text: Murray Engleheart.

Guns N' Roses

Not an exercise in hero worship

After the monumental success of their suitably epic 1991 twin album releases *Use Your Illusion I* and *II* and subsequent tour, Guns N' Roses chose a change of pace for their follow-up project. Slash later revealed that the title *'The Spaghetti Incident?'* was an inside joke referring to a food fight between Axl Rose and drummer Steven Adler. By 1994, an estranged Adler undertook legal proceedings against the band where an attorney referred to the food exchange as 'the spaghetti incident'. With its obligatory question mark and quotes, the title's relevance to a collection of punk and hardcore rock cover versions remains a mystery more than fifteen years later.

It's pretty much an accepted fact that Guns N' Roses are the next step in a lineage that began with the Stones and moved on to Aerosmith, the New York Dolls and Hanoi Rocks. You know, the almost graceful look of human demolition with a 'raunch and roll' factor on tilt. The finest exponents of that bad-arse subculture have traditionally been the key guitar figures like Keith Richards and Johnny Thunders who made a seemingly kamikaze lifestyle as essential as being vaguely in tune.

Though clearly a superior guitarist, Slash has been the major torch carrier for that tradition over the last six years and his own outlaw status is now carved in stone. Part of that standing, I always figured, was drawn from Thunders. It's a theory that would seem to be supported by the fact that the guy is represented on the Gunner's *'The Spaghetti Incident?'* album not only by the New York

Dolls' 'Human Being' but also with his own 'You Can't Put Your Arms Around a Memory', but Slash couldn't remember what he was doing when he heard Thunders went blue for the final time. And he didn't care.

'I didn't even play on that song because I hated that little fucker,' the quietly spoken Slash laughed venomously regarding 'You Can't Put Your Arms Around a Memory'. 'So I really wasn't all that concerned when he died. It wasn't an issue. It wasn't a memorable day. I didn't like him at all. We worked with him a couple of times. Not to talk out of disrespect for the deceased, but he's not one of my heroes. Put it that way. I did like the Dolls and stuff but I don't know what the nicest way to put it is. I just wasn't very interested.'

That pretty much kills off the notion that *'The Spaghetti Incident?'*, with its now infamous inclusion of Charles Manson's 'Look at Your Game Girl', is purely an exercise in hero worship. Word of an EP of covers first leaked out during the *Use Your Illusion* sessions and seemed to have been the joint brainchild of Duff McKagan and departed guitarist Izzy Stradlin. The fact that Izzy's guitar parts were re-recorded by new boy Gilby Clarke for what was by then a full album must have been the ultimate insult for Stradlin. But then he was reportedly paid a staggering two million dollars to fill in for the injured Clarke towards the end of the *Illusion* tour. *'The Spaghetti Incident?'* is a reconstitution, a regrouping of everything that Guns N' Roses represented up to and including *Appetite For Destruction*. Somehow it's also reharnessed whatever naïveté the band held in those earlier days, and allowed them to recast themselves as a great flat-out rock and roll entity. To many, it was the album the Gunners had to make.

'To tell you the truth, there was a lot of pressure on us when we were doing the *Illusion* records. There was a lot of fucking heavy shit that we'd just gotten through as far as the band were concerned and all our personal lives just to become a band again. We'd had such a hard time adjusting to whatever success came from our previous work. We managed to stay together as a band, even though we lost Steven Adler. And we'd basically already lost Izzy during the making of that record. There was a lot going on. The fact that we accomplished recording the whole thing and recording all that different material . . . We ended up using all of Izzy's material, even though he didn't even play on most of the record. We used all the songs that we like of his that we never used before and shit like that. It was just a very hard record to make. So when we did *'The Spaghetti Incident?'*, it was us jamming in the studio and putting it on tape. There was no pressure and there was no record company involvement. We booked our own studio time and just did it ourselves.

'We didn't even have to write the songs!' he laughs.

Obviously *'The Spaghetti Incident?'* invites comparison with Metallica's *Garage Days Re-Revisited* EP, which championed the likes of Budgie and the Misfits. But Metallica's audience at that time was nowhere near the size and breadth that GN'R boasts these days. For a band like the Damned, whose 'New Rose' is given a ripping Gunners treatment, the entire *Spaghetti* exercise could mean serious paydirt.

I must say though that, while I don't deny anyone their due, particularly as most of the artists featured here are also heroes of mine, I would feel less than comfortable if one of my kids wanted a Dead Boys lunch box because: a) it would cheapen what the band were about and b) because I like to consider, quite greedily, that some things should only be available for private worship.

'Well, you know,' Slash muses, 'it'd be pretty strange if too many of the bands on there became hip all of a sudden, you know? In all honesty, three quarters of the people we covered on this record, the kids don't even know who the fuck they are. Which is pretty sad considering what a powerful impact they had on rock and roll at the time. All of a sudden they just get shelved, just like that.'

But isn't that where people like GN'R can help out? Just as Radio Birdman were the Australian connection to the Stooges and the MC5 for those who couldn't read Lester Bangs raving about their virtues in *Creem* magazine in 1970? Slash wasn't sure.

'Well, yes and no. I suppose it depends on how interested people are. We made a point of making sure that nobody got confused as to who wrote the songs. Maybe some people will take it further and check out the originals. It was just a fun little side project for us. Realistically, that's all it was. But we took it seriously enough to make it sound good or at least what we thought sounded good. Where it goes from here is up to the people who listen to it.'

As for the title, Slash isn't giving much away.

'It's an inside joke. I refuse to divulge the information and tell exactly what it means. It has something to do with our ex-drummer.'

Speaking of which, the album boasts a stack of exes. The ghosts are everywhere: the Dead Boys' Stiv Bators, T.Rex's Marc Bolan, the Sex Pistols' Sid Vicious, and the New York Dolls' Johnny Thunders, Jerry Nolan and Billy Murcia. Maybe that was part of the attraction for the Gunners. After all, they very nearly ended up the same way.

'Um, yeah. Yeah, I guess so. I guess there's no real way to express it. I mean, I couldn't put in words what influences we got from some of the bands we put on that record. But some of the songs really represent . . . er . . . they're very close to our hearts as far as the shit that we've been through over the years. The fact that some of these people aren't around anymore, that's just a given,' he laughs. 'That has a lot to do with where we come from. The fact we're still around is just sort of a blessing.'

While the choice of some of the material on the album is fairly obvious – the Misfits, the New York Dolls, and a killer version of 'Down On The Farm' by English punks the UK Subs – the inclusion of the Skyliners' fifties hit 'Since I Don't Have You' is a shot from the back row of the ballpark. Slash heard Axl singing the song years ago and Axl said at the time that he wanted to cover it.

'All this time went by. I don't even remember exactly what happened, but we started playing it as an intro to "Sweet Child o' Mine". At the end of my guitar solo, I would play the beginning and Axl would sing a couple of lines from it and then I'd go into "Sweet Child o' Mine". So when we were touring in the States, we had a couple of days off. We had a day off in Boston and booked some time in a cheap studio. We rented some gear and I borrowed Gilby's guitar. So that's what that is. It's totally live. You can hear the fucking amp buzzing!'

The band also recorded a version of the Stooges' 'Down on the Street' that didn't make the album.

'Well, we never put vocal on it. There's also a version of . . . fuck, what was the other song? We did a Hanoi Rocks tune as well. Both have basic tracks done, but we never did any vocals on them. We decided not to do the Hanoi Rocks song because we didn't want to give Andy McCoy the money. Then we didn't do "Down on the Street" because "Raw Power" just sounded cooler.'

The highpoint of the album is a stunning version of the lyrically black 'Ain't It Fun', originally recorded by the Dead Boys and written by Dead Boy guitarist Cheetah Chrome – who is rumoured to be doing an album for Melbourne's Dog Meat label – and another rock and roll fatality Peter Laughner when both were in a Cleveland band called Rocket from the Tombs in the early seventies.

'Those lyrics on "Ain't It Fun" pretty much wrap up the experiences for Guns N' Roses and probably a lot of bands like us. That pretty much sums us up right there.'

It's almost a suicide note.

'It's more like a warning,' Slash says. 'Like, cut the crap, kid. This how it really goes.'

January 1994. Original text: Murray Engleheart.

Magic Dirt

Believe the hype

Another wonderful slice of street press advocacy: a step-by-step lesson in hype from a self-confessed fan. In the effort to impart just how remarkable Magic Dirt's second EP is, Andrew Stafford falls just shy of actually buying the record for you and placing it on high rotation in your house. You get the feeling, if he could do that, he would.

To this day – after a crack at the American market, stylistic shifts that prompted accusations of 'sell-out', a stint on a major label, and the death of founding member Dean Turner – Magic Dirt endure. Their fans (not to mention the 'oversalivating critics') wouldn't have it any other way.

Avid readers of *Time Off* will have noticed Liam Cale's singles challenge in his regular column last week. In reviewing the most excellent Spiderbait single 'Jesus' (for the second time, no less) our easily bored and sometimes splenetic critic frothed that 'unless in the remaining six weeks of 1994 someone can show me something better, Spiderbait have the song of the year – even if it is too bloody short'.

Now there's a challenge. Liam is almost correct: 'Jesus' is a killer song and every home should have that little black pearl of vinyl. But the remaining six weeks of the year have seen Magic Dirt burst forth with what is unmistakably the EP of the year. Folks, just gird your loins because it has not one but *two* songs that are not only longer than 'Jesus', but are indeed a slight-but-sure improvement on the thin bearded holy man! Hallelujah!

Called *Life Was Better*, the record sports a hot orange cover showing the band in an old Valiant that's probably at least as fast as the songs. A significant improvement on their previous outing, *Signs of Satanic Youth*, *Life Was Better* is more focused, better recorded, better played and contains better songs. Look, it's better, okay?

The band are better too. Ask bassist Dean Turner: 'Brilliant, actually! The record's out, this weekend we start touring, we've been rehearsing new songs, lots of stuff happening . . . everything's going really well.'

It sounds like more time was spent on making this EP better than the last.

'Actually, I think we spent less time, but that's because we knew what we wanted as soon as we went in the studio. Previously we would record and mix before realising we didn't like it, then we'd have to go back and remix it. We didn't do that on this one. We wanted more live sound and I think that's pretty much what we got. We rehearsed the songs a lot more and we knew what we wanted to do with overdubs, so when we went in there we automatically got them down faster.'

So, I hear you breathlessly pleading, just what are *better* songs? Well, there's 'Daddy', a favourite from the band's live set for some time now with an amazing spiralling guitar line courtesy of guitarist Daniel Herring. And then there's 'Amoxycillin', which marks Magic Dirt's first foray into the realm of pure pop, and damn it if Adalita Srsen hasn't improved her singing beyond all reasonable bounds since we last heard from her. These songs will burn themselves into your brain on your first listen. And let me remind you in case you've forgotten: they're both *better than Jesus*. But, given that everything's going so much better, why didn't that vaunted debut album come to fruition as the band had originally planned?

'Well, we only really had seven songs and we would have had to write the others pretty quickly. So we figured rather than do that we'd just put out an EP of really focused songs that we were really happy with. We didn't want to just throw an album together, so we thought we'd worry about it next year. And, in doing the EP, we've become aware of what we want to do on the album.'

One of the problems with doing everything so much *better* than everybody else is that you get mountains of *hype* poured upon you from oversalivating critics. Hope it doesn't put them off their game.

'We just tried to stay away. Because we live down in Geelong rather than Melbourne, we're away from a lot of that. We've got a really good manager working for us and the people at the label are really good. They keep all the shit away from us; they insulate us. All that hype stuff seems to be dying off a bit now anyway, so that's good. We stopped doing interviews for a while.'

So there you go: the word on hype from the band themselves. But the last word goes to yours truly and it's just to reiterate that *Life Was Better* is genius in motion, a totally rocking slab of bright orange cool. Liam may think I'm full of shit, but I've got ten bucks that says that my life was *better* when I heard this EP. So goddamn go – go *get it*.

November 1994. Original text: Andrew Stafford.

Pearl Jam

Vedder on *Vitalogy* and immortality

With the release of their debut effort, *Ten*, Pearl Jam became a global entity, lumbered as ringleaders of the grunge movement. Front man Eddie Vedder accepted his fate as a rock star, but was wary of the trappings fame would bring. Over the ensuing years, Pearl Jam broke the mould for what a stadium-sized rock band could achieve: from boycotting Ticketmaster in the United States to encouraging fans to bootleg any show they attended, all while Vedder consolidated his reputation as the voice of a new generation. Robert Hilburn is one of rock's great writers. He was with Johnny Cash when he recorded his Folsom Prison concert, he travelled with Bob Dylan on his first concert tour to Israel, and he was the first journalist summoned by Yoko Ono after John Lennon's murder. Here, Hilburn speaks to Vedder on the release of Pearl Jam's *Vitalogy*.

With the arrival of the magnificent *Vitalogy*, Pearl Jam are set to ascend even further up the rock pinnacle, if that were possible. *Vitalogy*, despite following less than a year after *Vs*, is their most coherent, daring and brilliant album yet, seeing the band break into an artistic stride the like of which hasn't been seen for years. The 'difficult third album', as Billy Bragg once called it, has proved effortless for Pearl Jam. Doubters will be converted and the converted will be transported.

Eddie Vedder pauses when asked if 'Immortality' – a song on the new Pearl Jam album about deep depression – was inspired by the suicide last April of Kurt Cobain. It's hard to tell whether

Vedder is surprised by the question or is simply sighing at its inevitability.

Vedder is the rock artist most closely compared to Cobain. Both have been hailed as key figures in a new generation of songwriters who reflect the alienation and anger that seems to characterise youth in the nineties. And 'Immortality' includes lines that certainly sound as if they were inspired by Cobain's death – there is even a reference to a cigar box on the floor, such as the one found next to Cobain's body in Seattle.

'No,' Vedder says finally. 'Immortality', he explains, is a look at his own delicate state of mind, written in the days before Cobain's death. The cigar box is simply where Vedder often keeps lots of tapes. But with lines like 'cannot find the comfort in this world' and 'some die just to live', everyone is going to assume it's about Kurt.

'It was written on tour in Atlanta. It's not about Kurt. Nothing on the album was written directly about Kurt and I don't feel like talking about him because it might be seen as exploitation. But I think there might be some things in the lyrics that you could read into and maybe will answer some questions or help you understand the pressures on someone who is on a parallel train.'

How were you feeling in the months surrounding Kurt's death, just when you were complaining about the pressures? Is it that hard for people to understand what is so difficult about being famous?

'I understand that. It is a tremendous privilege to be able to play music for a bunch of people. It's a great feeling, very humbling. But as far as putting up with the rest . . . the media and the way they exploit and scoop out your chest without leaving anything behind. Haven't we witnessed that in the OJ Simpson case? I was in Greece when that happened and I felt like renting billboards all over the United States saying, "Have you people lost your mind?" Everybody was kind of fascinated, but I was sick. I don't want any part of the whole celebrity trip.'

But you also complain about the business side of rock. What's so hard about dealing with that?

'Someone wrote a letter to a magazine the other day about Eddie "It's So Hard To Be A Rock Star" Vedder. Well, I just want to clarify it's not hard to be a rock star. If you want to go around fucking women and fleecing a bunch of teenagers of all their dough because they like your band and charge them the earth for t-shirts and concert tickets, that's easy. That's playing the game. What's hard is trying to stop playing the game . . . trying to treat people fairly and with respect. If someone bumps into me on the street, it could be worth something; someone might want to buy that story. Or if they bump into me hard enough, they can claim I hit them and they can sue me. You just feel that after a while you become a commodity rather than a person. It interferes with your life and the music.'

Vedder is less interested in the trials of rock stars than in the tensions of relationships and the exploitation of youth culture. To get away from his own rock world pressures, Vedder has largely stayed out of the spotlight for nearly seven months, during which he married his long time girlfriend, writer Beth Liebling. Some songs from *Vitalogy* seem to speak directly to the listener, where others take the role of a character.

'There are songs like "Better Man", where you create a fictional character the way James Taylor does in, say, "Mill Worker", and writing within the framework of someone else's head. That's really fulfilling because you feel like you're writing a story. Then there are other songs, like "Not For You", where there's no doubt about where it's coming from. It's straight from inside you, it is therapeutic.'

'Not For You' seems a pivotal song on the album. What about the line 'all that's sacred comes from youth'?

'I believe that is true, that there is something sacred about youth, and the song is about how youth is being sold and exploited. I think I felt like I had become part of that too. Maybe that's why sometimes I have a hard time with the television end of music and the media and magazines. When I pick up a magazine, I just count how many pages of ads before the first article starts. You go one, two . . . up to fifteen to twenty or more! And then, in the back, you have phone-sex ads. So I've pretty much had it. I don't want to be the travelling medicine show where we go out and do the song and dance and someone else drops the back of the wagon and starts selling crap. I don't want to use our music to sell anything, whether it's us or anyone else.'

Isn't 'Not For You' also directed at the music industry in general?

'There are a lot of middlemen, somewhere between the band and the audience. I know you need some people to help create a live show – and I'm not saying I don't appreciate these people – but in the last ten or fifteen years, there have been a lot of changes in music and somehow the percentages charged by the concert industry got out of hand. We don't want to be part of all the marketing tools or whatever, but believe me, we have been. That happened on the first album and that's probably even why we are where we are now, but it was hell, and I feel awful about it and I'm not going to do it anymore.'

On 'Nothingman', Vedder writes about a troubled relationship. Was that written before or after marriage?

'I wrote it before. I might bring something I know from the relationship to "Nothingman", but I'm thinking about someone else going through it, someone who fucked up. I didn't fuck up. The idea is about if you love someone and they love you, don't fuck up 'cause you are left with less than nothing. Relationships can be tough. There are times . . . I end up putting a lot of time into the music thing. I don't sleep at night; I think I'm probably a very difficult person to deal with. Things never seem to settle down and be normal and I think Beth has to deal with a lot. I don't want to get into our personal relationship, but at times there is tension. We are all selfish at heart, I guess. But I just know that without her, I'd be a kite without a string: a nothing man.'

Is 'Corduroy' also about a relationship?

'It is about a relationship, but not between two people. It's more one person's relationship with a million people. In fact, that song's almost a little too obvious for me. That's why instead of a lyric sheet we put in an X-ray of my teeth from last January and they are all in very bad shape, which was analogous to the rest of my head at the time.'

When people hear some of these songs, they probably think you sit in a dark room all day. Aren't there good days?

'Sure, I have good days. I had a good time last night. [US band] The Frogs were here and we were up until five in the morning. Everyone had wigs and masks on and we were all switching instruments. That kind of stuff is fun. I also feel good about the way our music is going.'

So there are good times?

'There are always good times. I've heard Krist and Dave – I hope they don't mind me repeating this – but I've heard them tell a number of people about all the happy times he had.'

Kurt?

'Right. I am sure that there were moments when he was happy, that everything wasn't depressing in his life. But it just seems like the negative somehow sticks with us, where the good seems to just kind of bounce off. You feel it for a second and then it's gone. I was trying to analyse it myself the other day. I should learn how to deal with it. Some day I will. It's just that music was the thing that always helped me and now a lot of the problems seem tied to the music. That's why it turns your world upside down. You feel like you want to protect the music and yourself and there are a lot of things that attack both.'

December 1994. Original text: Robert Hilburn.

REM

Michael Stipe goes for the jugular

In 1995, after a six-year hiatus from touring, REM had set their sights high: a world tour, new songs not on the latest record, a verbose front man. And Australia was to be the place where it all started, specifically Perth. It might say something about the band at the time that they chose one of the world's most isolated cities in which to return to performance. But the show itself was anything but low-key. This was REM rediscovering their mission as a rock band, a mission they have lost and regained a few times in the years since. It's interesting to note Stipe's attempts to shatter his esoteric air of mystery, but fifteen years later his enigma remains intact, despite liberal use of the word 'boner'.

Along the main drag of Hay Street, a special vibe is tangible. The people of Perth seem to be honoured that their city has been chosen. In one sweep around the mall, three different REM songs waft out of the stores. A rumoured 180 media people have gathered to cover the Big Event. Perhaps puzzled by the fuss, the individual members of REM would argue that theirs is simply a rock group. But the fact is that REM are much greater than self-image; the band are revered and respected by millions. And now they are here in Perth.

Prior to REM's first proper live performance in more than five years, Michael Stipe seems remarkably cool. His mood is one of excitement rather than dread. The thrill of touring, it seems, is still there for him and the pull of the stage is growing stronger and stronger.

On 1989's *Green* tour, Stipe tore his way across stages, writhing and jumping like a man possessed. At the time, he was the world leader pretend. But repeating the glory of the past is beneath REM; their world is one of constant evolution, not only in their music, but also in the live arena. When asked about the changes that would eventuate with a new show, Stipe's reply indicates that he wants to keep things as loose and as vibrant as possible.

'You know what,' he smirks, 'we haven't done it yet, so I can't really tell you. It's kind of a new thing for me. It's been five years since we last toured, so I've got no idea what it's going to be like. My plan for the full tour is just to stay in key, and try and keep the pitch right.'

REM's tour begins on Friday the thirteenth, though superstition doesn't unnerve Stipe in the slightest.

'Isn't that great?' he beams. 'It's good luck, actually. My grandfather was born on Friday the thirteenth and of course if he hadn't been born . . .' With a shrug, he trails off. Again you get the sense that, for guy about to embark on a world tour, Stipe comes across as ridiculously casual. Does he even remember life on the road and the rigours of a touring lifestyle?

'No, I mean, I've been travelling since the last tour a lot,' he replies, consciously separating the travel from performance. 'But I tend to go somewhere and stay there more than a day. I don't really remember. I did it for ten years of my adult life, so I think it should be cool. I'm just really excited to be doing it.'

In the pre-tour rehearsals, Stipe acquired a taste for good old-fashioned rockin': something he describes with great relish.

'They were pretty rowdy,' he laughs. 'We rehearsed in New York for a while, and we rehearsed in Atlanta for a while, and then Ireland. They were just a blast.'

Stipe gleefully relates the process of picking up some of their more relaxed-paced numbers from *Out of Time* and *Automatic for the People*.

'The only song that I know that is really working is "Try Not to Breathe" and that's just got this guitar on it that is really fucked up. I really like that song. Having never performed these songs before, it's like visiting an old room where you used to live ten years later. Now you don't live there anymore and the furniture is different. So it's kind of cool to do these songs now, particularly some of the stuff of *Automatic*. It's good to change it.'

In something of a pre-tour gesture of support, Stipe was the recipient of a goodwill message from one of his heroines, Patti Smith.

'Yeah, you know, I've blindly stolen from her for the last fifteen years,' he laughs. 'She wrote me a note that I got at the airport in Los Angeles just before we left. She was just saying she hopes we have a good tour and thanked me for all the nice things I've said about her. I was a walking boner for about eight hours. I mean, I really think she is one of the premier artists of my lifetime.'

While we're on the subject of boners, Stipe was recently quoted as saying that infiltrating the consciousness of his audience through his lyrics is 'the supreme boner'.

'It really is,' he says of his desire to deliver something personal to his audience, 'and it's not like it takes a lot of intelligence to learn how to articulate your thoughts to people. There's a little more than just clever word play involved.'

Certainly when it comes to conveying emotions, REM can take many cakes. With them, there is no deception. Even when you can't quite put your finger on exactly where Stipe is coming from, you inevitably arrive at a conclusion using the song's mood as a guide. It's open and honest, isn't it?

'Yeah, I think so. I don't have the typical American male hang-up of not being able to show my emotions. I just kind of go for the jugular. I despise that whole false emotionality that you find in Steven Spielberg movies. You can either hate it for what it is or you can decide to go along with it and allow yourself to be manipulated emotionally. That's okay. It's like jacking off. But I hope I'm not adding to all that. I hope I'm sidestepping that whole thing somehow. Somebody told me recently the first time they heard "You Are the Everything", they were lying back in the back of a car, looking at the stars. That was the most powerful thing to hear, especially when it comes from some Hispanic guy who just stopped me in a restaurant.'

A primary concern on REM's new album, *Monster*, is Stipe's assessment and condemnation of popular culture and consumerism. On 'King of Comedy', Stipe targets the corporate and wider society, but Stipe accepts that his observations on the industry now come from within. Despite its refrain ('I'm not commodity'), the song gives every indication that REM is mildly involved in the very system they rail against.

'Mildly?!' he says incredulously. 'We're smack bang in the middle of it! I'm just looking at the kinds of conditions we're living in and looking at myself and seeing where I can fit in. With something like "King of Comedy", it's a very cynical view of things commercial.'

Elsewhere on the record, Stipe dissects the mass media and especially clueless figures who bandy about brand names like 'Generation X' to describe youth culture.

'Yeah, "What's the Frequency Kenneth?" is more about media, rather than consumerism,' explains Stipe. 'Well, in a way it's like the buying and selling of a generation. Once again, I'm smack in the middle of it. I can't escape it.'

Tied in with this is REM's tendency towards political activism, but Stipe is exceedingly reluctant to wear the 'Voice of a Generation' tag.

'I don't like the position we are forced into, whether it's me or Kurt Cobain or whoever. Not only is it hard for the person and their band, but it's unfair to everyone else. I mean there are millions upon millions of black and Hispanic people in the United States who have never heard a Pearl Jam song. And the media expect Eddie Vedder to represent them?'

January 1995. Original text: Bob Gordon.

TISM

Oh Christ, a TISM interview

The title of this piece would seem to say it all. TISM (the shorter moniker for This Is Serious Mum) were a regular scourge of the music street press throughout the nineties. Much of this reputation stems from the band's standard interview technique of the time. It can be summarised like this: you fax them a list of questions and they fax back whatever the hell they like. Typical TISM interviews of the period dispense with the famously anonymous band members entirely in favour of hastily invented scenes with a cast of thousands: loopy right-wing propaganda from Oprah Winfrey, lewd humour from Michael Stipe, and deathly silences from Kurt Cobain (pun well and truly intended).

Away from the chaos and outrage, this 1995 interview stands out for the fact that it was conducted by phone, offering the briefest of insights into the satirical minds behind Australia's proudly low-brow and much more humorous response to the Residents. How wonderful that – for however fleeting the moment – it seemed appropriate to take the title 'Monsters of Rock' away from some crummy English festival in a castle and place it at the feet of a band who never saw themselves as anything more than a bunch of shit-stirrers.

I remember when I was a wee boy. Kiss were the biggest band in the world and Buck's Fizz weren't far behind. The mind boggles. The world watched with bated breath as it appeared that Richie Cunningham might actually be about to have a significant encounter with a member of the opposite sex in *Happy Days*. TISM were not even a glint in the sardonic eye of the unknown teenagers who now comprise the band, if indeed 'band' is the right word to describe what they would become.

Move to the present day. The wee boy is now a hack journalist. The unknown teenagers are still unknown, yet they – and only they – can truly claim the title 'Monsters of Rock' (Castle Donington be fucked). And meanwhile, Kiss continue to tour, sadly now without make-up.

Like any journalist on the scent of a good story, I threw facts and verifiable truth to the wind and rammed my point home. Was TISM's forcibly maintained anonymity analogous to that of Kiss's infamous mask in the late seventies? In short, are Melbourne's masked men of mayhem copping an act from the made-up rockers from New York City?

'I think there are probably more parallels between TISM and rock bands like Evian or Moving Pictures,' explains the band's Humphrey B Flaubert. 'Mediocre adult-oriented rock is what we do. It's just that we're so bad, the music comes out sounding alternative.'

TISM's orator extraordinaire, Ron Hitler-Barassi, continues:

'Oh, Kiss? They've gone right up the parabola, haven't they? Everyone used to slag off Kiss: Kiss are uncool, Kiss are no good. But now they're coming out the other end of the tunnel, aren't they? Kiss are almost cool again in a kitschy sort of way. We started off a little bit cool. We had about two weeks of being cool. What we find interesting about going interstate is that some people still think we're cool. You know, here you get the film directors and the cappuccino drinkers and the inner city *avant-garde* coming out to see us, but in Melbourne they wouldn't wipe their arse with us.'

So will TISM at some stage unmask themselves, *à la* that certain other disguised rock band we could name?

'I don't really know why Kiss unmasked,' says Humph. 'They turned out to be sort of hairy Italo-Americans with the carpeted chests and so forth. I think the single notable factor if we were to unmask would be the unnoticeableness of it all. We wouldn't really gain or lose anything. Well, put it this way: if you had a festering sore under a Band-Aid on your foot, you wouldn't show everybody, would you?'

'The thing I wonder about Kiss is,' says Hitler-Barassi, 'what if they haven't taken their masks off at all? I have this theory that for the first ten years of their career we were seeing their real selves and now they've just put on Italo-American masks.'

In a rare reversal of fortune, TISM are conducting this interview by telephone. The electric telephone is an impersonal medium at the best of times, yet in the case of TISM, it is a remarkably intimate forum. As an anonymity-preserving device, they normally respond only to faxed interviews, receiving a set of questions and butchering the answers as they see fit. The telephone, however, allows a modicum of focus to be maintained.

From where does the well of TISM's inspiration spring?

'Self-disgust,' says Hitler-Barassi. 'Inspiration is, I think, too grand a word. I think it's more grinding formularised schoolboy humour, poorly, ill-conceived witticisms, and trashy, repetitive, unimaginative drum rhythms. I think the word "inspiration" should be applied to bands like 1927 or Moving Pictures or . . . yes, even Kiss.'

And what of your current shows? What can we expect?

'We'd like to think our live shows are the same sort of facile, one-dimensional pop they've always been,' says Humph. 'Gimmick-ridden, shoddy, a lack of musicianship, trying to divert the audience's attention from our worthlessness. Just the same sort of shit we've been peddling for nearly ten years.'

In that nearly ten years, how many of TISM's initial ideas and visions have been realised?

'Surely none,' says Hitler-Barassi. 'We tried at the start to satirise things and have a satiric and intelligent and literary view of rock music. We were sort of inside it looking and laughing at it. But it didn't work in any way. No one got the joke, no one understood. People just slagged us off. Now we realise we were just uppity schoolboys in an adult world. And once we got to the

Year Twelve of Rock we bombed out. We bombed out because we were seduced by it. We started off thinking rock music was nothing but a wank, but now it's the best thing in our obscenely middle-class and pathetic lives.'

'Mind you,' adds Humph, 'we did get to meet Courtney Love. She told us we weren't allowed to walk in certain areas at the Big Day Out. That's always a beautiful experience. You see, being TISM, we never get told: "Yes, you may walk here," because no one ever recognises us. It's the best thing we ever did. It's fundamental to maintaining our sanity.'

You had the honesty to admit that the second record of *Great Trucking Songs of the Renaissance* wasn't as good as the first. What would you say to those who say that your most recent records are not as good as your early ones?

'Fantastic dead-on perceptiveness there,' says Humph. 'I was just about to say that the second record of *Renaissance* was better than *Hot Dogma*, and so on.'

'That's another thing Courtney told us at the Big Day Out,' adds Ron.

February 1995. Original text: Simon McKenzie.

The Flaming Lips

Beverly Hills 90210 might use jelly

Describing the music of the Flaming Lips poses a challenge for the most seasoned rock scribe, and Oklahoma's finest have inspired reams of 'experimental punk rock' and 'spacey neo-psychedelia'. The band hardly help with rococo song titles like 'Yeah I Know It's a Drag . . . But Wastin' Pigs Is Still Radical'. At the time of this interview, the band's first (and pretty much only) hit single, 'She Don't Use Jelly', was still filling airwaves and bad teen soap operas. With twelve years already under their belt, the Flaming Lips were about to find themselves financially and artistically secure enough to begin *really* experimenting with sounds and concepts, almost killing their fledgling commercial prospects with a four-disc box set where all four discs were designed to be played simultaneously.

It wasn't until the end of the decade that the Flaming Lips settled back into their current position as lovable eccentrics with a worldwide following and a reputation for enough over-the-top live theatrics.

The almost absurdly catchy song 'She Don't Use Jelly' has made the Flaming Lips an overnight sensation and rightly so. It's a song you just can't help but love. Far from an overnight success story for a young band from Oklahoma City, the Flaming Lips have in fact been plying their mercurial trade for well over a decade and have released six great records, many with songs better than 'She Don't Use Jelly' (if not as absurdly catchy). All that has changed is the Flaming Lips' sudden popularity, enough to secure them a guest appearance on *Beverly Hills 90210* and play live on *Letterman*.

Wait a minute. Excuse me? *Beverly Hills 90210*?

'Um . . . ah . . . I don't know how that came about,' says guitarist Ronald Jones. 'They needed a band and I think we were in the right spot. We played at some club they have in the show called the Peach Pit or something and we lip-synced to "She Don't Use Jelly". We were there at like ten in the morning although we didn't really need to be there until like twelve hours later. Still, I got to sit in a trailer and eat all day; that was fun. I don't know, I don't think too much of that one. The *Letterman Show* was real fun, though. For years and years, that show has kind of *been* American pop culture. My grandma watches it. I watched it when I was younger. None of us thought we'd ever end up on that show.'

Indeed not. From the first, eponymous EP in 1985 through seminal classic LPs like *Oh My Gawd!!!*, *In a Priest Driven Ambulance* and *Hit to Death in the Future Head*, obscurity seems to have beckoned somewhat enticingly to the Flaming Lips. Even the current album, *Transmissions from the Satellite Heart*, has been out for nearly two years, doing very little until 'She Don't Use Jelly' caught on like a fire in a heat bead factory.

'For the last four or five months that song's been kind of popular over here, but for a good year and a half or whatever, nothing like that was happening. We're working on another record now, but I've been alerted to the fact through previous people I've talked to today that the record only just came out there. Am I mistaken?'

It's been out a month or so.

'Wow. I was not aware of that. That record will be out two years here at the end of this June, so that's why we're recording. I thought the record had already been out in Australia. Maybe it was and it sold, like, ten copies or something. Maybe they've re-released it or released it officially. Anyway, we've been on the road almost non-stop here, doing what we do. And all that stuff that happened with "She Don't Use Jelly". I mean, it's nice that people finally get to hear it, but as far as why the song is suddenly everywhere . . . I don't know. I can't explain.'

As mystifying as it is to the Flaming Lips, you get the feeling that a hit record won't change much within the band. The two original members – guitarist and vocalist Wayne Coyne and bassist Michael Ivins – teamed with Jones and drummer Steven Drozd in 1992 to form their current incarnation. The mystery of the Flaming Lips' music – marrying sonic meltdowns to infectious melodies you can't quite eject from your mind – is not that they have found success, but rather that success has eluded them for so long.

It's not as though they haven't worked hard for it or anything.

'Me and Steven joined the band before the *Hit to Death* record was out. Because it took nine months to come out, we were already in the band and on the road. We made *Transmissions* while we were on the road and then, once it was out, we took it out on the road some more. That's what our life is like.'

Do you get sick of the constant touring?

'Oh, you know. It comes and it goes. Playing is fun, but sometimes endless travelling can wear you down. But for that one hour you're on stage and playing, that's amazing. It's the other twenty-three hours spent preparing . . . I don't know what to do about that.'

March 1995. Original text: Simon McKenzie.

Dinosaur Jr

No role model

After rising to fame as underground darlings during the eighties, Dinosaur Jr had become, by the turn of the decade, essentially a J Mascis solo project. The singer played most of the instruments himself in the studio and adopted a rhythm section for touring purposes. Strangely, this period coincided with the band's breakthrough to major label backing and exposure to broader audiences internationally. This interview took place following the release of their sixth studio album, *Without a Sound*, one of the most commercially successful albums of the band's career, though one that Mascis found difficult to write and record, overshadowed by his father's death around the same time.

You'd swear someone as lethargic as J Mascis would be happiest back in the sleepy Massachusetts college town of Amherst where he grew up. A place where time stands still, it's full of freaks and no one pressures if you want to smoke pot, drink Budweiser, listen to music or watch cable television all day. But since 1987, J has been living in New York. Mind you, J's corner of the city that never sleeps is a quiet, leafy area called Evelyn, near East Village, a neighbourhood full of retirees. Presumably many locals are a little hard of hearing, because no one has ever complained about the volume of Zeppelin, Sabbath and Purple records coming from his apartment.

'I don't go out . . . or I go out only at night,' Mascis drawls. 'The pace slows down a little then. Not much, though.'

So how true is the sleepy persona?

'I don't talk fast and I kind of think before I talk, so people think I'm stoned all the time. But, y'know, we've made a lot of records and we've done a lot of tours. I've produced a lot of records for other people or appeared on them. I couldn't have done all that if I really was just a couch potato.'

Those who know Mascis well will tell you he's right into competitive sports, particularly hockey, table tennis and video games. Since the age of twelve, J has suffered from migraines. Three times a year, he says, he suffers incredible pain in his eye. When it goes, he spends the next few days vomiting. As a result, he doesn't drink alcohol. His only drug of choice is Fiornal, a prescribed migraine suppressant.

J's band, Dinosaur Jr, are widely regarded as the first to take US hardcore and broaden it, with J taking inspiration from his older brother's Gram Parsons and Buffalo Springfield records. Says Thurston Moore: 'He is an incredibly gifted musician, more so than anyone else I know. He's a modern McCartney; he'll always be an influence. He has the most perfect understanding of music theory and logic of anyone I've ever met.'

Mascis never recovered from a skiing accident when he was ten. He broke both legs and stayed in his bedroom, listening to music endlessly. It made him a true social misfit. At school, he only spoke to the potheads and freaks who thought his attaching plastic animals to his clothes was cool and who understood when he told them all he wanted to do in life was to make a record. The rest of the school hated him with a vengeance.

The last time I spoke to Mascis (1990), he'd just rolled his station wagon on the way to a skiing holiday in Connecticut – he's a maniac driver – and been inspired to turn the experience into a song. The English twelve-inch version of 'Wagon' included an acoustic version of David Bowie's 'Quicksand' because that's what he was listening to on the radio when he crashed.

Does he see writing as a therapy?

'Gee man, that's hard to say.'

What was the massive force that took him from being a fan in the audience to a guy up on stage?

'It was some sort of attitude. It came from seeing people do nine-to-five jobs they hated, watching their lives getting slowly sucked away. I remember the first punk show I saw, it was an English band called 999, and it changed me forever. The bassist couldn't even play, he just jumped up and down. But he had an attitude. That was something the kids who were into music understood intuitively.'

Is there a specific event that inspired Mascis to sing about feeling the pain of the whole world, then nothing?

'Uh, no. I was just hanging out with a friend and we came up with the lines, I don't think they mean anything in particular . . . y'know, like, it's humour, but I don't think it means anything further. The records don't say a lot about me. Maybe they make a statement about where I was at when I made them. But the songs are not autobiographical. Not all of them, no.'

Dinosaur Jr's sixth album, *Without a Sound*, has seen Mascis embark on a round of touring with Mike Johnson on bass and drummer George Berz, the latter enlisted because he shared J's love for Deep Purple and Black Sabbath.

But music won't be the only thing on J Mascis's mind when he arrives in Australia. He plans to devote plenty of time to checking out the local golf courses. So what's his handicap?

'Thirty. I've been playing since I was a kid. I won a trophy when I was nine. I've still got it at home. My mom and my grandmother played.'

Spin magazine recently labelled Mascis 'God'. Was he flattered or horrified by the veneration?

'I wanted to barf. I tried to see the humour in it. People talk about this being the record that's going to break Dinosaur Jr, but I don't see it like that. We've always gone about it the wrong way if we wanted to make it big. Since I was a kid, I've always put up a wall around me. I didn't need to be liked then and I don't need to be liked now. If anyone sees me as a role model, I think it's sad.'

March 1995. Original text: Christie Eliezer.

Lou Reed

'Pablo Picasso was never called . . .'

Lou Reed doesn't care what you think of him. To do so would deny an essential ingredient of his Reed-ness. After all, this is the man whose now infamous encounter with gonzo rock journalist Lester Bangs was documented in an article titled 'Let Us Now Praise Famous Death Dwarves, or How I Slugged It out with Lou Reed and Stayed Awake'. A personal favourite comes from a 2008 interview with *New York Magazine* where Reed abruptly hangs up on the journalist, but not before calling him a 'fucking piece of shit'. The film director Wim Wenders claims to have seen Reed smile. Once.

Here we are treated to a generous helping of classic Lou crankiness, interrupted only by his sudden interest in this wild thing they're calling the 'Internet'. He uses 'electronic mail'! So enthusiastic is Reed for the technology, he's even setting up his own slice of technical jiggery-pokery called a 'World Wide Web site'.

While more often than not he makes inspired music, it's hard to consider Lou Reed a *likeable* character. A recent biographer, Victor Bockris, is on record saying, 'Lou Reed is an arsehole.'

Reed may also be one of the most gifted and erratically brilliant songwriters and rock and roll performers of the last thirty years, but the fact remains that, more often than not, he's an obnoxious, arrogant, self-obsessed piece of nastiness. Even Reed himself agrees, having once said:

'I've probably had more of a chance to make an asshole of myself than most people and I realise that. But then not everybody gets a chance to live out their nightmares for the vicarious pleasure of the public.'

The years have certainly not mellowed Reed or his ambitions one bit. A few minutes after I spoke with him, Reed mumbled and insulted his way through a phone interview conducted by an intelligent woman from Triple J. Towards the end, he sarcastically taunted, 'Why don't you ask me something like whether I'm looking forward to coming to Australia again?'

Told that this was a fairly uninteresting question, Reed hung up. Still, while his legendary intolerance remains, Reed shows absolutely no signs of slowing down his creative output either. Since his last studio album, *Magic and Loss*, he has contributed tracks to tribute albums for his friends Victoria Williams and the late Doc Pomus. He's re-recorded 'September Song' for a Kurt Weill documentary, and 'Egg Cream' for novelist Paul Auster's film *Blue in the Face*.

Reed also sang and played guitar on *Bright Red*, the current album for Laurie Anderson who's been his constant companion since the break-up of his marriage to Sylvia Morales. There's been collaboration with the Smithereens and appearances at a variety of shows, including the concert celebrating the thirtieth anniversary of Bob Dylan's association with Columbia Records.

Reed has published a book-length collection of lyrics and other writings, *Between Thought and Expression*, along with a three-CD retrospective box set covering his years with RCA Records. There have also been two recent biographies: Victor Bockris's scurrilous (and probably accurate) examination of Reed's life and a more fawning effort, *Waiting for the Man*, from English poet Jeremy Reed.

Acknowledging his achievements, the French Government awarded Reed with the rank of Chevalier in the Order of Arts and Letters. Oh yes, and there was that minor reunion tour with the Velvet Underground that may have ended in bitter acrimony, but resulted in a rather excellent live double album.

With all that activity and an income that's still supposedly over one million US dollars a year, it might be reasonable to assume that Reed would be fairly happy with his lot. If he is, he doesn't show it in the opening moments of our conversation. He sits in the offices of his management company, Sister Ray, in New York, and even though I'm on the phone on the other side of the world, he's intimidating.

Things start badly. Informed that one of his heroes, Vaclav Havel, President of the Czech Republic, was recently in Australia, there's a lengthy silence before Reed drawls in that unmistakeable Brooklyn accent, 'No kidding.'

Asked whether he's kept up communication with Havel since the two met some years ago, Reed says, 'Oh sure.'

The next few minutes continue in desultory fashion. Yes, he's about to do a new album. Yes, Hal Willner will be producing it. No, it's not the much-rumoured album of interpretations of other people's songs. Yes, he liked Willner's collaborations with 'Beat' writers Allen Ginsberg and William S Burroughs, along with his multi-artist tributes to Thelonious Monk and Kurt Weill. No, he never reads the books written about him. Yes, Bockris did attempt to elicit his involvement in the biography.

'Usually the vermin approach me, but they don't get the secretary.'

Mention of the Internet sparks a little more enthusiasm. Reed is rumoured to have posted messages to computer bulletin boards and news groups devoted to both his solo career and the Velvet Underground. While he won't be drawn on whether the messages were posted by the real Reed or an impostor, he does admit that he spends time surfing the net. He keeps in contact with Laurie Anderson while she's on tour via electronic mail, and is planning to put up his own World Wide Web site.

'Oh, it's amazing the amount of information that's there,' Reed drawls. 'You can find out what the weather's like in China, any of the latest discoveries. You can find out anything about anything.'

Mention of Reed's contribution to shows celebrating the

songs of Bob Dylan, the Who's Pete Townshend, and singer/songwriter Victoria Williams shifts Reed's attention level to 'animated': a mood that remains for the rest of the conversation.

'Those were all great fun,' he says. 'At Bob-Fest I did this really remarkable song he wrote called "Foot of Pride". It was easy for me to pick that song to do because we'd been touring that year and I swear I must have listened to that one song every day because it made me laugh out loud every time I heard it. I think it's one of the funniest single songs ever written by anyone anywhere, one of the truly, truly, great, great, great songs.

'The other thing you've got to understand, to my right was Booker T, behind me was Duck Dunn, and to the left was Steve Cropper for Christ's sake, and of course the wonderful GE Smith. I was in heaven. I couldn't even imagine more fun.'

Certainly the backstage footage seen on the concert video of the night gives the impression that Reed was uncharacteristically nervous before going on stage.

'I must have been trying to get a sympathy vote,' Reed says, laughing out loud for the first time. 'I was backstage with Johnny Cash and George Thorogood. Johnny Cash is this big guy and I was all in black too, except that I was wearing flaming orange shoes. Johnny Cash looked at me and I looked at him. He's all in black with black boots on and he says, "Well, Lou, I love your shoes." And I said, "John, I knew you would." And then I went on stage.'

Reed is also a voracious reader and seems pretty content talking about books, admitting (much to my delight) to enjoy a lot of contemporary crime fiction. As for the much-rumoured novel from Reed, he admits only to playing around with something for a while.

'But the same thing happened again in that they started turning into songs. That's what happens when you have a short attention span.'

Reed is currently reading a collection of short stories by Ruth Rendell and William S Burroughs's *A Book of Dreams*.

'When you run out of other books, there's always Burroughs.'

These days, Reed sees the author from time to time, having first met in the late seventies under stressed circumstances. Reed had been invited to Burroughs's apartment for drinks, but arrived an hour and a half later than expected, drunk and probably drugged, clutching a bottle of Scotch. He proceeded to abuse all the other guests. Burroughs appeared to be the only person in the room not offended. He and Reed traded stories about important matters like how to shoot heroin with a safety pin, should the need arise.

'I saw Burroughs a couple of months ago,' Reed says. 'He gave me this book about paintings and guns. It was so sweet of him. We were at a party for him and he autographed the book for me, so I really treasure that.'

An inquiry about the health of Burroughs, now in his eighties, is met with the loudest laugh of our conversation.

'He's going to be ahead of us all, you know,' Reed chuckles. 'Burroughs is an example to one and all: a pretty amazing guy. Talk about being ahead of your time.'

Just as we hang up Reed tells me it was nice talking. Coming from him it's a big compliment. Maybe he's not so bad after all. Ten minutes later he's dissecting the woman at Triple J with all the sensitivity of a demented, pathological surgeon. Oh, that's right. He *is* an arsehole. An extraordinarily talented arsehole.

April 1995. Original text: Stuart Coupe.

Nine Inch Nails

Trent Reznor gets theatrical

The Downward Spiral was the defining Nine Inch Nails album. On its release in 1994, the band were six years into 'their' career. Helmed by Trent Reznor, the industrial rock outfit drew thematic comparisons, at the time, to Pink Floyd circa *The Wall*. The album, NIN's second, was recorded in a studio built by Reznor in the Los Angeles house where Roman Polanski's wife, Sharon Tate, and four of her friends were murdered by Charles Manson's 'family' in 1969. After he met Sharon Tate's sister, Reznor's interest in the 'folklore' of the house vanished. 'I went home and cried that night,' he later admitted. As MTV embraced NIN, the band were booked to play the Woodstock revival concert. Broadcast on pay-per-view in the United States it is estimated 24 million people witnessed their performance. Reznor continues to fit the mould of twenty-first century musician, never afraid to tackle new technology or to come to blows with a major corporation.

While the Nine Inch Nails clan were unpacking their belongings after their collective move to New Orleans, one of the removalists approached Trent Reznor about an item in the truck. Trent had claimed the piece of criminal history before he left Le Pig Studios, birthplace of the hypnotic purgatory of *The Downward Spiral* and the site of the Manson Family's 1969 Beverly Hills killing field.

'The moving guy said "What the fuck do you have a door for?"' a relaxed and extremely pleasant Reznor laughs quietly. 'We told him and he said, "Oh man! Does it still have the blood on it?" That was kind of a consolation prize for getting ripped off for the amount of money we ended up paying to be there.'

Money, interestingly enough, was also at the centre of NIN's stunning, dawn-of-time-like performance at Woodstock. Nine Inch Nails (and to a lesser degree the Rollins Band) were the antithesis of the spirit of the event, and mud ended up being Reznor's holy water. The set will go down in rock history as some of the finest high drama rock action since Hendrix's guitar immolation at Monterey in 1967 and Iggy Pop's walk on a sea of hands at Cincinnati in 1970. For Nine Inch Nails, Woodstock was great theatre just waiting to happen.

'They offered us a lot of money and it offset the cost of an expensive tour,' Reznor says casually, as my mind boggles at the kind of moolah he must be referring to. 'It just erased all inhibitions and all sense of . . . it was probably the most nervous I've been in as long as I can remember, for some reason. I guess it was perceived as great theatre. For me it was a pretty true moment. When I got off stage, I felt like it worked, I felt like I connected. I mean, it didn't sound worth a shit. My high was blown when I actually heard the tape the next day.'

Last year, Nine Inch Nails grabbed the world by the balls and squeezed. *The Downward Spiral* hit the number one spot in the US in its first week of release and that virtually forced the MTV machine Reznor despises so much to desperately want to be his friend. It was the ultimate act of subversion, being in the belly of the beast and being given – no, fuck that – demanding the right to raise hell within what are usually safe, secure confines. A fringe benefit of that position was Oliver Stone, himself more maverick than cog, recruiting Reznor to compile the soundtrack collage for *Natural Born Killers*. Surprisingly, Reznor didn't think the inclusion of Leonard Cohen was 'worth a shit'. The kid that was intrigued by the echoes in his mind of Pink Floyd's *The Wall* – which he reckons without exaggeration he's played three million times – has hungrily thrown himself into some sort of alienation transfer process not dissimilar to what he loved in Pink Floyd's epic of negativity.

United States metal magazine *Rip* once ran an interview I did with AC/DC's Angus Young. In it, I referred to AC/DC as being the closest thing in modern music to Muddy Waters. Some soul took exception to this and fired off a letter to the mag saying if anyone was akin to Waters today, it was Trent Reznor. Yeah, it beat me, too. But the NIN central effigy is a sort of blues and according to Courtney Love, of all people, Reznor is playing the blues from a feminine standpoint.

'I know what she's saying, I think,' he begins thoughtfully. 'The degree of vulnerability is probably what she's reading as being feminine, because on every song there's a macho man perspective. But there's something creative as well. I don't mind an observation like that at all. It's unusually flattering for her to say something like that at all. She said that same thing to me, actually. She likened that to one of the reasons she liked our music because she saw similarities with how Kurt used to write. At the time, I took it as a compliment.'

Such discussion does little to lift the shroud that surrounds the inner workings of Trent Reznor, not that he has any desire to expose himself to the world anyway.

'What the public has seen of me is an intimate part of me, but it's not the whole me. I don't really care anymore if people understand or not. I've heard enough stupid shit about myself that I don't have the energy to try and rebut it anymore. In the future, I think you'll see fewer interviews and personality profiles. Here's my music and there are my videos and concerts. That's all you get of me. That's all I really want to let you know about. I don't want to have to sit here and talk about why I lived in the Tate house. It wasn't because someone got murdered there – I mean, that was interesting, but it doesn't justify spending nine thousand dollars a month in rent. It's a great place to record because it was on the side of a mountain and it was by itself and it was quiet and it was beautiful. No, I didn't fuck Courtney Love. No, I didn't . . . whatever. That stuff gets tiring to me.'

April 1995. Original text: Murray Engleheart.

Björk

'Euergheerghurg!'

With a genre-hopping taste almost as wide as her vocal range, Björk has built a reputation for confounding expectations. Following the break-up of her band, the Sugarcubes, Björk as a solo artist found herself the subject of unexpected critical and commercial success with her album *Debut* in 1993. Since then, she has continued to experiment furiously with her music. Not content with one artistic outlet, Björk has also made an impact as an actor, including a best actress gong at Cannes in 2000 for the musical film *Dancer in the Dark*. This conversation dates from 1995, on the release of her second album, *Post*.

Björk Gudmunsdottir would have us believe that cars and other modern appliances have spent eons hiding inside a mountain, waiting for dinosaurs and humans to retire gracefully so they can take over.

It is not the least rational proposal to be found on her most recent LP, *Post*. And her delivery still makes her subject matter seem positively mundane by comparison. Cutting a long intro short, to call Björk a unique talent is to err on the side of clueless understatement. Getting a handle on Iceland's first international household name requires a fairly probing explanation. Could we start at the beginning?

'I was born,' she explains obligingly, 'with an unreasonable amount of independence. My mother remembers me, when I was seven months old, I would learn to walk. And when I sat in her lap I would not lean up against her. I would stay on my own.'

All roundly rolling rrrr's and absurd tonal shifts, Björk's weird cockney-Nordic accent emphasises the fact that you are talking to someone destined to remain an alien no matter where she goes – even Reykjavik.

'When I was a little kid in Iceland, I was called the China Girl. In Iceland, people are blond and blue-eyed and I looked very different from everyone. And they had all this gossip about how an Eskimo came in this canoe and fucked my mum. My mum was flattered that they thought she has such an adventurous past, but even a thousand years back, there is not one foreigner in my family tree. Still they kept saying, "She's so strange, that girl, she must be a foreigner." Then I go to Europe and they say, "She's so strange, this girl, she must be from Iceland."

'I've never been able to do things the way other people do them. Part of it is because I can't and part of it is because I won't. I tried sometimes to do cover versions, some of the dodgy bands I used to be in, and sing like certain singers but it's just impossible for me. For me, for two singers to sing the same is sort of like two people having the same fingerprints. It doesn't make any sense to me.'

Easy to say when you're blessed with a voice that's not easily mistaken for any other sound on the planet, let alone another singer on the pop charts. But then Björk could easily have leaned on that asset and settled for a cushier gig, musically speaking.

Instead, having disbanded indie-oddball outfit the Sugarcubes in 1992, she set her sights on the usually mutually exclusive concepts of songwriting and ambient-techno. Always allowing room for radical digressions (big band swing, for instance), Björk treats the studio like a cyber-amusement park with an eighteen-piece orchestra and a hammer dulcimer in the corner.

'Another thing that you've got to understand is for me to make *Debut* and *Post*, I had to leave Iceland,' she is keen to explain. 'I thought I was going to live there forever – I love it to pieces. I had to leave all my family, all my friends, take my little boy [Sindri] with me too, take him from all his relatives and his school, learn another language, because I was on a mission to do a record. Just because I wanted to do a record, I bring out my scissors and cut away all the things I loved. And it would be kind of pointless to go to London and do another Kylie My-nogue record. I might as well stay home. It's already been done.

'I am definitely a visitor in London. I'm an immigrant here. Don't get me wrong, I love it, but I'm just here because I feel I can add something. I'm not being big-headed. I don't think the world will collapse if I wouldn't write songs, but if my songs weren't different from all the other songs, I might as well have stayed home and worked in the fish factory.

'The minute I lose the plot and do what's already been done, it's pointless, just from a practical point of view. No, Björk, you don't have to paint that closet, because it's already been painted. I stick to my guns with that.'

The philosophy extends to how the singer treats her own material in a live context. *Post* has undergone radical road metamorphosis throughout 1995, she says, to the point where she accidentally heard the LP in a hotel lobby in 'Eeesrrrruh-elle' (possibly Israel) and decided it was 'really crap'.

'*Post* wasn't really a big step forward,' she says. 'It was more doing the same things again, better and deeper. *Debut* is quite a polite album, kind of surfacy. You know when you visit people the first time and you're not exactly talking about periods or labour or when your mother committed suicide? You're more like [positively squeaks] "hello!"; you're in your good mood.

'On *Post*, I allowed myself to go a bit further. People tend to misunderstand that, like I have gone all depressive and need help, but it's more a question of feeling more relaxed to show more sides of me and being more . . . rrrrreal about the whole thing.'

Album number three is evolving, its composer says, but it remains under tight wraps inside her head. She already knows 'the centre, its main character, the nature of it', but remains undecided about whether to take the controls herself or call, once again, on the exceptional human resources at her disposal: Nellee Hooper,

Tricky, Marius de Vries and 808 State's Graham Massey, to name a few.

'Maybe I'm a coward, I should do it all because I know I can,' she sighs. 'Then the other angle is that there are gorgeous people out there and at the end of the day, the target of humankind is not to isolate oneself, but to communicate. That is the biggest challenge for humans, I think. It's easy to live on an island on your own and put the sugar where you want it to be and your shoes where you want them to be and wake up when you want to. That's very easy, but that is not the reason we are on this planet. It's more to learn to communicate and be able to live in a two-bedroom flat with forty people without arguing for forty years.

'I really thrive on working with other people. It's not because I haven't got ninety-seven ideas myself but there's that surprise element there. Like you say "green" and they go, "no, scissors!" And I'm like "euergheerghurg!" And I think in a way that's when true magic happens, because you're caught by surprise.'

Like everything at the megastar end of the spectrum, collaboration has become more complicated for Björk in the past year. For the first time, she has found herself on the expensive end of several lawsuits stemming from tentative collaborations and sample-borrowing technicalities.

'I've been sued three times this year and I've never, ever been accused of being unfair,' she mutters. 'I've always rather been accused of giving too much. That was very awful for me. And some were people I considered my closest friends. Things go a bit bonkers when people see all this money and all this power, suddenly. But I'm learning.

'I've become more organised,' she says when asked if life on magazine covers has changed her home-town Reykjavik outlook. 'I think it shows best when I go out with my mates in Iceland. Twenty of us go out to get drunk and I'm getting everyone taxis and making sure everyone's got drinks and nobody's puking in the toilet and making sure they get to kiss the right person – even though I'm hysterically legless myself. That's a talent I've developed in the last few years but apart from that, no, I haven't really changed.'

So will Björk branch out into other superstar pursuits along the lines of her rumoured acting role in *Tank Girl*?

'They offered it to me but I'm not going to act,' she says bluntly. 'I've been offered lots of things but I'm very aware that the world is full of dentists who want to be race car drivers. I want to be singer and I am a singer. And I am still grateful. If I stand up one morning and think I can do everything just because I can sing, I think I will start losing the plot. I am humbled towards the fact that I am doing the job I want to do. It is more rare than you think.'

June 1995. Original text: Michael Dwyer.

You Am I

Pilgrim's supreme rock and roll progress

You Am I remain one of Australia's more incendiary live bands. Still a trio in the early days, the group would make various sorties to America and the UK looking for a wider audience. This piece from Simon Wooldridge captures the band working their way through the mundane rigours of touring America, which, as Charlie Watts once famously observed, involves a lot of hanging around. You Am I were the first Australian band to have consecutive albums debut at number one. This interview took place shortly after the release of their classic *Hi Fi Way*.

A romantic mind's eye would place the scene closer to trashy road movie cliché than truth: a motor inn innocuously and somewhat predictably named Tempe Travelodge, a quiet room with drawn curtains and low-rent funnies on cable, and a rock band on the run. It's stinking hot in the middle of the dull Arizona desert, and You Am I singer/guitarist Tim Rogers is celebrating his first day off in living memory by not moving an inch from his air-conditioned cocoon. For an instant, he feigns ignorance, pretending he has no idea where the band have turned up today. Then he admits . . .

'We're in Tempe, Arizona, in a little motel,' he says. 'It's pretty barren, it's 112 degrees, I guess, about the equivalent to forty-five Celsius, really hot, dry, and pretty much desert. Rusty (Russell Hopkinson, drummer) and I are spending a day in. We're not venturing outside at all; we're just kicking around and looking at ourselves in the mirror. It's okay as long as we can attach the Sega to the TV.'

Rogers, Hopkinson and bassist Andy Kent are coasting through their third trip to America, a tour preceded by a high-profile support spot with Soundgarden and a recording session with Sonic Youth guitarist Lee Ranaldo. So far, Seattle, New York and Los Angeles have been highlights. Beyond that, Rogers outlines a simple daily routine.

'We arrive in the town at about four in the afternoon, you've got about two hours 'til sound check, so you look in the Yellow Pages to see if there's a good record store and you go there. Then you play the gig, and leave straightaway. It seems just to be a blend of playing the show, getting drunk, falling asleep in the early morning and then getting back in the van. It all blends a bit.'

Between adding to their already sizeable pop-culture collections and shopping for gas-stop memorabilia, You Am I play support to the Goo Goo Dolls, pop-punk veterans from Buffalo, NY, who've had a minor US alternative radio hit with the single 'Long Way Down'. If You Am I have a tough schedule, pity the poor Dolls, who've been on the road since January, and don't expect to get back home until Christmas. You Am I are taking this tour as an opportunity to relax, compared with May's Australian tour, their first after the release of the already legendary *Hi Fi Way* album: playing short sets to uninitiated punters makes a sweet change from the pressure that followed *Hi Fi Way*. The album was universally applauded, awarded five stars in *Juice* and *Rolling Stone*, eventually debuting at number one on the mainstream charts: certainly groundbreaking for a band that were playing to fifty punters at the Hopetown pub just five years ago. It's also a welcome opportunity to see how crowds react to the songs without the hype precedent. Rogers is enjoying the change.

'We've only got thirty- to forty-minute sets, so we just pack in as much as we can of the power-pop frenzy, try to look as good as possible and show off just to each other. The sets are very different. With the last tour at home we got into things like taking three guitars on the road, having a stage guy with us and playing a twenty-song set. Now we just turn up, turn everything on and go, which is really good fun. There's so much pressure off. It'll be good to get back home because we won't feel that pressure to make the show perfect any more. We'll just keep doing what we do now, which is the same thing the band did for the first three or four years anyway.'

Aside from answering questions about young grungesters Silverchair, who are all over the US airwaves and making amazing progress in the Billboard charts (up to forty-three from fifty-five after selling 27,000 copies last week), Rogers has been busy dealing with journalists puzzled by You Am I's music and face-value image.

'We've got our stock answer, because we knew when we got over here the first question would always be who are you, and the second would be if we know Silverchair. I get asked if I'm trying to look like Paul Westerberg or if I realise I look like him. A lot of bald guys come up to me saying,' Rogers adopts his best Yankee accent, '"Oh, I remember seeing the Who at the Fillmore . . ." They just seem a bit shocked that we don't have the soft-bit-then-heavy-bit sound or that we don't have noodly guitar solos. We are pretty much just an aggressive pop band. I don't know whether there are too many other bands doing that at the moment.

'I think there's a curiosity there because we look like something lifted from a 1965 copy of *Go-Set* magazine,' says Rogers in reference to Australia's earliest rock mag, notoriously the first base for Molly Meldrum. 'Maybe there's an interest factor there: that we're not swathed in tattoos and don't all have goatees.'

Rogers has taken the opportunity to catch up with old acquaintances in America, linking up with Screaming Trees and Soundgarden members in Seattle, Ranaldo in New York, and gate-crashing a Manhattan party with REM members in attendance. Beyond that, it's business as usual for the next three weeks.

'We're just trying to make every show fun at least for ourselves, if not a supreme rock and roll experience for the audience, which is of course what happens every time we ascend the stage.'

August 1995. Original text: Simon Wooldridge.

Dirty Three

On the road with the Dirty Three

On what may have been their first trip to Brisbane, the Dirty Three played Fortitude Valley's famous Ric's Bar. Simon McKenzie was one of the few in attendance. The next day it was like the young scribe had seen the equivalent of the Beatles at the Hamburg Star-Club. A lengthy live review singing the trio's praises followed and, to this day, McKenzie is on Warren Ellis's door list anywhere in the world. This time around, we tried the rock star interviewing rock star tack and the Go-Betweens' Robert Forster did the honours.

It's been a strange year for the Dirty Three, most of it spent abroad. Having risen to national prominence with their earth-shattering brand of wildly original instrumental rock, the Three – violinist Warren Ellis, guitarist Mick Turner and drummer Jim White – have been overseas since March, playing a host of shows on both sides of the Atlantic and inexorably attracting a huge international cult following. They've played everything from honky-tonk bars in Texas to amphitheatres in Greece, including shows with everybody from John Cale to Pavement and a 140-minute live soundtrack to a silent film led by friend and occasional stage guest Nick Cave. They've stunned audiences and other musicians across the northern hemisphere and they look to be damn near unstoppable.

The major question on everyone's mind in Australia is whether Jim White has got himself a new suit. Or is he still getting around in the same one?

'Well, I'm glad you asked that, because Jim's girlfriend came over and, in New York, she insisted that he throw that old jacket out. I must say, it was a day when the heavens opened, but he's got one that's almost identical again.'

A thousand ashings of Benson and Hedges, whiskey spilt all over it?

'Yeah, there was a definite characteristic about the old one that has not been missed in the car. But, at least Jim's still pretty much dressed in the same way.'

The Dirty Three are fresh from a string of performances on the Lollapalooza tour, where they played on the second stage for seven of the dates. What's the vibe on the tour? Is it a worthwhile gig to play?

'It's sort of interesting. The second stage is pretty much the same at any of those big things. It was hot. The second stage, in a lot of cases, was a long way away from the main stage. The main stages had like all seats in front of them, which really takes away from the point of a festival, I think. But some of the shows we did were really great. Other times when we played, hardly anyone turned up. But it was an interesting thing to be involved with. I mean, the highlight for me was meeting Nancy Sinatra in Los Angeles. That was the highlight, I think, for all of us.'

I've seen the *Playboy* spread on Nancy and there's something with her mouth. Has there been some sort of plastic surgery on her face that's done something with her mouth? Do you notice that close up?

'I didn't want to ask, Robert, I was too overawed by the whole experience.'

But could you see it?

'Well, I didn't want to stare, you know. But no, she looked perfect.'

What's your frame of mind? Are you completely road burned? Have you gone crazy or are you quite sane and on top of things?

'I've been through, I think, every sort of emotion possible in the last seven months. You know, from absolute ecstatic joy, from feeling great, to feeling an absolute shell of a man. It was a bit weird at first actually coming to terms with what we were doing.

This American tour has . . . it's been getting pretty exhausting, but we're sort of pacing ourselves a bit better, I think.'

So, with the entire world at the Dirty Three's feet, will they ever feel compelled to return to their native land?

'Don't worry. We're coming back in a few months to play some shows and finish the new record, if we don't finish it earlier. After that, I guess we'll base ourselves either in America or Europe for a while. We've sort of been invited to do a tour of Europe starting in February or March next year.'

Has your success surprised you at all?

'It's absolutely stunned me.'

But you must have thought it was a possibility.

'Oh, you know, not really. I really didn't, because our first record [self-titled] had been sent out to labels and no one had replied at all. No one responded. But in one three-week tour of the States, we had both a booking agent and a label approach us. Quite a few labels, actually, so after the non-reaction at home, I was genuinely surprised. We had a lot of support from other bands too that really helped us out. Pavement and Morphine both took us on a tour with them. The Bad Seeds took us to Israel. And then there was the European tour.'

Maybe what you're doing is showing a lot of Australian bands that they've got to get off their butts and get over there and just believe in themselves.

'Well that's the bottom line, isn't it? Believing in what you're doing and just going out there and seeing what happens and not having any false illusions. I've been completely amazed at what's happened for us. But I think you sort of have to show some initiative, especially in America. The music scene here's much more of a business, you know? They have to see you've got some conviction. They ask you how committed you are to what you're doing. I mean, I don't have a house anymore – I've left all that behind – what more do you want? You have to just get out there and do it. I guess the approach we took was just to go over there and show them what you can do.'

And there in the room, are there drinks going round? Is there a sort of a party atmosphere?

'Well, there's a bit of a party vibe going on. There are some mashed potatoes going round. There are some pork ribs. A few beers. You know, we fit quite nicely into American culture.'

October 1995. Original text: Robert Forster.

Meat Loaf

I just had a Diet Coke after that soapbox speech there

To be fair to Andrew Stafford, the challenge to squash Meat Loaf's stream-of-consciousness non-sequiturs into something resembling a properly constructed sentence – let alone a logical sequence of ideas – is just too daunting to consider seriously. When faced with such a task, you do what you have to do: trim the edges to meet the word limit and get that voice out of your head as quickly as possible.

As an aside, Mr Loaf references the now-defunct American political panel television show *Crossfire*, apparently forgetting for a moment that switching between that and *Hey Hey It's Saturday* would have been nigh on impossible without a VCR and a satellite dish. But that's just the kind of nitpicking that would prompt another soapbox rant.

Dateline: Some Thursday
Interview subject: Meat Loaf
Reason: Release of new album *Welcome to the Neighbourhood*
Disclaimer: All paragraph distinctions are arbitrary devices. Read this story as you might a Monty Python sketch. Mr Loaf's answers are roughly in order, though they have been edited heavily due to space constraints.
Surgeon General's Warning: Sedation advised before reading. Sedation mandatory after listening.

Time Off: This album is with us so soon! Only two years since *Bat Out of Hell II.*

Meat Loaf: But I don't understand your question – all this stuff has absolutely no bearing or relationship to what the record actually *is*! It has no bearing or relationship to *any* of that! The fact is that the record is here and the fact is that the record is AB-SO-LUTELY BRILLIANT and there are people who say it's the best record I've ever made! And I say, wait a second! *Bat Out of Hell* is a classic record. If you compare it to an orange, it is a perfect orange, hanging on a tree just waiting for someone to come along and do something with it. And about thirty-five million people have done something with that orange. With this record *Welcome to the Neighbourhood*, if *Bat Out of Hell* is an orange, *this* is an apple! And we're waiting to see how perfect that apple is. To me, the apple's perfect. And the bottom line is the buck stops here and for this record to be a success, it's *my* choice, and this record is a success right now if it doesn't sell one copy, because when I listen to it, I go, THIS RECORD IS GREAT. How do you judge how great your work is? There's only one way to judge how great your work is and that is this way: Did I give EV-ery-THING on *every* second that I had to give to this project? *There are no seconds* that are worth throwing away. And that's how you make a great album and that's how you become successful. It's not a matter of money, it's not a matter of how many records you sell, it's none of the above. That's it. THAT IS THE MEASURE OF TRUE SUCCESS.

[*At this point, the phone is apparently put aside for a moment.*]

Time Off: Right. Ah, thanks for that. Are you still there?

Meat Loaf: Yeah! I just had a drink of Diet Coke after that soapbox speech there. I should have been on Speakers' Corner in London.

Time Off: Right. Let's change tack now.

Meat Loaf: That would be a good idea on your part. I'm eating a cookie now.

Time Off: Do you get tired of performing?

Meat Loaf: You know what? When I think I have nothing more to learn and nothing more to give and I can't stand on the stage with any performer in the world – okay – and give it in exactly the same way . . . [*more in this vein for a while*] . . . I've been reading all these editorials about the ARIAs with these people going on about *it's time to move these old guys out and let these youngsters come in*. Fine. I have no problem with that. I have absolutely zero problem with that! BUT . . . just for the sake of moving some kid in, what about the *talent* part of it? . . . [*spluttering*] . . . You know? What about TALENT? Throw away Jimmy Barnes if you want! But make sure that you're not throwing the baby out with the bathwater . . . [*he turns to his publicist*] . . . I love that phrase.

[*About a thousand words redacted at this point.*]

You think of yourself as this: GOD GAVE ME THE ABILITY TO DO WHAT I DO. That's the bottom line here, and when HE says to me – not some editor at a newspaper – when HE says to me, you've done this long enough and it's time for you to go, that's when I'll go.

Time Off: Um. Yeah. There's a certain parody . . .

Meat Loaf: I didn't say parody! I didn't use the word parody! Don't put words in my mouth! You know what? I'm sitting around here thinking how I can be funny on television. And what's wrong with being funny? Nothing! So why is it that musicians can't be funny? *Who wrote* the famous rock and roll guidebook that says musicians must take themselves FAR too seriously? They must be MOODY, they must PRETEND to be intellectual and they are NEVER! EVER!! allowed to be funny!

Time Off: Can I finish my question please?

Meat Loaf: [*To publicist*] . . . He wants to finish his question. I think I've driven him nuts. Go ahead!

Time Off: I was going to suggest that Meat Loaf is almost a parody of rock and roll excess . . .

Meat Loaf: ABSOLUTELY! But what does *Star Wars* do? How about *ET*? How about *Hey Hey It's Saturday*? You tell me, what would people rather watch? *Crossfire*, with a bunch of politicians sitting there saying how the WORLD is being RUINED? Or would they rather switch over and watch *Hey Hey It's Saturday* and be friggin' entertained?

Time Off: Well, I'll take that as a rhetorical question.

Meat Loaf: [*With great gravitas*] . . . I think – you're *right*. AND . . . there is nothing wrong – THERE IS NOTHING WRONG – with BIG PRODUCTION! There is nothing in the world . . . we've suddenly come into the nineties where it's all ANTI–show business and if you're in show business then you must be a fool. You can't perform for these people; they don't want to be entertained. Baloney! I like to do LIGHT things, because I think that's enter-TAIN-ment. I don't want all this DEEP MEANING stuff, that's not part of rock and roll! Believe me, I know EXACTLY what I'm doing. I know exactly WHY I'm doing it. I haven't been doing it for twenty-eight years not to know. IT'S NOT A GUESS.

[*Long pause*]

Time Off: Meat Loaf?

Meat Loaf: Yes, dear?

Time Off: Thank you.

Meat Loaf: YOU'RE WELCOME.

October 1995. Original text: Andrew Stafford.

Beck

The dark album

Working on the album that would become the multimillion-selling *Odelay*, Beck was still precariously positioned as a potential one-hit wonder with a song that was never designed or marketed as anything of the sort. Despite his attempt to maintain a studied slacker calm, a sense of tension runs through his responses. Beck seems to know the music business better than he lets on. And he knows his future rests not on what he's done, but what he's about to do.

'Things are just kind of riding in neutral,' says Beck. 'Just rolling.'

It's a situation that would probably come as a relief. After years in utter obscurity, Beck's career took off like a rocket in late 1993 with the release of the strange, though very catchy, single 'Loser'. Only four hundred copies were made in its original American release, but the song was subsequently requested on radio so many times that Beck soon found himself atop the Billboard charts (calculated by number of radio plays rather than sales).

The song was quickly snapped up by major label DGC along with the accompanying (and much weirder) album *Mellow Gold*. Suddenly the twenty-four-year-old found himself the subject of much acclaim and acute psychobabble (some fools suggested the songwriter's hippie folk made him a kind of slacker Bob Dylan). For a songwriter whose one hit was more a novelty than a breakthrough, it was – and still is – a vulnerable position.

Incessant touring at least provided Beck with some kind of insulation against the nonsense going on all around him.

'I don't know, you know?' he says vaguely. 'Like as the song grew more and more popular, I was just touring and writing songs and doing what I always do, so I didn't get caught up in it. It seemed like something that would come and go. The only thing that was going to stay was the music and me making it, so I guess it didn't seem like it really was hyped. I hear that a lot, that it was hyped. The single, at least in America, was number one, but it was popular 'cause people liked it. They would call into the radio station wanting to hear it. It didn't get to number one because there were ads all over every magazine saying *you must listen to this*. There was no record company behind it forcing it down people's throats. It kind of grew by itself, before I was with any record company.

'I just didn't want to get caught up in stuff that's really not that important, the stuff that's really an illusion. The media creating this thing, they're the ones that create the hype. Myself, I don't judge music on how hyped or popular it is, I don't really plug into the streams where it gets forced down your throat. Of course, some of it you can't help but hear when it comes out of every shop and car window . . .'

'Loser' was like that.

'Yeah, I guess it was. It was funny and it was definitely weird, but you know, I guess people liked it and they wanted to hear it, so . . . I know how it is when radio grabs on to some new thing and just plays it to death. I thought it would have been cool if they picked a couple of the other songs and played those too, because it would have rounded the picture out a little bit.'

Enough then, of 'Loser'. Beck is back in the studio at last, currently mixing the 'Long-Awaited Follow-Up' to *Mellow Gold*.

'This is probably the first time we've gone in to record something knowing beforehand that it would be an album and people would hear it,' Beck says. 'But in the studio I get this kind of amnesia and forget that we are making a *record*. It just becomes the action of making music and being in the moment. The more acoustic stuff tends to be written in its own time, but a lot of times, especially with *Mellow Gold*, we'd go in and I'd start improvising. Then when it was done, we'd pack it away and not listen to it for five months. And then we'd dig it up and wonder what it is. You don't even remember that you did it and that gives you a clearer view. You can come back later and look at it with fresh eyes and ears. I guess we still have some tracks like that from the last record, but I think the last record was a little more silly,' he concludes with a laugh. 'It was definitely one of those situations where we were just goofing around and it didn't really matter. This time I guess there are fewer tendencies to be all-out silly. But it's not this bogus "this is my dark album, my mature work". I don't really buy that. It's three years later and this is a totally different record.'

And in between, there's been the touring.

'It was a strange way to get back into the creative side, because we'd been touring for a year, which felt more like five years. So being in a studio and writing songs again felt almost alien because we were just exhausted. You never know how exhausting it is to be running around all over the place, barely sleeping, and playing all these shows. All the energy that goes into that, it drains you. You hear about it but it amazes me how people do it and still stay inspired. It's almost a miracle that you can stay inspired and still love it and still be creative after doing all that travel and repetition. Once I'm back to making the record, it takes me a little while to land back on ground, before I lose this feeling that I have to go somewhere any second. It's like an unconscious mechanism that turns on after you've been touring for months and months.'

December 1995. Original text: Andrew Stafford.

Beastie Boys

Bring on the dancing bears

The Beastie Boys got their start fusing rock with hip-hop, or more specifically white rap with an element of punk to create a sound somewhere between Run DMC and the Sex Pistols. You could argue that, for a time, the Beastie Boys were the world's biggest hip-hop outfit. Rick Rubin was a fan and Madonna even took them on tour. The release of *Paul's Boutique* in 1989, with its byzantine wordplays, street cred, sampling and visual homage to New York's lower east side, continued the Beasties' ascent further into hero status. *Ill Comunication* tipped them into the big time again. At the time of this interview, Mike D groans about being 'so old', but adventures in running a label and making videos worth watching were still in the future. Now, with 1995 a distant memory, the Beasties have clocked up more than twenty-five years as a working unit.

With just the slightest hint of slack-jaw, the infamous man on the end of the phone – even in the long, gaping silences that follow greedy slurps of his watermelon juice – is still the pure embodiment of all that is stylish, sardonic and white-cool. The Beastie Boys' Mike D is also comfortably well versed in the art of the unruly.

'We've been described as controversial, angry and brattish,' he muses. 'I don't know how angry we are. Controversial, probably by default, although certainly not out of any kind of premeditation, or actually, somehow more due to people's reactions to what we're doing than in our original actions. Bratty? At times, maybe, but overall I think that's an overblown impression. If it's bratty to eat a watermelon while you're doing an interview, then I must be pretty bratty.'

He may be a notorious member of obnoxious mondo stars the Beastie Boys – who have always managed to drag outrage, anger and damage reports in their wake – but Mike D is also the owner of Grand Royal, a magazine and record label, husband to film director Tamara Davis, and part owner of the X-Large clothing company that funded Kim Gordon's X-Girl label. And, on a calm New York evening, Mike D is a vessel for the philosophies, thoughts and sentiments of an outfit spawned from a jokey, hardcore New York University band in the late seventies.

Following the success of their last album, *Ill Communication*, the Beasties are back in the studio recording their next opus, which Mike vaguely describes as 'us just trying to do something different. We're kind of like taking our time, so it might be a while. We've got to see where it goes and right now it's really too premature to judge.'

The Beastie Boys break barriers with a sniff of contempt, hardcore stews of snotty punk, hip-hop pulsing with rock energy and pure unadulterated fun.

'We may not be the best band in the world, but we definitely have the best time. There are too many misconceptions to address in the time for one interview, much less than the several hours you'd need. People think we're interested in doing lots of different kinds of music and they also seem to think that one of us is individually responsible for each different thing. Well, that isn't the case.

'There are also different camps who claim we're either completely talentless or ridiculously talented. Both are off base; I think we're neither. I mean, I don't know about talentless. I listen to other people and I'm in awe of them and think wow, they're really talented, but I never put us into that category. You know, there's a lot of music we listen to that's just so inspiring. Who knows?'

On the question of what people can expect from the band's forthcoming headline festival slots, the Beastie Boys, in typical fashion, are relying on spontaneity.

'I'm not really sure what people can expect, because we haven't started rehearsing yet. It'll be like a three-ringed circus: a lot of sideshow action going on. We'll break out the dancing bears, but they will be humanely treated. They're not going to be chained or caged or anything. In fact, they'll have their own first-class seats. We'll come to Australia and see what kind of native animals are around. We'll talk to the animals in the wilderness and try to coerce them into our show,' he laughs.

Jokes aside, the Beasties have, for the last year, seen life through the windows of their travelling home. Touring endlessly for *Ill Communication* left them at times closer to the edge than Mike cares to admit.

'We couldn't do that again,' he sighs. 'I think we're too old now, anyway. Now we're so old nothing fazes us. That's one of the reasons why we want to take a while with our next record. We're really not ready to head out into the whole circus again, you know.

'It's always ongoing and changing. It would be really hard for me to ignore our age and changing influences. I know it sounds completely hokey and corny, but really it's all about growing and expressing all you're going through . . . '

The fight for your right to party continues.

December 1995. Original text: Jayne Margetts.

Jeff Buckley

Spot the New Yorker

The difficulty with a Jeff Buckley interview is – much like Kurt Cobain – the ever-present temptation to read more into the words of a man whose time would be cut short. Though the following interview from 1996 includes references to both death and swimming, its inclusion here is not an exercise in morbid trainspotting, but rather an example of a young, literate musician discussing his inspirations and connecting with a growing audience. Which only makes the tragedy of his death all the more palpable.

'When can I go into the supermarket and buy what I need with my good looks?' says Jeff Buckley, reciting one of the lines from Allen Ginsberg's famous poem 'America'.

'America, I'm putting my queer shoulder to the wheel,' I add. Here we are, one of the most impressive new singer songwriter/rock and roll performers to emerge in recent years and a middle-aged rock critic sitting in New York on a cold December day trading favourite lines from a poem written in 1956.

Like this conversation, Buckley's 1994 album, *Grace*, was certainly a record that seemed to come from another time, and, in keeping with that sense, the soft-spoken Buckley is most at ease talking about poets and writers from the past. In lyrics, attitude and appearance Buckley could almost be viewed as a beat/jazz hipster born in the wrong era.

'I read as much as I can, but not as much as I should,' he says. 'I read just about anything that grabs my interest at the time. I read biographies and I have this book by Noam Chomsky. I like reading other people's poetry.

'The one I'm reading now is *Selected Poems* by Leonard Cohen. I like to go through my Ginsberg book. I like to sample Rimbaud here and there. With poems I can usually only take one at a time. It's not like a constant reading thread through one poet. I like to have that one poem in my brain. That's what poetry is for: you carry it with you. They are meant to be memorised and you just find relevance in your everyday life to them.'

Buckley explains his favourite Ginsberg poem is 'Kaddish' ('that's especially touching') and he likes his older 'sex poems' like 'Kral Majales' ('King of May'). My mention of *Holy Soul Jelly Roll*, the four-CD set of Ginsberg reading and singing, prompts Buckley to talk about what he feels is the importance of poetry being read (or in his case sung) aloud.

'That's the thing about the Beats . . . the twentieth century actually has a line of poets who are ecstatic in the classical sense even though they're very relevant to this time,' he says. 'Their stuff is meant to be spoken and shouted out in a room because it has a certain lyrical penetration as opposed to the literal.

'I also love Kerouac. I love to peruse lyrics as well: the Dylan songbook, the Patti Smith songbook. With anybody else's writing, I just look to see where the rhythm is.'

In the same way that many of Buckley's inspirations were misunderstood, at least in their formative years, there was a similar response to *Grace*. Heralded by many Australian critics as 'the album of the year/decade', its sales weren't as spectacular as hoped. Buckley probably did better in Australia than just about any other country, thanks to a merciless flogging the album received on Triple J and other alternative radio stations. That, combined with some incendiary live shows during a short promotional tour during the middle of last year, has laid the groundwork for Buckley's return to Australia this month for a more extensive thirteen-date tour.

'I don't think that all the reviewers really dig the album at all,' Buckley says of the reaction in America. 'Still, there are nice pockets of people who like the record and that enables us to tour.

'In terms of radio here, I would get comments back from radio programmers saying "it ain't going to fly" or "not our format" right through to "too mellow", "we threw it away" or even just a flat "it sucks". Some college stations played it; however, it didn't really fit in with what else they were playing, which is usually middle-of-the road alternative rock and lots of loud rocking stuff. So they really weren't into the experience, but that's cool.'

And as for more mainstream American radio stations? If college radio didn't embrace *Grace* it was hardly likely that those stations would play it either.

'No, the songs were too long and they didn't have any hooks,' Buckley laughs. 'It's all a question of taste. I have no idea. I don't know how their minds work and if I ever do find out, I'll hang myself from the nearest tree.'

Buckley's few shows in Australia were greeted with the sort of reviews that money can't buy, and demand for tickets for the upcoming tour suggests that word of mouth has more than doubled his audience. The general feeling was that no matter how good the record is, it pales in comparison with the live experience.

Aside from the shows, the highlight of Buckley's last visit to Australia was 'checking out Bondi Beach at sunrise, which was totally special, very beautiful.'

And how does Australia's most famous stretch of beach compare with those in America?

'There's nothing to compare with the sleazy majesty of a wash of hypodermic needles and human sewage,' he laughs as I try to work out whether he's referring to Bondi or the American coastline. 'It's pretty breathtaking, but I have to say it was a lot cleaner in Australia. I tried to swim, but the water was too cold. My nuts totally contracted into my body. It was too cold, and I can't surf, but it was a really pleasant place. We went there on the off hours. Later on, when it got hot, all the naked people came and crowded the beach. You could easily spot the New Yorkers walking through, fully clothed, dressed totally in black and asking for a light for our cigarettes.'

February 1996. Original text: Stuart Coupe.

Sex Pistols

How great they art

Whenever an interview with PiL came around John Lydon would invariably be asked one question: 'Will the Sex Pistols ever re-form?' The answer was always a resounding 'No'. By the mid-nineties there had been a cooling in the various Pistols camps and the original four-piece decided to tour to prove they could both play and pocket a few shackles. Their live album, which was dubbed *Filthy Lucre* after the tour of the same name, speaks volumes. On stage the band tore it up, but tension remained in the ranks and there have been various reunions and falling-outs since, as well as Julien Temple's fine documentary *The Filth and the Fury* and a well-publicised episode where the original foursome quite rightly turned down a spot in the Rock and Roll Hall of Fame.

The Sex Pistols changed rock and roll like Jesus changed Judaism. In 1976, they shook the music world, heading an out-with-the-old in-with-the-new movement called punk.

The Pistols didn't invent punk – if you want to, you could take punk and its attitude as far back as, say, Jerry Lee Lewis, certainly as far back as the Velvet Underground. Even so, punk as we know it – in all its glorious energy and attitude – really started with the New York scene of the Ramones, Patti Smith, Talking Heads, Television and Richard Hell, around 1974. The Sex Pistols, however, became the public face of punk, and its most famous exponents. Like Nirvana and their predecessors and peers, the Sex Pistols weren't alone – it's just that they made the definitive statement of the times.

That particular statement was called *Never Mind the Bollocks, Here's the Sex Pistols*. It ranks as one of the most incredible debut albums of all time and is often near the top of anybody's lists of the greatest albums ever. The band and the record raised hell and controversy was their constant companion. In the famous song 'Anarchy in the UK', Johnny Rotten (aka John Lydon) screams 'I am an Anti-Christ'. To the outraged middle classes of England, it sounded like gospel truth.

What makes it such a great record, though, is the fact that it still sounds utterly convincing and amazingly powerful, despite the fact that Western society and rock music have altered substantially since the seventies. It's timeless music, and its passion and conviction continue to astound – and will do so for many years to come.

It would prove to be the Pistols' one and only album: the band self-destructed in an ugly morass of mismanagement and acrimony. Their legend grew over the years, distorted by those who would turn the Pistols' legacy into an industry. The posthumous celebrity of the near-useless Sid Vicious didn't help, either. The band became synonymous with self-destruction and stupidity, while Vicious's dubious instrumental abilities and the posturing of former manager Malcolm McLaren saw them labelled as a band who couldn't play.

The Pistols *could* play, though, and bloody well. In June this year, the four founding members of the Sex Pistols – John Lydon, Steve Jones, Paul Cook and Glen Matlock – played their first show together in almost twenty years. They were back for the money, they said, but there was a daring glint in their eyes. What they were back for was posterity. They wanted to set the record straight, finish the job properly and prove they can play.

'We just finished the American tour a couple of days ago in Vancouver,' drummer Paul Cook says on the line from Los Angeles. 'It was great. Brilliant.'

Cook's assessment is to be expected – the band always were arrogant and cocky. There have been glowing reports from the

British and American shows, though. Even the negative reports have merely been along the lines of 'they shouldn't have re-formed'. Nobody is actually saying that they're not playing well.

'That's right, yeah,' Cook says, with obvious satisfaction. 'I think they're a bit pissed off by that. People were getting really cynical, especially in England. The press has been great in America, really, but it was a lot more cynical in England about it. They just didn't want to say how great we really are, that's all.'

How are the band feeling on stage?

'It's been great on stage, yeah. I mean, we didn't know what to expect either, when we started. We didn't rehearse, we just jumped in and said we were going to do a jump in at the deep end and see how it goes from there. But it's been fine, no problems at all.'

There's been talk of a Sex Pistols reunion for some years. Since the late eighties, offers of huge money have been made, but until this year the band were dismissive of re-formation rumours. So what was different this time?

'I don't know, really,' Cook says, 'just the timing, I suppose. It just felt right to do it now, you know? Before, I don't think, if we'd have done it five years ago or whatever, I don't think it would have worked. It was just when everybody felt comfortable with it, really.'

The band naturally had to go back to their groundbreaking album and relearn the songs. None of the members listened to the album very often during the intervening years, so it was something of a rediscovery for them.

'We haven't played them for fifteen years or whatever so it was the first time we'd played 'em. That's another good thing about it; we're playing the songs for the first time in a long time, which is why they still sound fresh, really. It isn't as if we've been playing them to death for the last ten or fifteen years and got tired of them.'

The re-formed Pistols' first show was in Finland, a warm-up affair that saw the band leave the stage a number of times during the set. It wasn't the Pistols being snotty punks, though – it was just that they had to take shelter.

'It was just in front of like, fifteen thousand drunks, basically,' Cook laughs. 'They were a bit rowdy, throwing bottles and shit. It was alright, we just used to walk off stage every now and then, have a rest and come back on.'

Their first show back in Britain was before thirty thousand people in London's Finsbury Park. It was more of a nerve-wracking affair, not least because the show was recorded for release as the *Filthy Lucre Live* album.

'That was only the third gig in of the whole tour,' Cook recalls, 'and we had to do the biggest show we've ever done by far, playing in front of our home crowd, if you like, in London. So that one was pretty stressful, but we came through it alright, you know. The live album sounds great, but don't get it until after you've seen us. It'll give the game away.'

October 1996. Original text: Simon McKenzie.

Silverchair

No complaints from the 'Chair

Newcastle trio Silverchair got their start winning a song competition through SBS's *Nomad* program. Initially called Innocent Criminals, Silverchair took their new moniker from a CS Lewis novel. Former journalist and Sony executive John Watson took on the band's management while John O'Donnell signed the group to his Murmur label, a Sony subsidiary. Their first album, *Frogstomp*, was a hit in America and a great deal of expectation was placed on the follow-up, *Freak Show*. The band launched the album with a show for media and guests under a Big Top in Sydney. Here Simon McKenzie tackles reticent front man Daniel Johns.

Silverchair's Daniel Johns used to be a nightmare to interview. Around the time of the 'Tomorrow' single, it was hard to get much more than a sentence out of him: the combined result of shyness with simple teenage introspection. These days, the eighteen-year-old Johns is a more experienced and communicative talker – without giving too much away to strangers.

Meanwhile, Silverchair's second album, *Freak Show*, exhibits a far more profound development and maturity, both musically and lyrically. It's the work of a band starting to realise that there's a whole universe of possibilities out there, some ready to be explored by the Newcastle trio. On *Freak Show*, you'll find haunting ballads, raging thrash, Indian instruments, sonic freakouts, strings and quiet interludes: an impressive and promising willingness to experiment. There are still obvious comparisons if you want to make them, but listen to it on its own terms and you'll find it hard not to be impressed.

'I think it's just natural progression, wanting to experiment and try different stuff on different songs,' Johns explains. 'The first album, we were a bit scared to try shit, because we were a bit studio-frightened. When we got in there, we didn't really know what to do. We just turned all the amps up to ten and played – which was good for a first album, good to have a really raw, rough-sounding album. I think that's kind of perfect for a first album. It set the stage to give us a lot of room to experiment with different instruments and sounds on this album.'

Lyrically, *Freak Show* is a long way from alienation- or angst-by-numbers. It's easy to see someone questioning the tumult the band members' lives have been thrown into as a result of having to grow up in public. Like all writers, Johns looks at what he wrote when he was younger and isn't all that proud.

'A lot of the lyrics on the first album, a lot of the songs, were written at a really early age, like thirteen or fourteen,' he says, 'so we weren't happy with a lot of the songs on the first album, but we needed them to make an album's worth of songs. On this album the songs are a lot more recent, they're a lot more personal lyrics, so I'm a lot more happy with them.'

With a little more time under their belts to adjust to their status as an album-making band, Silverchair have started to produce songs at a consistent rate, without having to go back to their first songwriting efforts in order to fill a record. Now that they're getting used to the recording studio, though, they're also finding out how much time can be spent in there.

'It was an easy record to write; I don't know about an easy record to make. We experimented with a lot of different sounds and instruments, so it took a while to get things right,' says Johns. 'The first album, we took nine days to do it, which was pretty quick. This album we took four weeks, because we wanted to experiment a bit. So in some ways this was easier, but it was more time-consuming and a bit more stressful, just because you wanted everything to be right.'

One of *Freak Show*'s most positive attributes is that, despite the fact it's such a different record to their debut, *Frogstomp*, it's still recognisably Silverchair. The fact that their group identity is strong enough to show through a work of such progression bodes well for the future indeed. The fact that they're capable of such progression is also a good omen and Johns thinks it might win them some more fans, although he happily admits they may lose a few as well.

'With a lot of people who didn't actually like the first album, a lot of them like this new one,' he says. 'But we're expecting it to happen the other way as well – a lot of people who like the first album won't like this one. But I think the majority of people who like the first album will have grown with us, so they'll like this one too.'

A lot of people did like the first album, by the way: about two and a half million of them. Johns and his bandmates – drummer Ben Gillies and bassist Chris Joannou – may be living in the same place they were two years ago, but they're not really living the same life.

'Yeah, your life changes a bit,' says Johns. 'I never really went out anyway, I wasn't really a social person, but I wouldn't be able to go out as much as I used to if I wanted to. But we're not going to complain. Too many bands try and get successful and then, once they get there, just complain about it. We're not that kind of band.'

February 1997. Original text: Simon McKenzie.

Bruce Springsteen

The highway is alive tonight

Bruce Springsteen first toured Australia on the back of the *Born in the USA* hyperbole in 1985. By the time he returned in 1997, he'd disbanded the E Street Band and was travelling light with an acoustic guitar, showcasing material from his then current album, *The Ghost of Tom Joad*. Sean Sennett met Springsteen in the street a few days prior to Bruce beginning his tour and the pair spoke at length about music. When Springsteen heard the following night that Sennett wrote about music and owned an independent magazine, he invited him backstage after the show to chat further, this time with the tape recorder on. The relationship has seen Sennett continue to interview Springsteen in various locations on numerous occasions.

It's getting close to midnight. Bruce Springsteen has turned in the second of two killer Brisbane performances. On the road for a year, Bruce has literally brought *The Ghost of Tom Joad* alive to a respectful local audience.

After the show, Springsteen returned to the foot of the stage to sign autographs for the faithful. One fan had driven twelve hundred kilometres. Another had flown in from Singapore. Nobody had been disappointed.

Hearing Springsteen in 1997 is an intense experience. The songs from *Tom Joad* deal with some of life's bigger issues. But this is a Springsteen show so the audience is also treated to dollops of humour, and genuine warmth is shared between the performer and those beyond the footlights.

Sitting in the backstage area, there's a real buzz in the air. The roadies pack up the guitars and prepare to send them to Sydney for the next series of dates. I'm lucky enough to be sitting in a dressing room with Springsteen's manager, Jon Landau. The bespectacled Landau has just finished sharing a Paul Simon anecdote when Springsteen himself enters. Weary from the performance, Springsteen is obviously moved by the capacity house reaction and the potency of what transpired on stage.

'We had a real good audience,' he begins in his familiar New Jersey drawl. 'This is a nice building, it's real tight. There's a good sound here and when you have an audience like that, they make you feel safe. That's when you can really risk what you're doing. They were a really focused crowd, listening intensely. It was great; I really enjoyed it.'

The bulk of the material from Springsteen's eleventh studio album – named after the protagonist in John Steinbeck's *The Grapes of Wrath* – would be demanding for any audience. Springsteen was taken by both Steinbeck's book and John Ford's classic film adaptation. Taking its cue from the book, Springsteen's album deals with the plight of the immigrant, updating the trials of the underprivileged for modern ears. The songs themselves – and the occasional monologues between them – deal with Mexicans trying to get across the American border. Darker tales take on isolation, theft, murder, violence, drug running and deprivation of liberty. Despite the tone of the evening, Springsteen, with his unique gifts as both narrator and singer, manages to make the performance a uniquely uplifting one.

'That's what I've come to do with my stories,' he says. 'I just want the audience to take a walk in these shoes for a while and discover what it says about themselves. Basically, all my songs are about how we treat ourselves and how we treat one another. So the audience has to be willing to take that trip. It can be pretty harrowing. You're asking them to go places they may not be completely comfortable with. It's pretty dark. If you make that kind of journey, something happens. You feel like you've been somewhere. All of those images, and all that geography, somehow it's all inside you: the deserts, the mountains, even the Mexican immigrants. That's what I want to accomplish. That's what I want to try to leave with people. In some ways it brings you as much a connection to yourself as to the outside world. It brings that slightly heightened sense of experience. I hope it works.'

The last time Springsteen was in town, he had a great band behind him. With the E Streeters in tow, Bruce concocted an amazing amount of light and shade in his performance. This time, Springsteen performed the entire two-hour-plus set with an acoustic guitar as his sole prop. From that one acoustic, Springsteen can muster more venom than others can achieve with a wall of Marshall stacks. Hearing Springsteen perform 'Johnny 99' or 'Darkness on the Edge of Town' is both intense and entrancing. At times he metaphorically beats the guitar within an inch of its life. Then, on 'If I Should Fall Behind', he exerts a rare delicacy. To achieve this, Springsteen relies on a number of tuning variants.

'I've made them up as I've gone, depending on necessity,' he explains. 'There's nothing too fancy going on. I use a few tunings some people wouldn't use, but they're song specific. A lot of it is D-tuning or G-tuning. It allows me to accompany myself and to keep the colours of the evening changing musically. I'm working with limited resources, so the tunings are a way of keeping people's ears fresh.

'The new version of "Born in the USA" I'm doing is modal. It's a modal blues, connected with very eastern sounding music. In the introduction to the song, you hear Robert Johnson, and then you hear the sound of Vietnamese music. I wanted to try and mix those two things together. The combination of twelve-string and modal tuning allows you to combine that east-west feel. It creates a setting for a song about worlds colliding and what happened.'

The last time Springsteen released a purely acoustic album was 1982's *Nebraska*, recorded on a $1000 Tascam recorder at Bruce's home. During the current tour, *Nebraska* plays an important part.

Besides the title track, Bruce's current live sets are likely to include 'Johnny 99', 'Atlantic City', 'Mansion on the Hill' and 'Highway Patrolman'.

During those *Nebraska* sessions, Springsteen effectively sowed the seeds for what would become *Born in the USA*. It was this period where Bruce wrote and recorded sparse versions of the songs 'Born in the USA', 'Pink Cadillac', 'Downbound Train' and 'Darlington County'. Later the tracks were re-recorded with the band and the results resonated globally. Springsteen doubts that *The Ghost of Tom Joad* will lead to a similar juggernaut.

'That's not going to happen this time. I don't know if that will ever happen again for me. But I'm sure I'll play with the band again at some point and have fun with it. We did a couple of shows about a year ago and it was fun playing some of the old tunes. I don't know if I'd want to do it for a living right now, though.

'Occasionally, I'll go out in a club and play. Melissa Etheridge was playing some night I was in town and she came by and asked me to come over and play. So I walked right off the small stage and went directly to the arena where she was playing and I came out and sang "Pink Cadillac" with her. It was fun and I enjoyed it, but I didn't miss it.'

The acoustic storyteller is where Bruce's mind-set is currently most comfortable.

'I'd just love to continue on in this vein for another record at least. That's if I come up with the songs. I've got a nice song "Brothers under the Bridge" and another one called "Long Time Coming". I've got some things sitting around. I'll see what happens when I get home.'

Describing 'Brothers under the Bridge' as a 'nice song' is something of an understatement. Over the course of his two nights in Brisbane, much of the post-show audience chatter pegged that track as a clear highlight. The song traces the story of a young woman who finds her father, a Vietnam veteran, living in a communal environment with other vets on the edge of the desert. In the style of Tony Joe White's 'High Sheriff of Calhoun Parish',

Springsteen has the listener on the hook and then lets the image and the music slip from your grasp.

'Well,' he ponders for a second, 'it's a funny thing. I try to leave the music inconclusive. I tell a story. You enter into somebody's life-in-progress. You hear their story for a while. Then, like lives do, they go on. You go on your way and they go on theirs. That's what I try to do with most of the stories I tell. I rarely try to tie them up. Otherwise they can sound one-dimensional or phony. You want a character to end up living and breathing. If you create a character, in some fashion, they will go on past the end of the song.'

When Jon Landau was a rock critic in the early seventies, he dubbed Bruce 'the future of rock and roll'. To a certain extent he was right. In the eighties, Springsteen encapsulated the ultimate heights of the rock star myth. Various audiences over the period have anointed him as the successor to the likes of Woody Guthrie, Elvis Presley and Bob Dylan – a canon as varied and prestigious as they come. But Springsteen, to his credit, has always been Springsteen.

'You see these people as your mentors, your heroes, or your influences,' he begins with typical consideration. 'I was lucky because I got to come along and carry whatever flame I was going to be able to carry. In a certain sense, I may see connections over the course of the night to all those people and the work they've done. It couldn't exist without them. You hope some kid will come along and think "this guy was really good" and want to play the guitar. That's a thing you're trying to do.'

At the end of our chat, Springsteen hauls himself out a sunken sofa and starts to pack his travel bag.

'From here, I go home,' he smiles. 'Then I've got a couple of months where I'm going to try and record some of the material I have. Then I go to Europe for about three weeks. Then I take the summer off and hang out with the kids.'

February 1997. Original text: Sean Sennett.

Paul McCartney

It came in a vision

With the release of the Beatles' *Anthology* series, Paul McCartney took a short holiday from releasing solo records. The *Anthology* project saw the surviving Beatles and their producer, George Martin, revisit everything the band had ever committed to tape. After three years of informal chats with McCartney's London-based PR, Sean Sennett was invited to meet the artist at his Soho office to discuss his then current solo album, *Flaming Pie*. Prior to this, McCartney had never done an Australian street press interview. The album received some of the strongest reviews of McCartney's solo career.

Ensconced in his Soho Square office, Paul McCartney looks relaxed and happy. Comfortable with his past and confident about the future, McCartney is back in style. In a time where the whole world seems to be in love with everything Fab, McCartney is in vogue again. His latest calling card is *Flaming Pie*: an album written in the main while he was hanging out with George and Ringo while working on the Beatles' *Anthology* project. It was during this period that McCartney got an EMI 'memo' to cool his heels.

'I'd been officially laid off, as it were, for a couple of years,' he recalls. 'I thought, "Oh God, I don't get to do anything." Then I thought, "No, as a member of the Beatles, I get to do massive things for the next couple of years." Three double CDs later, it was a hell of a thing – twenty million sales and stuff. It was huge. When a [new] song came along, I didn't suppress it. I just kept it up my sleeve.'

Flaming Pie has a pedigree that links back to the likes of

McCartney's first solo albums from the early seventies, *McCartney* and *Ram*.

The title of the album strikes a chord with ardent Beatles enthusiasts. Thirty-odd years ago, when pressed on the dubious origins of the name 'Beatles' by the *Mersey Beat* newspaper, John Lennon replied:

'It came in a vision: a man appeared on a flaming pie and said unto them: "From this day on, you are Beatles with an A." "Thank you, Mister Man," they said, thanking him.'

'The idea for the title arrived while we were doing the *Anthology*,' explains McCartney. 'People would ask whether I had a new album coming out. When I'd say yeah, they'd ask what it's called so I always said *Flaming Pie*. Whether they were young or old, whether they knew the Beatles or not, they'd all nod and smile. I kind of like that reaction. It's a quirky little title and, for Beatles fans, there's a big story behind it.'

Flaming Pie notched a number one on the UK charts. In Australia, the album debuted last week at number six. In the United States, McCartney scored his highest first-week sales in twenty-six years.

'I don't normally count,' says McCartney – and you wonder if he's bluffing. 'It's always somebody else that counts. I don't really know how many sales the Beatles did or anything, but it's fantastic. A lot of people from England, big stars, have not been doing well in America this year. People like George Michael – who normally does very well in America – haven't made much of an impression. I wondered what was going on and whether we would do alright. The only ones making it over there are those bloody Spice Girls!' he laughs. 'One of them has just broken her ankle and [adopting a cockney accent] it wasn't me . . . I swear it wasn't me, I never touched 'er, Guv.'

If the Beatles experience had any sort of sway on *Flaming Pie*, it's that it reacquainted McCartney with the beauty of speed and simplicity. Trying to write another 'Blackbird' while Linda prepared lunch, he came up with the acoustic 'Somedays'.

'I'm from the generation that didn't really have a lot of time in the studio,' McCartney continues. 'In the old days at EMI, everyone would come in at 10:30am to 1:30pm. We'd have an hour off. You had two three-hour sessions. I remember recording "Michelle". I'd written it on acoustic guitar. Me and the guys played it through for George Martin. We had an hour just playing it. Because I'd been playing guitar, I overdubbed the bass. By the time I'd done that, George Martin said "Super, Paul" and that was it.'

The *Anthology* project, coupled with the break from recording seemed rejuvenating for McCartney. Hearing virtually everything the Beatles ever did can't have hurt either.

'I think that's so important,' he says of the 'lay off'. 'You've got to give your brain – or your body or your life or whatever – a little gap occasionally. That's what happens when you're younger: eighteen, nineteen, twenty. You've sort of finished school and there's a little time before you decide what you're going to do. You read *On the Road* by Jack Kerouac or whatever. And you're aware there's a world out there. I think a little break like that is exciting. It reminds me of a computer that will suddenly tell you you've filled up ninety-eight per cent of the thing. There's no more room. Erase some stuff. So you go ahead and erase.

Despite his own feelings and the success of 'Free As a Bird', McCartney can't offer any concrete plans for further 'reunions'.

'I don't think we will [do anything else],' he offers candidly. 'The thing is, on "Free As a Bird" we had John. John was one of the constituents to that project. If someone had just handed us a song John had written, just piano notes and some lyrics, I don't think we would have done it. It was the fact that John was *there* – in inverted commas. So I said to the other guys at the time, "Let's pretend we've nearly finished an album. We've got one more track to do and John's gone off to Spain on holiday or something."

'We could say, "Bloody hell, wouldn't you know? He's out of time." We'd have to bring him into time, because he would vary his tempo a bit. We'd say, "Oh God, he's a bit out of tune too – we'll have to fix that."

'We could talk irreverently like that because it was as if he was there in the next booth doing the vocals. I could keep hearing him in the headphones, so it was like he was there. We could record with that in mind and play off his vocal. I could sing along with it, I could answer it or whatever we needed to do.

'It would be a completely different kettle of fish if you think of just the three of us. Now there's a big hole where John is supposed to be. Okay, George and I can sing. I can play bass. It could be a neat little trio. It'd work. The trouble is for us it wouldn't. For us, we'd keep asking ourselves, "Where's John?"'

July 1997. Original text: Sean Sennett.

Henry Rollins

The world according to Hank

Henry Rollins earned his stripes as the powerful front man with Black Flag. Then there's been the Rollins Band, the books he's written, the films he's been in, the television and radio work, and the publishing company he founded. Strangely, Rollins is now almost as famous as a spoken word artist as he is for anything else. A terrific orator, Rollins is a great interviewee too. Here he recounts how he first trod the boards without the safety net of a band. After downing a virtual Amazon forest in praise of Rollins's gifts – and never turning down a publicist's request to interview the great man – we were a little miffed after running a gushing feature to hear Hank rant at a show on how he hated the media. C'mon, Hank, we're not all bad.

Henry 'Hank' Rollins is something of a paradox. He may be all muscle, bulging veins, tattoos and angst-rock on the outside, but a different engine drives within.

Henry Rollins is actually very polite, funny, amiable and intelligent. Not only is he a musician, but also an actor and a music and book publisher in his own right. Basically, he's everything you'd expect him not to be.

In many ways, the 'real' Henry Rollins has emerged via his spoken word shows, where his revealing exhortations cover some extensive ground – everything from light aeroplanes to racism. And when Henry Rollins says something, it's pretty damn convincing.

But Henry Rollins – 'spoken word artiste' – is not a new

phenomenon. He's been doing such performances – with ever increasing gusto – for nearly fifteen years.

'I started doing talking shows in '83, actually,' Rollins says down the phone line from Los Angeles. 'It wasn't my idea at all. I went to shows put on by a promoter called Harvey Kubernik. Harvey was getting guys and girls from bands to get on stage and do stuff that they don't usually do. Like if you're in a band and play guitar, this time you're going to have to read something you wrote or play harmonica. Whatever it is, you can't do something you normally do. You have to be thrown off balance to a certain extent. He was doing one of these shows every week and they were really, really comin' off well. There were a lot of people and the line-ups kept getting more interesting because people in bands would go to the venue with requests: let me do this or that. So I went one night and I thought it was great. Harvey came up to me and asked if I wanted to do something. And I said, man yeah! I didn't know what I was going to do but it looked like so much fun. So he gave me like ten or twenty minutes for the next show.

'The next week I went on stage and I told this story about being at band practice in this pretty bad neighbourhood where there's a lot of gang activity and what it was like to hang out with these Samoan gangster type guys who kind of dug our band and would hang out at like band practice. Afterwards, people wanted to know when my next show was. And I said, I don't know, I think it's just a one-off. I did some more of those shows and then ended up doing whole nights just by myself in clubs in Los Angeles. I drew pretty well and I started selling places out. I'd do this between band tours and then, by the summer of '85, I was just going out by myself.

'I was reading from things I'd written a lot in those days until, little by little, I graduated to just going up and telling stories and kind of editorialising. Now I have a set in mind – things I want to talk about and stories I want to tell. But I also leave lots of room in the set just to kind of wing it.'

Do you come up with some of your best material when you're winging it?

'No,' he laughs. 'I think I do best when I come out with six or seven good stories and just knock 'em out.'

Did you know you were capable of doing this back then?

'No, but it sure came easily. As far as anything I've ever done, it's the thing that's come the most easily to me as far as any kind of performance or writing or being in a band or something. This is the thing I just took to and felt very at home with very quickly, almost immediately, because I have no fear on stage at all. I do over a hundred shows a year – for seventeen years. There's not a whole lot that trips me out up there because I spend about a third of each year up on stage or on my way to it.

'I've been around the world twice this year already – two complete laps around the earth. And I've seen quite a few interesting things on the way; inspiration is there all the time.'

The *Won't Sleep, Won't Shut Up* spoken word tour of Australia is Henry's first here since 1992 and he's happy to be heading back after his recent band tour.

'I'm looking forward to doing the shows. I've done quite a few talking shows in Australia before and it's been great. I like it very much in Australia – it'll be my tenth trip there. I'm doing a show almost every night. I'll be there for ten days. I think I'm doing like eight shows or something.

'That's such a great place you have down there. It's clean, it's beautiful and you have lots of space for everybody. Sometimes I get so cynical, when someone tells me how the world should be I just want to scream fuck you hippie! But Australia is different. It's not the kind of place that makes you want to scream at hippies.'

Taking his inspiration from his travels around the world, everyday life and personal feelings and emotions, there's very little that doesn't crop up in a Rollins spoken word show. Henry declares that there's absolutely nothing that he won't touch. As a result, his shows are a roller-coaster of emotions. One minute you'll be laughing like a hyena and the next you'll be trying to sink into your chair out of sheer guilt.

'I think you should try to mix it up because life is a gamut of emotions,' he explains. 'It's like all the colours on the palette. So why shouldn't this tiny slice of life I'm bringing to you on the stage be the same? I just try and provide a well-balanced meal, basically. I'm sure people would like just nine hours of comedy but they're going to have to go somewhere else. I just don't want to be the one providing it.

'I think the best way to influence others is by example. When I've been influenced by others, it's by their good example. I think everyone does it and you don't have to be some guy on stage. If you do right and you're a good person, your actions will rub off on other people. It basically just makes the world a better place, you know, once inch at a time.'

Would the world be a better place if people were just good to each other?

'Yeah, if everybody had the opportunity to be good to each other,' he says. 'It's easy for a millionaire to be philanthropic and feel great about the world because he wakes up every-day and his ass is secure. But if you're waking up in a ghetto, how full of joy are you going to be? And how much do you want to listen when you watch the TV and the President says if you don't take drugs you can be anything you want to be. Say no to drugs. How does that play to the sixteen-year-old kid living in the ghetto? Can he be anything he wants if he just doesn't do drugs? So if he gets off crack, can he be the President? Being nice isn't everything. For a lot of people, being a nice person is . . . well, they'll just say fuck you and be done with it.

'In America, at least, the role of a criminal has been built into the fabric and into the guts of the machine so much, we need criminals to make the economy work. Without criminals the system would malfunction. The transmission would drop out on the highway. That's why, I think, a lot of ghettos are just like crime recruitment centres. Jails are crime schools. You go in a burglar, you come out a murderer. It's like karate. You go in a white belt, you come out a green belt, blue belt up to black belt. Before you know it, you'll be an elite criminal.

'Governments rely on people's fear to keep them in line: fear and uncertainty. How do you control millions of people unless you divide and conquer them? If you have white and black tension in America you can always make people believe whatever. You can always have bad whitey and black guy deranged: one guy mad and the other guy scared shitless and everything can just run in this nice fearsome circle where the calm cool people in the eye of the hurricane are making the money and setting the precedents. This is all entry level shit. I know you know all this shit. I'm just saying in America, at least, you watch it every day.'

Having appeared in several movies, Henry readily admits that Hollywood provides him with a lot of worthy material.

'Every movie I've ever been involved in there's been a good story in that. Actors are hilarious, man. They're probably the most fucked-up people I have met in my life. I'm not saying it's not a legitimate art, but what an intense way to go about your life. It's fun every once in a while for me but I don't see how anyone could do it as a full-time job. That just blows me away. The better an actor is, the better they are at erasing themselves into a part. What they do for a living, it just makes them . . . really intense. Their job is basically to be super-self-aware. You just meet these people with incredible idiosyncrasies. They can't switch it off. The camera is always on them.'

Despite his misgivings, though, Rollins is preparing to return to Hollywood soon.

'I've got some meetings this week for a couple of films. I'm not the biggest fan of being an actor because: a) I'm not very good and b) being an actor is pretty weird. But these two movies are in a time where I don't really have anything to do. One is in January if it comes off and I can get the job. It's a part I'd like and it's a part I think I can do. In January, there's nothing really for me to do and I don't really want any time off. Relaxing in my apartment is good for about five days and then I figure I did that, now it's time to go and get something done. So if I can get work in January or February, that'd be great. So I'm hopin' it works out.'

So you like to keep busy?

'Life's short, do shit. Hey, I should sell that to Nike!'

Yeah, they'd probably give you a couple of million for that.

'Hey, they've given it to everybody else. They given you your million yet?'

October 1997. Original text: Matt Connors.

Regurgitator

I like your old stuff better than your new stuff

Regurgitator were an almost accidental band. With all three members already in several other bands, Regurgitator remained a side project until Ben Ely submitted a demo of his primary project, Pangaea, to manager Paul Curtis. The cassette's flip side had tracks performed by Ely with Quan Yeomans and Martin Lee. The rest – as they might say – is very loud history. This interview with singer and guitarist Quan Yeomans took place shortly before the release of Regurgitator's second album, *Unit*. Though the album would ultimately provide the band's greatest success – earning triple platinum status – Yeomans here is quite understandably anxious at how such a radical departure from their previous work would be received.

Regurgitator's second album is one which will confound – and perhaps alienate – many of the so-called die hard 'Gurge fans who love nothing better than the *Hamburger* EP and similar strident thrashouts like 'FSO'. *Unit* is a record drenched in lightweight synthpop, straight out of the eighties. The band's biting humour is still there, but the serrated riffs and funky bass rhythms are far less evident.

Even for a band that can pump out bursts of metal, interspersed with Dre-styled rap, before tying it all up with a hardcore explosion at the end, *Unit* is an unexpectedly adventurous excursion.

The track '!' (or 'The Song Formerly Known As') sounds – unsurprisingly – like a lost track from Prince's mid-eighties songbook; 'World of Sleaze' kicks in with a Diesel lick before launching into an anthemic chorus of Tourettian satire; 'New Stuff' sports a sugar-coated chorus with a Laurie Anderson vocal effect whacked over the top for good measure; and 'Polyester Girl' plays on the bass groove from the Jacksons' 'Blame It on the Boogie'. Although the band still rock out on 'Everyday Formula', 'I Piss Alone' and '1234', the album heralds a real shift towards the retro. If the *Tron* influences in the video for 'Everyday Formula' aren't proof enough, go take a decko at the bad taste cover for the single, complete with scanned-in Bowie hairstyles. It's as 1982 as Pac Man and Malcolm Fraser.

Sitting in the boardroom at the Warner Music Milton offices, Quan Yeomans explains why the band have steered towards accessible pop.

'Well, you get old,' he says with a laugh. 'It just sounded refreshing after hearing so much nineties stuff for so long. It was time to do a retro album. I haven't got much to be angsty about. And metal is just so out at the moment. We thought we'd give this a go. The thing about the eighties was that people didn't care. They were willing to try anything out. They didn't really know what was hip and cool. Everything was really new. Now you have to look and be a certain way to be a star – a thousand Mariah Careys indistinguishable from one another because they're all trying to be exactly the same. In the eighties, it was everyday people. People with fucked-up hair and bad clothing sense. It was really cool.

'I've got eighties records at home,' Quan continues. 'Scritti Politti, *Purple Rain*, the Cars, Cyndi Lauper – that kind of thing. That kind of music was a bit of an embarrassment for people for a long time, so to speak. But I think it's now that people are starting to look at it again. They're starting to think it's not too bad. It's really quite good. A lot of good songs were written back then. And there was a heap of one hit wonders.'

It was also a time marked by a heavy dose of conservatism, courtesy of superpower conflict, the outbreak of HIV/AIDS in the Western world, economic rationalism, and the constant threat of nuclear war. Strange then that the hallmark of eighties music was over-the-top performers and fashions: gender benders like Boy George and Marilyn, androgynous New Romantics, poncy big hair metal, and deathly pale Goths. Railing against the predominant political and social orthodoxy, the decade's pop culture was curiously in-your-face. The nineties, and especially grunge rock, are ironically reactionary in comparison.

'Everyone was doing their thing,' Quan agrees. 'I think you need that certain level of oppression to get the juices flowing, if you know what I mean. At the moment, in this country at least, it's too easy for people to get up there in jeans, look at their shoelaces and play rock music. It's a bit dull. But with any luck, things will move towards entertainment on a different level. Look at Prince. There's no one in Australia doing that at all. Flamboyance is what's missing, I think. That camp thing. People are too concerned about being a man or a woman and being in between is kind of a funny thing for a lot of people.'

Unit was written and recorded over a six-week period down in Fortitude Valley at the old Constance Street practice studios. The band grabbed a load of equipment, fixed the joint up a bit and got down to the business at hand. Where their first album, *Tu-Plang*, was recorded in Bangkok in a fortnight, this time the band were determined to stay close to home and record on familiar territory.

'We didn't really want to go away with this one,' Quan says. 'We've been touring a bit and we wanted it to be a bit more homely. We used a lot of keyboards and a computer to do a lot of sequencing. It's important to use the technology that's around or you'll get left behind. Electronic music is still moving ahead. The technology is amazing. They're coming up with machines that do the most twisted things with sound. It's unheard of.

'We worked with Magoo again; it was the same situation. He's easy to work with. We know each other well. We were more focused this time. Not much jamming went on in the course of the record. One person wrote the bulk of the material and then we went in and recorded it. We knew what we wanted. I certainly did. Ben was a bit more floating, but we concreted the songs later on. We wanted to record and mix three at a time, but ended up just doing one at a time towards the end. We'd just record it, listen to it, see what it needed, then add bits and mix it. We worked at a different pace than we normally do.'

Two songs that stand out on an initial listen to the album are 'New Stuff' and 'World of Sleaze', the latter of which could well be regarded as 'I Sucked a Lot of Cock . . . (Part Two)' thanks to its delightfully offensive chorus, taking the piss in typically sardonic style. But where 'I Sucked a Lot of Cock . . .' paid out on the band themselves, 'New Stuff' gives it back to the fans who keep yelling out for more *Hamburger* material. With a chorus that sweetly chimes 'I like your old stuff better than your new stuff', you can't ignore their point about people wanting to hear the same old stuff at every gig.

'I think it was one of the reasons why Ben wrote that song,' explains Quan. 'It's a universal thing that happens to bands that change or are perceived to have changed. I think we're at a point where it's difficult for us to change without pissing off a lot of people.'

A recent all-ages gig is a case in point. Plenty of punters were shouting out for the familiar old stuff while the band playfully debuted a lot of the *Unit* set to the young Brisbane crowd. And when the band recently went down to Melbourne to add a soundtrack to the play *Raised by Wolves*, they ended up playing their usual set instead of the one-off soundtrack they'd intended to perform. Quan describes it as an embarrassing ordeal, but he puts it down to experience. In the coming months, you'll see some changes at the shows with the permanent addition of Shane Rudkin on keyboards and a shift away from the band's early songs, perhaps permanently. But while some out there in shitsville scream 'sell out' at everything post-*New*, the band refuse to be all that bothered that people might lose interest in their music.

'When you play old songs, you get bored,' he says. 'We're also at a point of evolving our live shows to the point where it'll be something completely different to what we've done before. We might find it hard to mix in the old songs. It's going to be a lot less intense, I think. We might put on some costumes and just try to enjoy ourselves.'

While the band have set dates all around the country, it looks like Quan has lost interest in the whole 'let's set America on fire' trip.

'We toured America but it was a bit ho-hum,' he admits. 'It was the first level kind of thing. People have heard of you but now we have to decide whether we want to push it, move over there for six months and do the You Am I thing. Besides, I expect *Unit* would be a little bit lame for the Americans. It might be a little too early for them to go back to the eighties.

'I'd like to tour Japan because their culture is so interesting. If you want to make a lot of money, America is the place to go but it doesn't interest me that much, culturally. We've only been to Europe once and it'd be good to go back there once the record is released and we get a bit of airplay. It would be good to go one more time, at least. But Japan? Now *that* would be really appealing.'

November 1997. Original text: Geoff Nicholson.

U2

Making music to blow their minds

By 1997, U2 were already two decades into their career. With the release of *Pop*, the band were thought to have released a commercial blip. In a São Paulo bar, drummer Larry Mullen confessed – to the record company's chagrin – the album had only sold six million copies. Rushed to meet a tour deadline, *Pop* never fully satisfied the band and, years later, they were still remixing tunes like 'Discothèque' when a compilation of the period appeared.

The subsequent *PopMart* tour was the most ambitious of U2's career, with a stage set now best remembered for hosting a giant lemon, which, in a manner befitting Spinal Tap, refused to open in Sydney and trapped the band inside.

Standing in a São Paulo soccer stadium with 85,000 Brazilians singing 'One' in unison, you'd be forgiven for thinking U2 were the biggest rock band in the world. Since the turn of the decade, U2 have pushed their music into uncharted territory. While a majority of the Live Aid stadium stars were turned into dinosaurs by grunge, U2 kept creeping forward playing tricks with traditional song structures and new technology.

The albums *Achtung Baby*, *Zooropa* and *Pop* form a remarkable trilogy. The band are currently conquering the globe with their latest tour, *PopMart*. Where *ZooTV* splattered the audience with a myriad of images and misinformation, *PopMart* hinges on a core of great pop songs, albeit set against the pure spectacle that is the world's largest TV screen. When the group first flicked

PopMart's on-switch in the Las Vegas desert last year, concerned locals in nearby towns reported fears of an alien invasion.

Visual effects include a thirty-metre golden arch and a similarly sized toothpick, topped off with a giant olive. Then there's the real masterpiece of the set design, a lemon that doubles as the world's largest disco ball.

Behind the gadgets lies a formidable body of work. Witnessing the *PopMart* experience in action, there's a rare feeling of being in the moment. Despite the artistic twist and turns U2 have taken since *The Joshua Tree*, *PopMart* provides a unique thread through the group's past and future. It is bold and obtuse, but, somehow, entirely logical.

Relaxing after the São Paulo gig in his latest Fidel Castro 'day wear', Bono puffs on a Marlboro, studies the ice in his drink and seems genuinely pleased with where *PopMart* places U2 in the current scheme of things.

'If the word pop means anything,' he says evenly, 'it means "in the moment". That's it. That's what we're about. You know, on all our records, going back to *The Joshua Tree*, we tried to capture the feeling of the time. For *The Joshua Tree*, we felt America was everywhere, so that's where we went to make that record. With *Achtung Baby* we went to Berlin. At the time, Europe was happening. It was all the chaos and confusion of the wall coming down. We thought we could plunder it. With *Pop* we thought, here we are living in a time where "ephemera" is everything. Glossy magazines are everything. The surface and fun are the order of the day.

'While enjoying the face of right now, what else is going on? There are deeper questions in the record and in the show, but at the same time we wanted *PopMart* to look totally fresh.'

At the dawn of the nineties, many were reluctant to see U2 change. Here was a band that sold twenty million copies of *The Joshua Tree* alone.

'When we arrived in our plastic pants with a bunch of television sets on *ZooTV*,' Bono continues, 'we sailed our ship against a tidal wave of American music, namely hip-hop and grunge. It was the short pants and sneakers brigade. At the time we looked out of sync, but now, looking back, a lot of bands are thinking, okay, that was a clue.

'*PopMart* feels the same to me. It's brightly coloured and bold. I do believe in it.'

To create *PopMart*'s television set, U2 rode at the forefront of LED technology. A unique series of small lights creates one giant TV. At times, you can peer right through the screen. Other times, you can't take your eyes away.

The music on *Pop*, the album, is similarly cutting edge. Where tracks like 'Staring at the Sun' and 'Last Night on Earth' could have sounded like classic U2, the band have opted instead to dress them up. 'Mofo' and 'Discothèque' see the foursome messing with beats and screwing with traditional arrangements. At the dawn of the new millennium, *Pop* seems the perfect soundtrack.

'I think there've been some very exciting developments that we caught on to,' continues the group's bassist Adam Clayton. 'Looping and the whole digital process of sound liberates you. It allows you to create a rhythmic structure that, in terms of the development of rock and roll, hasn't really happened in twenty or thirty years.

'With sequencers and computers, there is now a shitload of new rhythms that you can mess around with. Equally so, you can take little bits of melody and orchestration and lay them in under what you're doing. We've embraced that as well as more traditional forms of songwriting.'

To a man, U2 see their music as the centrepiece of the show. Clayton describes the group as 'the heart under the arch'.

'For us,' agrees the Edge, 'this show, in the end, is about music. That's what we set out to do in the very beginning. It might sound bizarre when you consider the elaborate nature of the production. When we put this show together, in our minds, the core and the heart of it would be the music and the songs themselves.'

After the excesses of *ZooTV*, many critics tipped a return to basics. A stripped-back acoustic record seemed a logical option. U2 rallied in the other direction.

'It was a bit scary,' continues the Edge. 'I think we realised we had an opportunity to do something big, again, now. The predictable, and maybe the sensible thing, would be to scale it down after *ZooTV* and get back to grassroots. We thought, well, why should we do that? That's not the real challenge. We thought we should push it even further. We knew it was a big gamble, but I guess that's where we live. We're not interested in doing the safe thing. We're interested in doing the thing that seems the most vital, the most challenging and the most inspiring. For us, that means doing things that have never been done before. That's really important. In some ways, that's the only reason to do anything. This tour is an example of that.'

PopMart takes the opportunity to fuse U2's brand of pop music with pop art. One highlight is during 'Bullet the Blue Sky'. While the band crank out the tune, the giant *PopMart* TV displays an animated bent on Roy Lichtenstein's famous fighter plane sequence.

'I'm not sure that we see ourselves as a university,' continues Clayton, 'in a way, for us, the pop art thing is just threads interlinking. We were very lucky that Lichtenstein was still alive at the start of the tour. He was very generous and didn't mind us animating his images. That hadn't been done before. And we had a very good relationship with Keith Haring's people. They allowed us to use some of his animated images. So, these are all things that kind of connect for us.'

'Apparently, if you work with U2,' ponders Bono aloud, 'you die that year. Allen Ginsberg, William S Burroughs, Roy Lichtenstein: all these fantastic people, they're all gone now. A year ago we were collaborators. It's so extraordinary. Roy Lichtenstein was the premier pop artist, next to Warhol. I'm so proud he wanted to work with us. He wanted to be part of the show. He got it.'

Bono describes U2 as a 'working band'. Twenty years into the game, U2 aren't thinking about a greatest hits–style tour. The

PopMart set features roughly nine new songs, some of which are among the finest the group have committed to tape. The rest of the set tends to feature such staples as 'I Will Follow', 'New Year's Day', 'Sunday Bloody Sunday', 'Pride (In the Name of Love)', 'Where the Streets Have No Name', 'Mysterious Ways' . . . the list could go on.

'For *PopMart*,' says Clayton, 'we wanted to use the new record as the core of the show. I think we've managed to hold on to that, even as we worked back through the catalogue. We go back as far as the first record; we wanted to show an emotional journey. On *ZooTV* we accepted that the presentation was big and bright. It was sensory overload. This time around, even though we have a huge screen and that, we wanted the songs and the emotions to be the strength. I think Bono achieves that in the way he performs. Having pushed technology to the fore, we feel we can now let the same technology support and embellish the band. We can move in and out of it as we need to.'

Hearing the mix of old and new tracks in Brazil against such a stunning visual backdrop is a moving experience. U2's early nineties 'reinvention' was, artistically, a godsend. With the broad hats and pony tails gone, creating new on-stage personas has proven crucial to the band's growth.

'I think we quite consciously, around the time of the *Achtung Baby* record, reclaimed a certain territory that up until that point we hadn't been allowed into,' explains the Edge. 'I'm talking about the more humorous and ironic side of things. Bono, in particular, felt a bit suffocated by people's concepts of who he was, and what he was about as an artist, singer and lyricist. It was important for us to reclaim the right to add humour to what we did and to be able to take the piss out of ourselves. We wanted people to go down the road with us on that, and be comfortable with the seeming contradiction of singing a song like "Bad" or "Sunday Bloody Sunday" as well as something mad like "The Fly". We're in a much more comfortable situation now where we can write something that is on a really personal and serious level and do like we did tonight and goof around with some mad cover versions thrown in the middle like "Black Betty". That would have been against the law for us ten years ago. We can do it now and people get it.

'I guess that's a very longwinded way of adopting a persona or, as Bono has, to create the freedom to move in and out of character. MacPhisto was part of that. The Fly was part of that. These characters were important little stepping stones to get into a position we're in now.'

'I think the issue of persona,' says Clayton, 'is that they each accentuate a part of yourself anyway. Rather than wear ladies underwear on stage, it's a lot more interesting if the persona is an exaggerated version of you. I'd prefer to see that than some false cartoon persona that makes you seem more interesting than you really are.'

'Somebody once said,' adds Edge, 'I think it might have been Lester Bangs, that rock and roll, by its very nature, is a created thing. There's no such thing as a rock and roll star who hasn't, in some way, created himself. I'm sure that's true of us. We come from Dublin and it's a slightly different culture there to London or New York where everyone on the street seems to have figured out a persona for him- or herself. But, despite that, I'm sure there's a natural side of the process there that we're still plugged into. My attitude is I don't really care if someone is a self-creation. I'm more interested in whether their self-creation is good or bad. Jack Nicholson certainly didn't wake up as himself. He is himself because he's decided to be that person. And he happens to be an interesting one.'

If anyone has embraced the idea of a new persona, it's Bono. In *PopMart* he's the superhero, the boxer and, essentially, himself. Like Sinatra, Bono's autobiography is in the set list.

'Absolutely,' he exults. 'That's all it is. I don't even think I'm a very good storyteller. I think our songs are less stories than overheard conversations. Listening is like you're walking in on a conversation. Of course, for me, I can't just sing the tunes. It's just not like that. Performing is like you're telling your life story. I wish

I were a better songwriter. I wish I were more comfortable writing in the third person, but I can't. So I write what I can write in the first person.'

Despite all the success and global adulation, U2 remain on a simple mission: to create good music. Or as the Edge says:

'To make music to blow our minds.'

The credo hasn't changed since 1978.

'I don't think we have changed,' he says. 'People talk about how U2 reinvented themselves and evolved beyond recognition, but the core of what we do, the essence of our beliefs and the driving force behind the band, is exactly the same as it was when we started out. If there has been an evolution, it's been because of experience and openness. We're very inquisitive people. We're prepared to take on whatever we find out there. I think having an open mind is just oxygen. If you don't have that, you might as well forget it.'

February 1998. Original text: Sean Sennett.

Oasis

Champagne Super-poseurs?

Prior to the release of 1997's *Be Here Now*, Oasis could do no wrong. With *Definitely Maybe* and *(What's the Story) Morning Glory?* behind them, Noel Gallagher was seemingly writing anthems at will. Restarting a trend that had begun to fade with the advent of CD singles, even Oasis's B-sides were worth hearing. Nothing lasts forever and Gallagher's frailty as a writer was evident with the long-winded, and at times lumbering, *Be Here Now*. Strangely, more than a decade since its release, *Be Here Now*, without the weight of expectation it received in 1997, holds up reasonably well. Gallagher was aware he'd had his entire life to write Oasis's debut album, substantially less time for the near flawless *Morning Glory* and what must have seemed, in comparison, a matter of weeks for *Be Here Now*.

Backstage in a Palm Beach dressing room, Gallagher was surrounded by cloying hangers-on laughing at the 'Chief's' jokes and nodding in agreement as he sagely considered sampling a robotic toy monkey that a roadie had brought into the room for the start of the next album. The show that night in Florida was poor and worse was to follow in Australia when Liam stormed off stage in Brisbane leaving the band to limp to the end of an already lacklustre set. Thankfully, a reinvented Oasis were to find form again as a live outfit and Noel, even with his masterwork behind him, was still able to pull off flourishes of the old magic. Talking again a couple of years after this article, a sober Noel had no recollection at all of visiting Florida.

After a couple of false starts, the Oasis circus has finally made it to town, touring on the back of their third album, *Be Here Now*. The album, depending on who you talk to, has sold up to eight million copies worldwide. Despite their personal antics and boorish behaviour, the group are still a big draw.

Noel Gallagher, who nurses an ego bigger than most, is the group's epicentre. It's Noel who writes the songs, produces the albums and carries the grand vision. Apart from manipulating the mainstream media into falling prostrate whenever he opens his mouth, Noel's real gift is his way with a song. Under his belt already are such seminal nineties anthems as 'Wonderwall', 'Live Forever' and 'Don't Look Back in Anger'.

He's also been accused, more than once, of 'liberating' other people's ideas. 'Stand by Me' from *Be Here Now* bears more than a passing resemblance to Bowie's 'All the Young Dudes'. There are many others, but don't write Noel off too quickly. If songwriting was as simple as rehashing old ideas, every kid who ever strummed a tennis racquet would be chalking up number one singles. To his credit, whenever Gallagher has been charged with theft, he always pleads guilty.

'It's an easy way for me not to talk about the music,' he explains in his typical Manchester brogue. 'I'm left-handed and I play the guitar right-handed, so I'm dyslexic. So when I write the lyrics, it's only me that understands them. Someone else has to rewrite them and fill in the words. I find it hard. That's why I never do guitar magazines. I haven't got a fucking clue what I'm doing, so it's easy for me to say I pinched it. It saves me doing interviews. I suppose I'm a bit shy in talking about it, really. I don't know where it comes from. I think you can be too clever about music. I can't play piano, but I've written about ten songs on piano.

'I think *Be Here Now* contains some of the best songs of the three albums we've done, but I think there are great songs on all three of the albums. I don't think there's been a great album since *Definitely Maybe*, anyway. That, to me, was the last great British album.'

Apart from the current single, 'All Around the World', Noel

wrote the bulk of *Be Here Now* in only a week. As yet, he hasn't composed anything for a follow-up album, and can't see himself writing much more than a note to the milkman before England's spring of 1999 (after he's enjoyed Christmas and watched the World Cup). Writing on the road is rarely an option.

'I try not to, really. When you're on the road, you're never in the right frame of mind to write. I tend to gather ideas on the road. I haven't been doing much lately; this has been our most intense tour with interviews and things. I've done more interviews on this tour than I've done in my life. Everyone else in the band is refusing to do them.'

When Gallagher gets on a roll with a song, he likes to finish it quickly. If an idea doesn't eventually morph into a fully-fledged song in a short period, Gallagher seldom keeps it around too long.

'If a song takes more than two days to write, I'll bin it. I won't take two years to write a song – fuck that. They either come really quickly, or they don't come at all. There's no point forcing these things.

'The best time to write for me is when I first open my eyes in the morning. I've written some of my best things first thing in the morning – there's all these things going through your mind. "Champagne Supernova" started like that.

'In the morning, you've had nothing to eat, you're a bit sleepy, you haven't watched the telly and you've had no time to be influenced by anything. It just comes straight off. You think about what you were dreaming about. I think "Some Might Say" was written very early in the morning.

'I hone things for about a month. Usually, I've got a load of music and a load of melodies, and then I start to write the words at the very end, really. I don't really like writing lyrics.

'I think it's all about feel,' he says of the process. 'It's about the way the song feels, as opposed to what the lyrics mean. It's like "I Am the Walrus", what does that mean? Absolutely fuck all, but you know what he's going on about. In some ways, you know what he's trying to say. I'm not academically trained, or anything like that.

I think, if I know what it means, everybody else is going to have a grasp at it. I'm as intelligent . . . or unintelligent as anybody else.

'I got my spark off music between the ages of nine and eighteen. That's gone now. The only things that inspire me are magazines and television. I'm running out of things to be inspired by. Other people inspire me. Stand-up comedians are usually good for lyrics.'

For his own listening pleasure, Gallagher is currently grooving to late sixties psychedelic rock, early seventies punk, the Seeds ('they invented punk rock in 1964') and the Stooges.

'We've just made a big complex rock record,' he explains. 'I suppose I'm just getting excited at listening to no overdubs on records. I'm listening to sound. On *Be Here Now* there must be at least seventeen tracks of guitars. It's taking the piss, really.

I was twenty-nine when I recorded it – the fucking ego was going out of control. I'm in one of the biggest bands in the world, nobody was there to tell me to stop putting guitars on. I was producing the album as well. Looking back on it now, it's a bit over the top – but I wouldn't say it was a mistake.

'The songs are quite long as well. People were telling me I can't have seven-minute singles. You know, they won't play them on the radio and all. I was drunk in the studio thinking how dare they, don't they know who I am? I'm Noel Gallagher for Christ's sake, they'll play my records.'

'I was a year younger. I was daft. That's why all the songs are long. Next time I'll be taking a more rational approach. I'll probably get a producer to sit alongside me to tell me when to fuck off home.'

Thanks Noel.

'Cheers, mate.'

March 1998. Original text: Sean Sennett.

Custard

Check the bottom line

'How do slow sales fit within a hit-driven multinational? Discuss.'

Such is Dave McCormack's poser in this 1998 interview, reflecting the state of Australian music at the time. Popular indie bands on the Au Go Go or RooArt record labels had been swallowed up by multinationals intent on scraping off the cream and shifting larger and larger units across the nation. After years of plying their trade on community stations and Triple J, Custard had found themselves broadcasting to an unsuspecting 'general' public from commercial radio networks and staring down the barrel of an industry that places a high regard on sales. It was a sink-or-swim moment for many Australian (formerly) independent artists.

Custard's Dave McCormack has a problem. A serious problem. Dave suffers from something we might call axe-omotosis: a condition that afflicts countless musicians around the world. The symptoms? There's really only one: an obsessive collection of guitars to the point where the owner can't quite figure out what to do with them all.

'I don't know, I probably own twenty or so,' he admits. 'I've cut way back; I've given a lot away: at least five or six. See, I play the Telecaster for a while and I think that's all well and good. But then I see a Stratocaster and I've just got to get me one of those. So if I've got a Tele and a Strat, the next obvious choice is the Jazzmaster, of course. But even though the Jazzmaster sounds great, it's a little fiddly so I figure the only solution is to get another Telecaster. Eric Drew Feldman says Telecaster, Grant

McLennan says Stratocaster, Glenn Thompson says Jazzmaster. Now these are three people I pay attention to and here they are all saying something different! So I don't know. I think I've got to get away from the Jazzmaster. It's just too fiddly. It looks great and it's by far the best sounding guitar.'

As McCormack lapses into a frustrated silence, Thompson walks into the room and takes up the conversation slack.

'You know my choice,' he says.

'I know your choice and I respect that,' Dave replies. 'It's just when you go on tour, you can only really take two. See, I've got that other Squire Stratocaster with the Humbucker. Really nice. Remember that? The blond and cream one. You know the one! The Presidents tour!'

'You own it?' Glenn asks indignantly.

'Yeah, it's mine! The creamy one!'

'Well, why not just use that one?'

'No.' Dave shakes his head. 'No, I'm going to use the dual Stratocaster attack on the next tour. Imagine that, nothing but Strats!'

And Dave buys all these guitars himself?

'We've got some very dear friends at Fender Australia, who are wonderful, beautiful Christian people who always make sure we're happy.'

'And they've got far too many of their own,' Glenn deadpans.

'Yeah, they've got heaps,' Dave nods.

A dual Strat attack it is, then. Everyone in the room breathes a sigh of relief at the news as Custard's *Music Is Crap Tour* begins tonight.

'This is the third big tour since we released *We Have the Technology*,' Dave says. 'We generally do one tour a single with maybe a few other little things in between.'

More than a standard excursion, the *Music Is Crap Tour* is something of a victory dance for Custard, paying homage to their highest-selling single to date: the Thompson-penned 'Music Is Crap'. Glenn says he, more than anyone else, is flummoxed by the single's success.

'You just hear it on the radio and you think it's ridiculous,' he cringes.

'It sounds great on the radio,' Dave retorts.

'It's being played on Triple M,' Glenn ponders. 'And SeaFM.'

Dave and Glenn seem pleased with the single's success and agree that the more airplay from all areas, the better.

'This is a song I had before I joined Custard,' Glenn says. 'The version on the record is pretty similar to what I originally wrote. There are only three chords in it so there's not much else you can do.'

'You added that new middle bit,' says Dave.

'Yeah, I've got the original taped version, I'd like to hear that,' Glenn says.

'But why mess with pop perfection?' Dave asks.

The conversation soon turns to the *We Have the Technology* album, which Dave says is still moving along very nicely, thank you very much.

'Wasn't it selling twenty or thirty a week or something a while back?' Dave says.

'First it was twenty or thirty a day. Now it's only twenty or thirty a week!' Glenn says, 'What are you doing?'

'Okay, it was selling somewhere between twenty and a hundred and fifty a week a couple of weeks ago,' Dave says.

'I was initially disappointed with the album's sales, more on behalf of BMG. You know, with the people they're used to looking after over there, they looked at our album and thought this is going to be massive. They didn't know any better.'

'Yeah, they expected it to go Gold,' Glenn adds.

'But that's not the way things work with us,' says Dave. 'Our records sell year after year – well, sort of. We still sell *Wahooti Fandango* and *Wisenheimer* and stuff. How do slow sales fit within a hit-driven multinational? Discuss.'

But Custard have never been a band to do things by the book, whatever that book may be. For instance, there's the recent 'Custaro Press Release Scandal'. Accusations flew that Glenn was trying to change the band's name to Custaro by producing ambiguous artwork for the cover of *We Have the Technology* (squint and the 'D' in Custard looks kind of like an 'O'). Rather than deny, the band ran with it.

The press release issued for the 'Music Is Crap' single announced that the band were changing their name to Custaro. At the very bottom, the press release said words to the effect: 'Custard think music is crap and so is the above information about the band changing their name.'

Not surprisingly, certain sections of the Australian music press fell for it.

'I really don't know what I prefer now,' Dave cracks. 'Before it all, I preferred Custard, but I don't know. I like Custaro, I think it's good.'

'I spoke to a few people on the phone and informed them to go to the bottom line,' Glenn says. 'People love the idea of change, though, that's why they take the bait.'

'And who's to say we haven't changed,' Dave jests. 'If you went to a court of law . . . '

At this stage, amidst much laughter, Dave heads off on some wild tangent. Suffice to say, the name *is* Custard, but don't discount Custaro just yet. As with all things Custard, you can never be too sure what the bottom line is.

April 1998. Original text: Matt Connors.

SixFtHick

Don't mess with the 'Hick

There are bands that aspire to become household names, recording artists ubiquitous on radio, television and in glossy magazines: the kind of bands your mother has heard of. Then there are the bands that seek a different kind of success, the working bands that are considered primarily a live act who shuttle through the capitals, pack out small venues and dives everywhere, and build a loyal (and sometimes rabid) following almost through sheer bloody-mindedness. Your mother has definitely not heard of them and that's the way they like it. For these bands, street press is a kind of spiritual home.

SixFtHick are one of those bands.

When co-editor Simon Groth saw the band play some years ago to a ridiculously stuffed and sweaty room, he wondered why they used two front men (the twin vocal attack of Geoff and Ben Corbett). He didn't wonder for long. Part way through the set, one Corbett climbed onto the bar and performed a blind faith stage dive into a miraculously empty space and onto the concrete floor. In such circumstances, it's handy to have a spare front man. The diving Corbett disappeared for a few songs, while the band forged on with his brother taking solo vocal duties, until he reappeared apparently unharmed to finish the show.

When you go to a SixFtHick show, you can really never be sure of what you're going to get. Actually, you can never really be too sure of anything with this band. Bred on a straight diet of 'countrified rock and roll', dust balls and hay, the band are about as unpredictable as they are entertaining. Many a show has left the audience with raised eyebrows and slightly damaged eardrums.

Their debut EP, *Cousins* (a name that still pretty well says it all), started their tradition of poking just a tiny bit of fun at country life. Fortunately, this attitude does not make the band sound like a bunch of city boys with snakeskin boots on. Far from it.

Geoff Corbett, one half of the band's vocal capacity, speaks up on life within the band.

'We played this gig in Lismore a few weeks ago and these three drunk guys started causing all this trouble. They were thrown out once, but somehow they got back into the venue a second time. After the show, we had just packed up and Ben (Geoff's brother and the band's other vocalist) saw these same three guys picking on this little Asian dude. As he walked past, one of the guys said, "What would you know? You don't even come from around here." Anyway, Ben just couldn't help himself and blurted out, "Oh you guys are nice Aussie blokes, aren't ya?"

'So the big one came over to him and said, "Want to make something of it?" Ben just anticipated his punch and used some karate on the guy. It was full on. Ben has been working out a lot lately and the proof was there to see. The guy fell apart. The little Asian dude was really thankful, he said those guys had been picking on him all night. It was gutless of them, really. I mean, you think people in the Lismore area would all be into accepting different cultures and all that, but I guess not.'

This year, SixFtHick join the Livid line-up for the very first time; something that has brought a collective smile to the band.

'Livid will be great,' Geoff says. 'The line-up has a few great bands on it: the 5.6.7.8s, the Hellacopters, and a few of the other bands will be cool to see. I think some of this year's choices are kind of surprising, but that just makes it more interesting to go along. We are on the Loudmouth Stage, which seems like the right place for us to play.'

September 1998. Original text: Dave Gendel.

The Living End

The End is just beginning

The Living End cracked the charts wide open with their double A-side 'Prisoner of Society/Second Solution'. The rockabilly three-piece had an early incarnation as the Runaway Boys, virtually a tribute to America's Stray Cats. With a stripped-back kit, double bass and Chris Cheney's roaring Gretsch, the band drew a line of influences that ranged from the early days of Sun Studios through to Eddie Cochran, Brian Setzer and, oddly, the Cure. The band played with gusto and their live gigs, as well as their recordings, caught the imagination of the country. Before the Living End were signed, legend has it that a high-profile major label A&R man left a Sydney gig prior to seeing the band saying 'rockabilly would never catch on'. Famous last words.

It's hard to write about the Living End without getting caught up in a slice of genuine excitement. Only once in every few years does a band manage to shake the ennui out of the youth and have them screaming some kind of inflammatory message en masse. There's nothing quite like a genuine revolution, even if it does take place in the privacy of your own bedroom with the headphones on.

'Prisoner of Society' is a bit like a first kiss. There's an explosion of the senses taking place. Later on, after you've done it all before and sucked a thousand tongues, it either has to be really good or you need to be senselessly drunk to get off on it. Thankfully, the Living End fall into the former category. If you can get over a few obvious reference points, then you're going to hear some invigorating energy going down as well as getting a dose of personal catharsis. Am I overdoing it a bit here? Hell, I just like the bloody record to the point of playing 'Prisoner of Society' at full tilt early in the morning as my neighbours head off to work. I'm a funny guy.

But you always feel a bit of a dweeb telling musicians how much you like their record when they've heard it all before, especially from professional bullshit artists. Keep it together, Geoff. Don't make a fool of yourself.

'It was totally unexpected,' vocalist Chris Cheney says when asked if he had a sneaking suspicion that the band's 'Prisoner/ Second Solution' single might go fucking ballistic. 'It was released quite a while ago now. It didn't do anything for ages until we went on tour with Bodyjar and sold a few copies at the gig. Then we did our own little gigs and travelled around. It wasn't until two or three months after it was released that both songs on the single got radio play. Then it went bang and skyrocketed up the charts.

'It was strange because after it was released we played in Sydney at the Annandale to twenty or thirty people. It was just another EP. We thought we'd just tour on it for a little while and then do something else. But it went "Bang!" and we couldn't believe it.

'I think the song has connected with a lot of people because of that timeless thing about rock and roll where you write teen songs. Eddie Cochran, Elvis and the Who used to write all about teenagers doing their own thing and the youth becoming the leaders. I think that's still apparent today.'

The double A-side single ultimately blitzkrieged its way into the national top five and has since gone double platinum. Sensibly, the Melbourne three-piece headed into Sing Sing Studio with Lindsay Gravina to record an album which certainly proves the band is more than just a one hit wonder.

But, in an interesting move, they finished the recording and headed over to the USA to play on the Vans Warped tour and get the album mixed by Jerry Finn. Chris says the decision to go overseas made sure the band kept a level head while all the hype was going down.

'We were pretty much totally unknown,' he explains. 'We hadn't had anything released. We released a pack of our first two EPs – *Hellbound* and *It's for Your Own Good* – over there to show people what we were on about. Then we did the tour and played to people who didn't know who we were. But we got some good feedback and it was a good introduction. We don't know how it's selling but it was good to play over there.

'We were knocked back into shape. All of a sudden we were playing to people that weren't yelling out for songs. They were standing there waiting for us to impress them. It was good because we sort of had to play well and get down to basics. We had to remember how we started out here in Australia. It was good to have to do that.'

It was also pretty wise, which is how Chris is taking on the question about how the band could well be remembered for what many people assume is their first single. No matter if they release five albums, there's always going to be someone out there who goes: 'You guys sold out, man! All your records suck. Except the first one. Man, I used to get soooo wasted and listen to that song, man!'

'Unfortunately, I think that's going to happen,' he says about the possibility of being pigeonholed. 'We've had such a success and did so well in the charts. The question is how do we top this? I try not to worry about it too much because I'll go insane. I can see that it'll be a reference point for many people. But at least we have a reference point. It would be great if the album took over from that so that we can show people what we can do.'

October 1998. Original text: Geoff Nicholson.

Billy Bragg

A mirror image in song

Billy Bragg has never been afraid of 'mixing pop and politics'. An astute songwriter, author and social commentator, Bragg, with the beauty of hindsight, was the perfect choice to bring long-forgotten lyrics written by American troubadour Woody Guthrie back to life. The collaboration between Bragg's melodies and the reams of text Guthrie's daughter Nora gave him led to the *Mermaid Avenue* album. Bragg brought alt-country outfit Wilco along for the ride. The union between Bragg and Wilco front man Jeff Tweedy didn't run smoothly, and, although a second album of collaborations with Guthrie's lyrics was released, a third, to this day, remains 'in the can'.

Woody Guthrie was a visionary, a pioneer of what would eventually become known as the quintessential singer/songwriter, and an inspiration to a generation. None were more inspired than one Robert Allen Zimmerman. On hearing Guthrie's records in college, Zimmerman packed his bags and headed to New York City to meet his idol. Along the way he changed his name to Bob Dylan. The effect Guthrie had on Dylan and those that followed resonates to this day.

The original protest singer, Woody was best known for writing 'This Land Is Your Land' – a radical counterblast to Irving Berlin's cloying 'God Bless America'. Another song, 1948's 'Plane Wreck at Los Gatos (Deportees)', was written in response to the death of a planeload of immigrant workers. Throughout his life, Guthrie staged an ongoing musical protest against social injustice.

Woody Guthrie died in 1967 of Huntington's Disease. He left behind reams of words crammed into notebooks and packed in shoeboxes alongside hundreds of finished lyrics and poems. For years, legend had it that Guthrie had written more than two thousand songs. The Woody Guthrie archives now verify the number was no idle boast.

Guthrie only recorded four hundred songs in his lifetime. The 'tunes' for the remaining songs were never committed to tape; they simply wafted away into the ether. In the modern world, connotations of who Woody Guthrie was as a man are largely conjured by the music he left behind. The recordings that do exist portray him as an ardent political thinker. Viewed today, the majority of his songs espouse his left-wing views.

But there was another side to Guthrie's writing. It was a side well represented in those notebooks and shoeboxes.

His daughter Nora Guthrie dreamed of breathing life into the old lyrics. In Billy Bragg, she thought she'd found Woody's kindred spirit. Aware of Bragg's politics and his way with a tune, Nora contacted the Bard of Barking and offered him the chance to salvage the text from Woody's fading pages and turn them back into songs.

Bragg jumped at the opportunity. He first showcased his new 'Woody' tunes in 1996 before an audience that included Bruce Springsteen, Arlo Guthrie, the Indigo Girls and Dave Pirner (Soul Asylum).

'I was at a seminar about the life and work of Woody,' says Bragg, 'that coincided with the official opening of the archives. It was hosted by the Rock and Roll Hall of Fame at a university in Cleveland. One workshop dealt with his politics, another dealt with his influence on other musicians. Nora invited me along to perform, which I did partly because it gave me an opportunity to play for people who admired Woody and who had worked with him, like members of the Almanac Singers. I got to cop a vibe off them. If they liked what I was doing, then great. If they didn't, it was going to inspire me more. It was a good way to dip my toe in the water. I didn't come to the project as an expert on Woody Guthrie. The weekend represented a gathering of people to whom Woody was important. Me, I felt like a bit of an outsider to this group. The experience was constructive.'

Bragg is keen to point out that Nora Guthrie was the real prime mover behind what would eventually become *Mermaid Avenue*. She was fuelled by a desire to let a contemporary audience grasp another side of her complex father.

'She always knew they existed,' explains Bragg of the songs, 'but she never paid too much attention to them. They were around the house when she was a child. The way I understand it, from what she's told me, her mother was the person who realised that Woody Guthrie was a genius. In some ways, she persuaded him. It was Nora's mother who convinced him to write *Bound for Glory* [his autobiography] in 1942. She had a much greater view of what Woody did than Woody. She kept everything.

'When she died in the early eighties, Nora looked at what was left. She found these songs like "Ingrid Bergman" and thought to herself, "Woody Guthrie wrote love songs?" When I first read that lyric, I thought Woody Guthrie surely never wrote songs like this. It was an epiphany when she looked in that box. She realised the Woody Guthrie she knew, or thought she knew, wasn't actually the whole person. There was more. She never really knew him. By the time she was five- or six-years-old, he was ill and not really around. She never saw him perform.'

Sadly, the tunes that belonged to Woody's unrecorded songs simply disappeared from memory. That was the catch for Bragg. He may have been handed a goldmine of lyrics, but he had to come up with the melodies to put life back into them.

'On many of them, at the bottom, he types "words and music by Woody Guthrie". You can see by the meter of the lyric that there's the suggestion of a rhythm and a melody there. Some of them are not strictly songs. "Another Man Done Gone", I don't think there was ever a tune to that. If you look at it, it doesn't rhyme. When I wrote the music for it, I had to give it a form.

"She Came Along to Me", that doesn't rhyme either. Both of those are more stream-of-consciousness. I wouldn't say they're poems, strictly speaking. To write music for "She Came Along to Me", I had to sit at my own typewriter and retype it into a shape that I could sing. Consequently, I had to lose a couple of lines. Instead of writing "ten thousand songs I could sing you about her", Woody writes "ten thousand books of just about this size could I write about you". You can't open a song with a line as unwieldy as that. With Nora's permission, I edited it, slightly.'

After beginning the project on his own, Bragg felt the need for a collaborator. Jeff Tweedy and his band, Wilco, were drafted in to the project.

'My audience was coming up to me after shows and they couldn't tell if I'd written a song or if Woody had – this was when I was trying them out at gigs. I told them that all the new songs they'd heard were Woody songs, because I hadn't written any new songs. It made me think that I was doing well with Woody's songs, because my audience was connecting at one hearing. But I also realised that the Woody Guthrie material that I was selecting reflected my own sensibilities as a songwriter. There was a possibility that I was picking only one "Woody Guthrie". By ignoring the others, I might miss something. It became really important to me to involve other musicians, and to get another songwriter into the archives to choose songs.'

What makes the finished work even more rounded is the inclusion of former 10,000 Maniacs singer, Natalie Merchant.

'Natalie didn't have the chance to get involved at the writing stage, because she was busy with her own album. But I thought there needed to be a female voice in this. Some of the lyrics were written from a female perspective. If you look at a lyric like "Birds and Ships", there's a distinctly feminine aspect to what Woody was writing. A lot of his songs had been sung by ensembles like the Almanac Singers that included female singers; that was part of the tradition. So I felt it was important to involve Natalie.'

On the American artistic landscape, the spectre of Woody

Guthrie looms large. His influence is still regarded highly by many American writers today. Not surprisingly, Bragg too rates Woody as something of a giant.

'I rate Dylan a better songwriter than Woody Guthrie. But Dylan, for all the things he did, never wrote a book like *Bound for Glory*. That puts Woody apart from being just a singer/songwriter. That's not to take anything away from Dylan; he's the *ultimate* singer/songwriter. But in some ways, you can't really compare Guthrie to Dylan, they don't belong in the same category. At the same time, you can't compare Woody to John Steinbeck. Steinbeck was a better writer and novelist, but John Steinbeck never wrote "This Land Is Your Land".

Woody Guthrie to me is a one-off. He's a lyrical poet who happened to write books and songs and draw. He's not just a songwriter. He's not just a great novelist. The man was a unique figure of his time. He's the first singer/songwriter known to us. It was done in the blues, but he gave us an insight into the emotional state of the singer that went beyond "I'm upset today/because my woman left me". He wrote about his own human condition, which twenty-five years later became the meat and potatoes of the singer/songwriter. Woody was doing that when nobody else was going in that deep. He was holding a mirror up to himself. He was looking at his own depths of despair. And in 1942, 1945, 1948 . . . that was a revelation. People just weren't doing that.'

November 1998. Original text: Sean Sennett.

Spiderbait

Eclecticism crash

Spiderbait's early career was marked by a wall of fuzzed-up punk tunes played at breakneck speed. But by the end of the nineties, the band had built a huge popular following on the basis of two great albums – *Ivy and the Big Apples* and *Grand Slam* – the latter of which relied as much on the vocal talents of Janet English and Kram Maher as it did on its genre-bending tracks. In this article, two years after the band's triumphant number one slot in the Triple J Hottest 100 (with 'Buy Me a Pony'), Janet discusses *Grand Slam*'s broader sound palette and the influence of the members' various side projects.

There's a scene from the film *The World According to Garp* where Robin Williams is just about to buy a house. He's standing outside with the agent when a light aircraft crashes into the upper storey. He buys it immediately, figuring the house's karmic account is well in his favour.

Janet English says she felt similarly 'pre-disastered' after a traumatic incident in the final stages of Spiderbait's new album, *Grand Slam*. The happy catastrophe occurred about ten thousand metres above the ground between Sydney and Brisbane last October.

'There was this huge explosion and the plane dropped and everyone just freaked. One of the engines blew up and we had to make an emergency landing with fire engines on the runway and the whole bit,' the female third of Spiderbait says, lingering shock still evident in her tone.

'I already had this full-on fear about plane crashes so I was absolutely beside myself. I thought I was going to die. I was just thinking what a bloody stupid way to go. Surprisingly, my music career was the last thing on my mind. I just thought I wasn't going to see all my friends and family again. It seemed like such a waste.'

The ordeal ended safely enough, but the fact that Spiderbait had to fly to Japan with Regurgitator three days later was the source of some panic for the mild-mannered bass player. Then the *Garp* effect kicked in.

'I just felt like I was invincible,' she says. 'There was this incredible shock, then this euphoria that lasted a couple of weeks. I felt like nothing was a problem. Everything paled by comparison and making a record seemed like a piece of cake.'

It was a valuable shift in attitude. *Grand Slam*, the far-flung trio's genre-hopping slab of fab new tunes, was not an easy record to make. With English, drummer Mark 'Kram' Maher and guitarist Damian 'Whitt' Whitty now living in three different cities on Australia's east coast, it had been a much more protracted and stressful experience than usual.

'I'm surprised it turned out to be such a happy sounding record 'cause we definitely didn't feel very happy a lot of the time,' English says. 'We all got along really well but we were all away from home so there was a lot of air travel and we had plenty of technical problems too. Tape machines were breaking, we had trouble with computers initially and Kram and I were both really exhausted coming out of our other records.'

The two singers' respective holiday bands turned out to be a bonus in the long run. *Grand Slam* carries obvious shades of English's techno dabblings with Quan Yeomans of Regurgitator on their Happyland album. Maher's interaction with Tumbleweed's Richie Lewis on the Hot Rollers project was also the catalyst for new ideas and directions.

'It's funny, people have been pointing the finger and accusing me of being influenced by Happyland and I'm like, well yeah, I was half of that band, after all,' she says with a laugh. 'I guess some of Kram's melodic folkie stuff from the Hot Rollers crept in there as well. You can bland your life out listening to one style of music. I guess we try and make the ultimate mix tape of songs we liked when we were growing up. There is no subject or musical style that is taboo, it's just a matter of whether it's good enough as a song. When we started out ten years ago, we were perceived as this raucous hardcore punk band and I found that quite restrictive after a while. Now we feel we can push ourselves musically in so many more directions.'

Increasingly, Spiderbait's eclecticism is a cornerstone of their work. The overt Gary Glitter styling of *Grand Slam*'s first single, 'Shazam!', barely gives a clue as to the terrain covered within. Their road between beefy grunge and sugary pop is well travelled, but few fans could have expected Maher's Jimmy Webb–inspired crooner, 'By The Time I Get To Howlong'.

One of the most arresting tracks is Janet's 'Glokenpop', a delightful piece of ear candy that, on closer inspection, yields some of her most cynical lyrics. Like their smash single of 1997, 'Buy Me A Pony', it's typical of Spiderbait's baffling tendency to dump on the modern music industry while standing directly under the bucket. How do they reconcile their work with their attitude?

'It's a dilemma,' English sighs, 'but there it is. I'm a big fan of sweet pop music. It wasn't especially having a dig at that style of music. I think people have got to realise by now we're a cynical bunch of people and we're going to comment on whatever situation we find ourselves in. It's not like we're going to stop making music. We'll keep doing what we love doing and so we're going to exist in this industry that's full of some dodgy people and dodgy ideas. This is our little way of reconciling to that, justifying what we're doing.'

The combination of staunch indie spirit and adventurous musicality has made Spiderbait one of the critical darlings of Australia's current rock crop. Having debuted in the national top ten this month to sustained critical applause, *Grand Slam* is another milestone in the offbeat Finley trio's unlikely mainstream crossover.

'When we started out, the mainstream was Noiseworks and

Baby Animals – and they served their purpose,' English says. 'Even INXS were pretty innovative and interesting in their time, but I do feel strange that we've become so popular. It's flattering to be in this situation where people are receiving your records well and being appreciative of what you're doing, but it's not going to change what we do.'

May 1999. Original text: Michael Dwyer.

Red Hot Chili Peppers

Rolling out of the garage

Spinal Tap had their problems with drummers; for the Red Hot Chili Peppers, it has always been their guitarists (at last count, they have had nine in total). After original guitarist Hillel Slovak's death in 1988, the band's most permanent and successful strummer has been John Frusciante, despite his sometimes tenuous and fractious relationship with the band. This 1999 interview marks Frusciante's return to the fold after years in the wilderness and a not-entirely-unrelated return to form for the Californian funk masters with the album *Californication.*

According to legend, Red Hot Chili Peppers bassist Flea once passed out at the feet of Malcolm McLaren. It happened in 1987, during discussions about the one-time manager of the New York Dolls and the Sex Pistols producing the Chili Pepper's album, *The Uplift Mofo Party Plan*.

Although the talks proved fruitless, they nonetheless provided Flea with a slice of rock and roll lore. Twelve years on, the man seated before me in the Warner Music Sydney offices is not that happily fallen soul, nor is he the famed loony of the Peppers' live set. Flea is quietly and intensely contented.

Perhaps it's because one of his best friends, guitarist John Frusciante, is back in the Chili Peppers fold, where he belongs. Frusciante left the band during a pre-Australian tour of Japan in 1992 and his re-emergence couldn't be better framed than on the band's new album, the glorious *Californication*.

'If you eliminated *One Hot Minute* and made another record

after *Blood Sugar Sex Magik*, it would be this record,' says Flea, aka thirty-six-year-old Michael Balzary, between sips of herbal tea.

'This record picked up right where we left off with *Blood Sugar* and I think we've grown a lot. It's a much more dynamic record. It's got a much more diverse array of sounds and feelings. It's just very happy for us. It's a very happy thing.'

The rehiring of a healthy Frusciante and the amicable walking of his dark lord predecessor, Dave Navarro, took place in April last year. The reunited band's first gig with Frusciante was at the tiny two hundred–seater 9:30 Club in Washington DC. The next day they played at the far grander Tibetan Freedom concert. By that evening, all the Gods knew they were back.

'The Dave thing just wasn't working out,' Flea continues. 'Not his fault, not our fault; it just wasn't working chemically. It wasn't a tangible thing where I can say we did this or he did that, it just wasn't working and we parted ways with him. We'd been pretty inactive for about a year. Dave and I had been in Jane's Addiction and then I asked John if he wanted to come back to the band and he said yes. We started working with him and it was just like "Boom!" right away. We started writing songs and then we cut the record. It was very easy, very fluid, very creative.

'It just feels like a rebirth. Right now we're in a really good place. There's a great feeling. I don't like to say the word "rebirth" because I don't feel like we've gone anywhere, we've always been a band. But having Frusciante back . . . I just think he's the best guitar player in the world and so it's a real exciting thing for us. Everything's just great right now.'

It sure as hell sounds like it. Despite 'da funk' component, the Chili Peppers have always been makers of a cosmic American soul music, all very much of their own unique design (or maybe lack of design). *Californication* restates that alchemy like a true second coming.

From the gloriously fucked-up bass that opens 'Around the World' and the blazing, hit-the-lights power of 'Parallel Universe' to the gorgeous smash hit 'Scar Tissue', it's Magik all over again, even if the blood types have seen some changes.

'During the writing in my garage we'd just be like, fuck, yeah! This is great! During the recording, we'd play it and listen back through the speakers and go "Fuck yeah!" all over again. The record is a very live record. It's basically just us three or four guys in there playing. We'd play it and go out and listen to it in the speakers, check it off, and move on to the next! It was a very rewarding experience. I feel like it's the best record we've ever made, for sure.'

The album's title – or rather the possible implications of it – was something with which Flea initially wrestled.

'At first, personally, I was a little hesitant about the title because I feel like we always get pegged as these California sex guys,' he laughs. 'But the song "Californication" is pretty much about the pervasive influence of Hollywood on the world and the sickness of it. Really! It's not about us guys being macho Californian studs at all. That's the last thing it's about. So I was a little bit worried about it being misinterpreted in that way. But then you look at the cover and it has the sort of Californian dream of having a swimming pool and then it's all upside down and the sky is in the pool and the ocean is in the sky. I like it. I think it's nice. It's an interesting sounding word.'

That inverted world on the album cover would probably have suited the departed Navarro just fine. He's long been Mr Deadly Nightshade, the last of the Hollywood Vampires, and he wouldn't have it any other way. The Chili Peppers, on the other hand, have their dark places, but overall they're a life-affirming force. Little wonder their teaming wasn't long-lived.

'I can't say that because I feel like everyone has a dark and light side. And Dave romances the darkness and he finds that attractive and dresses all in black. He's very like that. So I don't particularly see him as darker than the next person. I can't really say why it didn't work out. Maybe you understand it better than me, I don't know. I just know it's a lot easier to play with John, just naturally easy. With Dave I know we always – both of us – had to really kind of work to get into a place where we could create, as opposed to okay, let's play and go do it. It was never a flowing natural thing.'

Rick Rubin was again the control room master for *Californication*, as he probably will be for the band's next ten albums.

'What's great about Rick is that he works with a pretty wide variety of acts and I don't feel like he has "the Rick Rubin sound". He just brings out the best of the act that he works with. He wants to make them sound like they sound. And that's how I feel this record sounds: it just sounds like us. It sounds like us playing in my garage.'

June 1999. Original text: Murray Engleheart.

Joe Strummer

You with Joe Strummer? Well are you?

The late Joe Strummer remains one of rock's great twentieth-century icons. After the Clash disbanded, Strummer took a brief stab at a solo career. With the commercial and critical failure of his solo debut, *Earthquake Weather*, Strummer went, in the rock and roll sense, relatively quiet. He took on acting roles, the highlight being his stint in Jim Jarmusch's *Mystery Train*. He enjoyed a brief tenure with the Pogues and even had a BBC radio program that reflected his eclectic taste, aptly titled 'London Calling'. Life as a front man beckoned again in the mid-nineties and Strummer put together a new band, the Mescaleros. Back in the studio and with the road ahead of him, Strummer signed a deal with Los Angeles punk label Hellcat. Living with an undiagnosed congenital heart defect, Strummer died suddenly at his home in 2002.

Joe Strummer knew he was still carrying a rock and roll torch that could be seen for some distance when he took his band, the Mescaleros, to Hamburg last year. The show was in the same venue that hosted an infamous series of riots during the Clash's visits to the region, incidents that subsequently saw Strummer banned from the precinct between 1980 and 1993. His return – armed with a set peppered with Clash classics such as 'London Calling' and 'White Man In Hammersmith Palais' – had the old bare-knuckled punks from 1977 literally in tears.

'In Germany, they take punk rock very seriously indeed,' Strummer instructs at 3:30am, London time. 'You with me?' he laughs. 'You with me?' he repeats far more seriously. 'This sounds ridiculous, but people feel proud because they went to all three riots while they were growing up. There was a year between each one so there are people in Hamburg who were fifteen at the first one, sixteen at the second and seventeen at the third. If you were there – whew! – you get as many birds as you want. I tell you, the show kicked off great. I've never seen anything like it in my life.'

Did you get a bit misty yourself?

'Absolutely,' he laughs quietly, as if close to tears again at the memory. 'I'm afraid so, sad as it seems. But then what really got me laughing again was the paper they have, the tabloid like the *New York Post* or whatever. They printed an anniversary picture of the original riot in that morning's paper. It basically looked like loads of fat blokes fighting. Your memory plays tricks. This is the only time you're ever going to hear me boast, right? By chance I'm striking a remarkably good pose in the middle of this mayhem. Somehow, I'm standing in the middle pointing down at the floor, caught in a good aspect!' he roars with laughter. 'This is a once-off moment. Let me boast, hey?'

For my rusty old studded wristband, Strummer can have all the latitude he wants, even though feverish last minute tour rehearsals have already meant his call came through several hours later than scheduled. Strummer was worried I would be 'mad as hell' and asked if he could call me back after he got himself together. He called me 'babe' and hung up. We reconnected a few minutes later. The Mescaleros – in classic Strummer rebel fashion they take their name from a fearsome American Indian tribe in an old William Holden movie – are Strummer's first band proper since the Clash.

The jumper lead for the bonding came with Strummer's introduction to Pulp and Elastica guitarist Antony Genn. A recording contract with Hellcat Records by Rancid's Tim Armstrong sealed the deal.

'I met a person I could collaborate with,' Strummer says of the band's formation. 'That pretty much really is the fundamental jump there. I kind of drifted for a few years and then I saw Antony working at sessions and I realised he had a mind on him. He said to me, in fact exactly what he said was, "Come on, you're Joe Strummer! You should be making a record!" So I said, "Let's rock!"'

And they did. The resulting album, *Rock Art and the X-Ray Style* – Strummer's first since 1989's *Earthquake Weather* – acts as if the Clash's 1982 effort, *Combat Rock*, never existed. Instead, it harks back to the grabs of punk rock from *Sandinista!* only in a more easily digestible dose.

'We got into the studio and all we knew was that we wouldn't make a ramalama-punk-ding-dong, you with me? Although I love it, I didn't want a Ramones sound. We wanted to do a sort of 1999 groove, rather than pretend it's still 1978. Really, we knew nothing. We didn't. I know it sounds kind of disappointing but we're just like idiots that throw mud at the wall and when it looks good we keep it. When it doesn't we sort of scrape it off. Really, that's it. What keeps us going, what identifies us or makes us exist, is the calls we make: which bit of mud to scrape off and which to leave on. If there's any kind of talent going on here it's about making good calls.'

The album's title is rooted in that same technique and ended up being the cornerstone of the entire project.

'It's another ridiculous thing, like the William Holden cowboy movie. You with me? Get this. I'm down in the dumps – this is about five years ago – and I tried to get a group going with Richard Norris from the Grid. Some of the tracks have ended up on this record. Anyway, I go and see my neighbour and he's got an old 1930s book on archaeology. Chapter Six was "Rock Art and the X-Ray Style". I thought that's it!

'It gave me something to focus on because even though it's just a bloody phrase and you could write it on a piece of paper and the wind would blow it away, it still gives your fantasy thing an identity. They painted shapes of animals in cave paintings and then after many thousands of years they began to paint the bones visible through the animals. The professors decided to call this the X-Ray Style. I immediately went in a corner and wrote "The X-Ray Style", the song, that afternoon. Things like that turn you on, you know?'

If you pay attention, you can hear the big beat that turned Strummer onto rock and roll in the first place. It's just a pity his heroes don't remember.

'There's this Bo Diddley song and it's about him asleep in his house and some cats come to his back door and wake him up. So he had to go out on his back porch at night. It's a terrific Bo Diddley song in my book and so I sang it to Bo. I said, "Bo, do you remember this one?" I sang a couple of lines. He went, "Nope." I said "Come on, Bo!" And sang him some more and he went, "Nope." So I sang him the whole song and he went "I never heard that brother in my life!" And I've got it on a Bo Diddley album in my house!' Strummer roars. 'That's the way it goes, mate. That's longevity. I haven't got over it yet.'

January 2000. Original text: Murray Engleheart.

Pink Floyd

Rebuilding *The Wall*

When Roger Waters left Pink Floyd, it led to one of the bitterest estrangements in rock history. Post–Syd Barrett, Waters largely steered the band creatively. On leaving the group, he assumed Pink Floyd was 'over'. David Gilmour had other ideas and kept the brand going with two more albums and live dates under the Pink Floyd moniker, much to Waters's disgust. It was a surprise to many when an olive branch of sorts was offered and Waters helped the band promote a live version of their masterwork of alienation, *The Wall*. Sean Sennett received a call out of the blue from Sony Music asking if he'd be interested in chatting to Waters about the release. A few hours later Roger was on the line.

'If you find yourself at a Pink Floyd show,' Roger Waters once said, 'you'll see my wall, my flying pig and their dry ice.'

Waters was once at the controls of the Pink Floyd that became a global commodity. It was Waters's vision – after the loss of Syd Barrett in the late sixties – that inspired and drove albums as famous as *Wish You Were Here*, *The Dark Side of the Moon* and their double-album opus, *The Wall*. After *The Final Cut* in 1983, Waters left the group. With his departure, he naturally assumed that Pink Floyd would be no more. They would simply break up, he thought.

'Well, it kind of did,' he deadpans from Paris, 'but a few of the bits went on calling itself Pink Floyd. But that's old history. There's not a lot to be said about it really.'

What has drawn Waters back into the Pink Floyd fold is a series of interviews to promote the new live album, *Is There Anybody Out*

There?, a live recording of *The Wall*, released to coincide with the original album's twentieth anniversary. For Waters, it's a purely retrospective mission – he hardly feels as if he's back in the band again.

'It doesn't feel like that to me,' he says. 'I feel like I'm talking about a piece of work I did twenty years ago. This in no sense includes me in what Dave (Gilmour) and Nick (Mason) are doing now, I would hope.'

Waters has been vilified by the other members of Pink Floyd as a control freak and many feel that it was Waters-as-taskmaster that nearly broke the band during the recording of the original *Wall* album. He sacked keyboard whiz Rick Wright and rumour had it drummer Mason was to be next. His relationship with guitarist Gilmour was similarly tenuous.

Despite the passing of time and the still lingering acrimony with his former band mates, Waters doesn't believe he's that much different from the young man who dreamed up one of rock music's finest concepts.

'Twenty years of psychotherapy later,' he says, 'I think I understand a bit more about who I am and I'm more content to inhabit this shell than I was then. But otherwise, I haven't changed. I'm quite clear about who made the record. The work remains in one's heart and one's memory.'

Since leaving Pink Floyd, Waters has toured America and Europe, playing to enthusiastic crowds. In 1980, he was lured into performing *The Wall* in its entirety. Ten years later, Waters performed the album in Berlin. Now, in 2000, promoters are again asking the question.

'I was actually asked to do it over summer as a kind of millennium thing,' he explains. 'The suggestion was that we could do it somewhere in North America and there'd be a big pilgrimage, an audience of a million people and it'd be free. I was vaguely attracted to the idea when they started talking about it being free. But then I thought how could it be free? Somebody had to pay for it. It'd cost a fortune to put on a show that size. So I asked, "If the audience doesn't pay, who does?"

'They said they'd get corporate America to pay in some form or another. I thought that could be alright, but how would that work? Would they write us a big cheque and send us on our way? I don't want Coca-Cola written all over the bricks. Then I started to discover what they actually mean by "free". Rock and roll is being infiltrated by corporate America and corporate Europe.'

So instead of a performance comes a live album, eagerly awaited by Floyd fanatics all over the globe.

'I think it'll just be an interesting addition to people's collections,' Waters says matter-of-factly. 'It's an interesting kind of historical document. Maybe the performance will have something the studio record didn't. It is a live album, not a "pretend" live album. Whatever happened is what went down in the mixes.'

April 2000. Original text: Sean Sennett.

Queens of the Stone Age

Solid gold hell

It was a long way from Palm Desert, California, when Murray Engleheart caught up with Queens of the Stone Age's Josh Homme. After the break-up of Kyuss and a stint as tour guitarist for Screaming Trees, Homme formed his new band in 1997. The moniker was coined by QOTSA producer Chris Goss as far back as 1992 while working with Kyuss. Latching on to the name, Homme believed 'Kings' was too 'macho'. Critics have often labelled the band 'stoner rock', a tag Homme rejects. He prefers 'robot rock' in deference to QOTSA's driving, near repetitive, way with a riff. Dave Grohl was such a fan of the band that he later signed on to play drums on *Songs for the Deaf. Rated R* was the band's second album. Subsequently, Homme has had tours of duty with Eagles of Death Metal and Them Crooked Vultures.

Queens of the Stone Age leader Josh Homme has had several constant companions since he was about fifteen. On tour, they don't receive a wage, and their meals and accommodation aren't an issue. Stuff like hardcore punk band Charged GBH's *Leather, Bristles, Studs and Acne*, Discharge's *Never Again*, the Misfits' *Legacy of Brutality* and any given Black Flag disc will bed down just about anywhere. Homme just needs a bit of space occasionally to re-enact the manic downstroke of his hero, GBH guitarist Jock Blyth.

The sheer bulk of the Stooges' recent *Complete Fun House Sessions* doesn't lend itself to endless visits to the world's departure lounges, but Homme carries its impact with him at all times.

'It's fucking excellent!' the singer and guitarist drawls from the back of a tour bus in Glasgow, Scotland, between hard pulls on a cigarette and the snotty noises of the flu. 'You hear the lyric changes and all these fuck-ups and you really realise what totally shitty musicians they were, which is really cool for me. It's like the perfect enigma.'

Enigmas are something in which Homme is well versed. He called time on his band Kyuss in 1995 at the absolute peak of their power and popularity. Since then, against a backdrop of the K-band's ever-expanding mythology, he's become a great deal more than just the dude who played guitar through a bass amp for the stoner kings, with devastating sonic effect.

Homme has taken on the proportions of a lightning rod and is almost a beer-and-weed spiritual leader. His creative and directive efforts on the now legendary musical collective series *The Desert Sessions* has become the stuff of stoner folklore, while influential types such as Dave Grohl and Billy Corgan think that the Queens are cool as all shit. Which they are.

Two years after the release of their self-titled debut album and with the joys of their label going bankrupt finally behind them, comes the Queens' new slab, *Rated R*, which is doubly titled 'Feel Good Hit of the Summer'. It was recorded in the same studio in Los Angeles where Kyuss pushed out their crushing final three albums – a figure with which Homme seems quite comfortable.

'This is part of a three-record cycle for me in establishing what the Queens are and what we do,' he says. 'Obviously, the first record I had to step away from Kyuss but not too far. I had to establish that we also carry a sound with us that's our own, but it's not Kyuss. Then on this one it's like I've got to fan the music out so it's like, look, we're going to play everything that sounds good under the umbrella of our sound. And the for third one, you'll just have to wait and see.'

Rated R makes it plain that there's no such animal as a template for QOTSA. There's the stuttering pit frenzy and drone of the alternate title cut, with former Judas Priest, near-operatic lung-man Rob Halford on back-ups, the quirky pop of 'Auto Pilot', the sweeping abrasive majesty of 'In The Fade' with Homme's buddy and former Screaming Tree Mark Lanegan ('one of the best voices ever') on lead vocals, and the flat out rush of 'Lightning Song'. There's also lap steel, vibes and even a free jazz rave-up *à la* Sun Ra's John Gilmore on the extended blow-out of the closer, 'I Think I Lost My Headache'. Little wonder Homme is at a loss to define the body of work as a whole.

'To be honest with you I have no idea because I want to be outside of all the cliques so much that I don't know what my clique is,' he says. 'I need something vague like rock and roll, you know what I mean? But for me lots of people claim to be an outsider their whole life! And I'm like, fuck, you lucky bastard! I *want* to be an outsider!

'My goals are the same that they've always been with Kyuss as well and now with Queens. That is, that each record has to be a complete record. The songs can't copy each other. They have to have their own personality and they have to flow together as one, like the record is one song. If we only have seven good songs then our record's only going to be seven songs long. Like *Fun House* is what, seven songs? Eight songs max? I don't need seventy-two minutes of music.

'I hear bands say, well, we're giving people value for their money and I question whether that's the case at seventy-two minutes. I don't want to have to dig for veins of gold in the side of a giant mountain. I just want the fucking gold! You know what I mean? Give it to me! Quit fucking with me! If it's on a cassette, rewind that motherfucker! Like, I'm not going to torture you with my visions of life for over an hour. I'd rather torture you with them for forty-five minutes!'

July 2000. Original text: Murray Engleheart.

Coldplay

Making grown men cry

Before Gwyneth, before Apple and certainly long before Moses, Coldplay were just another band on the brink of the big time. Celebrity magazine fodder was light years into the future and front man Chris Martin was just another bloke with loads of great songs and lots of hair to boot. With the release of their debut album, *Parachutes*, the rest of the world could hear ripples of what was happening in England and Europe. Championed early by the *NME*, it was obvious that Coldplay were going to be a group to watch. The world did sit up and listen, and Coldplay have been flooding the radio waves ever since. Here the band are caught as near-fledglings on the cusp of something special.

We all know the story. It's as familiar as your own reflection. Young British band burst from the back lots brandishing a bounteous barrel-load of bewitching 'choons'.

The UK music press loves 'em. Glowing live reviews, rapturous album reviews and front cover exposure ensues. Then everyone loves 'em. Somewhere, someone mentions 'the new Beatles'.

Yes, readers, that's exactly where our latest Pommie protagonists, Coldplay, find themselves residing. They're the UK's *next big thing*. This time, though, you may be wise to believe the hype. Coldplay look, feel and sound like the real deal, representing the most promising band to emerge from the UK since Radiohead gave us *Pablo Honey* back in 1993.

What's worse is they're just mere whippersnappers: guitarist and vocalist Chris Martin and lead guitarist Jonny Buckland are twenty-two, drummer Will Champion and bassist Guy Berryman twenty-one. It would be enough to make a sad old music hack green with envy if the band didn't come across as such genuine lads.

As Chris Martin explains, so far 2000 has been an incredible whirlwind of a ride.

'We've been in a state of confusion, really,' he says. 'We've been just going around Europe, really, like on one-off gigs, in countries we've never been to before. I don't know; it's been a bit weird. We've just been playing and talking constantly. More talking than playing, probably.'

Coldplay's four members met in 1996 at college in London and soon discovered that special chemistry unique to few bands.

'I realised we had something straightaway,' Martin admits. 'At first it was just me and Jonny, our guitarist, and as soon as we sat down to write together it just felt absolutely right; it felt brilliant. I can't explain how exciting it felt and I realised I'd met someone who makes me play better and write better stuff. It was the same when each of us joined. Do you know what I mean? We were each inspired by the rest of the band and that's what is amazing.'

Following the release of an independent EP (*Safety*) and single ('Brothers & Sisters'), Parlophone Records snapped Coldplay up, quickly releasing *The Blue Room* EP. While the momentum had been building, it's their debut album, *Parachutes*, that has truly fired Coldplay's mercurial rise to indie pin-up status. But, despite appearances, it hasn't come easy.

'To be honest, recording the album was quite painful. We were all really trying to put everything into it and there was a lot of tension a lot of days – just in general, not between anyone in particular. I think we were all very proud that we actually got through it and actually did finish our album. There were certainly a few days where it looked like it just wasn't going to get done, like we were going to split up or something. There were a lot of songs that we went through that didn't make it to the album. I don't think we were really going to split up . . . it just wasn't as easy as we'd imagined to record an album.'

Interestingly, Martin claims to have heard *Parachutes* just the once.

'I just can't listen to our music because I have a fear that I won't like it. I've only listened to it once to check that it all sounded right and that was that. But the thing is that we hear them just about every night, the songs.'

Coldplay's recent run of live shows has given Martin plenty of opportunity, with dates in continental Europe and Japan, as well as two of the UK's biggest summer festivals: Glastonbury and T in the Park.

'They were two of the most exciting gigs we've ever done, purely because of the crowds. It's a whole other world, really. We just couldn't believe it, especially T in the Park. You know when you watch some video of a band live and they sort of pan out across the crowd with the cameras? It was just like that; it was really exciting. Shit, maybe we're actually doing alright!

'We still think of ourselves as a sort of struggling band, you know. But in Britain, that's not really true anymore. Every time we go on stage we're surprised to see anyone there at all.'

Do the audiences know the songs now?

'Yeah. I think when I go see a band, it always helps if I know some of the songs. You have to listen to our songs a few times to get them, I think. The main thing really is that we've got a song called "Yellow" which radio was really nice to. Radio One especially was amazing so lots of people know that song when we play.'

Is it true that grown men were crying during your T in the Park slot?

'I have no idea about that. Probably because it was so hot,' he laughs.

September 2000. Original text: Matt Connors.

PJ Harvey

The 'dark woman of rock' syndrome

Hailing from a sleepy seaside town in England's west country, PJ Harvey quickly made a name for herself (and her eponymous band) with a raucous blend of punk, blues and grunge. The band's debut album, *Dry*, earned rave reviews in both Britain and the United States, with *Rolling Stone* naming Polly Jean best new artist of 1992. By the mid-nineties, Harvey had shed her band and built a reputation for elaborate and theatrical stage performances, typically wearing frocks and smudged make-up, a look she herself labelled 'Joan Crawford on acid'.

This interview in late 2000 saw Harvey emerging from her darker, experimental work to embrace what she later described as 'absolute beauty'. The resulting album, *Stories from the City, Stories from the Sea*, would prove one of Harvey's most commercially successful to date.

When Olivia Newton-John knifed her lover on the Banks of the Ohio, it was a tragic, momentary lapse of reason. She wailed her way through the song before rediscovering her senses along with her feminine poise in the final verse.

Twenty-five years later, when Nick Cave chose Polly Jean Harvey to wield the penknife in their 1996 duet, 'Henry Lee', it was more like typecasting.

She always was a scary piece of work, the slight, raven-haired banshee from the Dorset rock trio bearing her name, PJ Harvey. Their first record of 1992, *Dry*, found her striding stages in trousers, of all things, spitting strife over an aggressive musical attack rooted more in the swampy blues of Robert Johnson and Howlin' Wolf than any obvious female precedent.

Even the forbidding scowl of New York punk poet Patti Smith made for a superficial comparison. The lack of a convenient pigeonhole for such an eloquent, androgynous and evidently furious woman led to wild acclaim for PJ Harvey in underground music quarters. In others, misunderstanding verging on alarm still reigns.

'I think the most ridiculous misconception about me has to be this kind of angry-woman, man-hating feminist angle, which really isn't an issue with me,' Harvey reflects cheerfully. 'Really! I'm not exaggerating. Interviewers are scared of me. Men are scared of me. It's very strange.

'Once you're saddled with something it's very hard to shift it,' she sighs dismissively. 'So I'm securely fastened within my dark woman of rock syndrome.'

From this distance, the delusion is not one of rock's greater mysteries. The closest Harvey has come to a hit in Australia is 'Down by the Water', a nightmarish piece which finds her whispering for a drowned daughter on another shady riverbank. Once again, it doesn't sound like an accident.

But now it appears that 'the axe-wielding bitch character from hell' (her own, ironic description) may have exorcised her sombre preoccupations with her 1998 album, *Is This Desire?*, a particularly grim cycle populated by ghostly seductresses and tortured saints dancing towards doom in Biblical clothing.

It's a relief as much as a surprise to find this year's PJ Harvey arriving in a neon-lit jungle of skyscrapers with pistol drawn and cops on her tail, running red lights through the mean streets of Manhattan. If we can judge her state of mind by the characters she plays, *Stories from the City, Stories from the Sea* is where England's diva of angst takes flight and comes close to taming her tormentors.

'Yes, it was kind of a decision on my part,' she says of the adrenaline charge of her sixth album (she's long been PJ Harvey's sole constant, though original drummer Rob Ellis was recently reinstated).

'I write songs all the time so I had quite a backlog – that's the way I usually work – and then according to how I feel, what kind of record I feel it's time to make, I'll choose the songs that feel right. I felt that after *To Bring You My Love* (1995) and *Is This Desire?*, a lot of the music had been very atmospheric and very low and quite heavy going. I felt like I needed a blast of energy, really.'

Physical exhaustion was the official explanation for Harvey's late scratching from her 1996 tour of Australia aboard the annual Big Day Out summer roadshow. Rumours of nervous breakdowns came in its wake, along with speculation about drugs, anorexia and the lingering damage of her affair with Cave, who was confirmed for the same tour (much of his last album, *The Boatman's Call*, is reputedly about her).

But all that seems like a previous lifetime as the thirty-year-old tourist gleefully describes the view from her hotel window in Oporto, Portugal, an early stop on the tour that will bring her to Australia at last in January. Her manner is warm, her slightly posh, West Country accent a girlish lilt as she paints a picture of boats dancing under Alec Eiffel's bridge.

'It's very, very beautiful,' she coos, as bubbly as Kylie Minogue on a quiet day.

The romance of overseas adventure is all over *Stories from the City, Stories from the Sea*. The record began taking shape during a month-long stint in New York in 1998, where Harvey played a modern Mary Magdalene in Hal Hartley's film *The Book of Life*. With all its inherent excitement and danger, the city towers through the completed album.

'I'm a very creative, romantic person that lives in my imagination, looks for the romance in everything, 'cause that's what I'm drawn to,' she says. 'So I do think it is a romantic picture of the city, but that's such a beautiful way to see anywhere, I think. It was the longest I'd spent in New York and I began to get a bit of a taste for the kind of energy and inspiration that I felt there. I was even writing these songs during filming, some of them. I felt a real rush of creativity. It felt like personally – not just creatively, but personally – it felt like a space where I could grow and learn a lot.'

Driven mainly by restlessness, she says, Harvey moved to New York for much of 1999 before returning to her home near Bridport, on the south coast of England, to draw together the strings of her latest project. As usual, they're woven too loosely to divulge specifics about the transcontinental love affair that forms the album's thematic heart.

Most intriguing of all is Harvey's duet with Radiohead's Thom Yorke, 'This Mess We're In', which poses a threatening centrepiece to the affair while revealing precisely nothing. It's almost as if Harvey had written a detailed dialogue describing the lovers' rise and fall, then pared it back to rest on the power of suggestion.

'Yeah, that is very much the way I work. I tend to start off with a large amount of information in my lyrics and I do the process of stripping back and taking away what isn't needed to leave the song more powerful, really, more direct.'

It's tempting to wonder if this process reflects Harvey's response to her own public image. Her guarded privacy has been a recurring issue in her career, one punctuated by long absences from the spotlight.

'I don't know if it's so much that,' she demurs politely. 'When I'm writing songs I'm purely looking at it from what I think is going to make the strongest song and what I am drawn to. I've always been drawn to simplicity in music and seeing what isn't needed, taking away things to leave as little as possible 'cause that's just the way I prefer to hear things. I do think that songwriting is a mixture of reality and fiction, autobiography and imagination. There are elements of that in every song. There are elements of myself and elements of my extended self, if you like. I don't feel it's a matter of becoming a different person, it's more a matter of extending my own realms into different possibilities to what is concrete and is real.'

The cult of celebrity seeks a more literal relationship between a star and her work, of course, which is probably why Polly Harvey has developed a reputation for caginess in interviews. Some observers have linked the emotional problems of her last few years to invasive media attention, but, ironically, her reticence has flowered into a mystique unparalleled by her female peers.

'I see interviews as a very necessary part of making my music available to people, but I do find it difficult, I don't enjoy having to explain why I've done things or what I'm like as a person. It's very uncomfortable.

'I think it's the same with any artist,' she continues, 'whether it's with paints, music . . . whatever you're trying to create or explore involves a lot of private thought and often that comes from people who are very deep thinkers, very private people. It can be very awkward to have to explain that in a public situation. That happens in rock music more than anywhere else. People are really aware of image. Rock and roll is seen as sexy, so you get this sexy image as well. It's just so much media onslaught. It's not listening to music anymore at all. I don't know if it ever was, actually.'

As a performer, Polly Harvey has dabbled in a range of guises from the gender-negating garb of the early nineties to the dazzling, red satin evening wear she was packing around the time of her cancelled Australian tour of 1996. What should we expect when PJ Harvey finally makes that long-delayed visit to Australia?

'It's very high energy, very rock, very loud, very in-yer-face,' she says, relishing each word like long-denied pleasures. 'Mmmm. Quite glamorous – but not theatrical. Very nice frocks, very nice shoes, very high heels.'

October 2000. Original text: Michael Dwyer.

Augie March

There is no such band: Augie take stock

Augie March's early career was marked by setbacks, frustrations and grief. For a band that embraced the beauty of sadness in their lyrics and arrangements, a certain discontent with the commercial music world was probably expected, but the unexpected death of tour keyboardist (and intended full band member) Rob Dawson was a blow from which the band struggled to recover. In this 2001 interview with ever-affable Augie drummer Dave Williams, the pain of that loss is still raw.

It would take another five years and two albums before Augie March, almost accidentally, achieved major label mainstream triumph in the form of 'One Crowded Hour', a song that compromised little on the band's established sensibilities. Success, it seems, had stalked Augie March, rather than the other way around.

Brisbane Augie March fans could be well inclined to think the Victorian four-piece have been giving us the short shrift. Barring their Livid and Big Day Out performances, headlining shows in the region have been rarer than imports of British beef. As Augie March drummer David Williams apologises for the cancellation of two local shows last year, he admits it makes the prospect of their *There Is No Such Tour* dates even more appealing.

'It's good to be heading up north again,' he says. 'Yes, we haven't quite made it a couple of times . . . I can't actually remember the last tour we did get up there but, hey, we're going to be up there soon. We made it as far as the Gold Coast for the Big Day Out.'

Recent events make it easier to forgive Augie March. Midway through the promotional cycle for their stunning *Sunset Studies* album, the band were rocked by the death of keyboardist Rob Dawson in a car accident in early January.

'It's been pretty tough since the death,' Williams admits. 'We're still finding our feet. It was devastating and it still is, but it's good to be able to play and just get back on the horse.'

Williams says the band made the decision to do the Big Day Out shows on the advice of friends, despite having no time to grieve for their departed band member.

'People we spoke to – friends of ours – who've been in similar situations when they were touring and stuff, they just said from their experience the best thing is just to get back into it as soon as everyone feels like they can. There's no point wallowing in grief anyway. It wouldn't do any good. We just decided to continue with the Big Day Out and it was a positive thing. Everyone enjoyed it, but there was a bit of a sombre mood. The single we've released ['There Is No Such Place'] is dedicated to him and I think on this tour we'll still be thinking of him the whole time.'

Have you replaced Rob?

'At the moment, we've just decided to go the four-piece. I think in the future we'll want to have someone there because the reason Rob was asked to join in the first place was we composed some keyboards for the album, which were intrinsic in the songs. I think that will continue to happen, but we're just not ready yet. Rob really did bring an element that wasn't there before and in the future maybe we'll explore that again. We'll have to do a bit of improvisation to get around the sudden lack of keyboards for now. I think it will be alright, but he's sorely missed – I think that's the bottom line – we miss his sound. I think with the songs, we'll be pretty tired of them anyway by the end of this tour, so we'll be looking forward to playing some new songs.'

Much has been made of Augie March in Australian music circles, where they've attracted praise from both punters and pundits alike, largely for creating a sound that's both fresh and intelligent.

'I'd like to think intelligence is the reason why,' Williams laughs. 'I guess I'm not really sure. I suppose we're just offering something a bit different to the four-to-the-floor. We want to be a bit subtler about the way we convey our music. We want to be able to go really soft, but still beat people over the head and get really loud too when we need to. We want to use the dynamics; we don't want to be a flat line. We're just offering something different and you don't need to be that different for people to take notice of you.'

Williams agrees that some of the acclaim needs to be attributed to the lyrics and sweetly maudlin vocals of front man Glenn Richards.

'I believe on our chat site that's a real realm, where the lyrics are debated and people write essays about what they think songs are about. I think Glenn enjoys that, you know. I think he likes listening to music that can be interpreted in many different ways. He really does take lyrics seriously. The words are just as important – maybe more important – than the music. His favourite type of music is stuff you can learn things from and is wordy in its content.'

Augie March plan to release one more single from *Sunset Studies* (though they are still undecided on which track) and hope to record again later this year. Williams says an all-ages tour is also a consideration. Whatever they do, the memory of Rob Dawson is likely to play a part. Already, Williams admits, Dawson's death has made them prioritise their goals.

'We haven't really spoken about it to each other in a formal sense, but I'm sure it did bring everything sharply into focus. There's a real long-term vision with the band and this experience just made us want to strive for it more, I think. It's sort of galvanised our push to go somewhere.'

March 2001. Original text: Matt Connors.

Kiss

Tales of the bizarre!

Gene Simmons has never been shy about making a buck. The Kiss bassist sees himself as a shrewd businessman and now fans can buy everything from Kiss plectrums for the big gig to a Kiss casket for the big sleep. To give them their due, the band were never afraid to push the onstage envelope. Wearing masks was an ingenious idea. Taking the masks off wasn't. Putting the paintwork back on and giving fans a case of high-voltage nostalgia has worked a treat. While Kiss line-ups have changed over the years, Simmons and vocalist Paul Stanley have never lost sight of their dream of making the band live up to the hype on stage. Just ask anyone who's seen them perform 'I Was Made for Lovin' You' or 'Love Gun' in concert. When we enquired what Michael Dwyer thought of the tour for which he interviewed Simmons, he deadpanned, 'They've got four great songs, and they only play three of them.'

It was the night of February 9, 1997. My make-up had done its dash by the time Paul Stanley climactically smashed his guitar on the blood-spattered stage of Perth's Burswood Dome. A good quarter of my Ace Frehley paint job was flaking down my shirt. No matter. When the finale firebombs had fizzed out, I only had to drive my mate Bob home – he was Paul Stanley, curly wig, genuine chest hair and all – and hit the showers.

Sadly, my old car wasn't up for that challenge. But the road service guy was a pro. He looked at me, looked at Bob, raised his eyebrows almost imperceptibly, stuck his torch under the hood and said, 'So what's the problem?'

Gene Simmons chuckles softly at the story: another one for the archives. Tales of the bizarre have been this bass-wielding sleazebag's lifeblood since he first stuck his unfeasibly long tongue out of his grease-painted face nearly thirty years ago.

'I'll tell you a moment,' he volunteers in response. 'We played Dodger Stadium in Los Angeles for the '98 tour. It was the first 3D tour in history. Everybody blowing out their minds behind those 3D glasses. Now this was Halloween night so on the way back from the show, as you can imagine, traffic was completely stopped. We were on Sunset Boulevard three blocks from the hotel and the streets were filled with people from Star Wars and Star Trek, Frankenstein's monster – and some Kiss people as well.

'So we're in the van in full make-up, full outfits and we looked at each other and said, well, why don't we walk? They won't know it's us.'

The odd catcall aside, Simmons reports, the four towering rock superheroes tottered home on twenty-centimetre heels, unharmed. It's a neat illustration of what an integrated fixture Kiss have become on the cultural landscape. Luke Skywalker, Spiderman, Dracula and Elmer Fudd: Kiss are in rarefied company and it seems unlikely the band's final bow next month will change that. But like the Fantastic Four, Kiss will live on.

'The idea that you stop making records doesn't mean the end of the band 'cause the band have always been more than just showing off the new song we just wrote,' Simmons says. 'We're also superheroes and all this other stuff. In our comic books, we don't even have guitars.

'There's a Kiss theme park being worked on, along with a cartoon show, a casino . . . there are already 2500 licences out there. Kiss the entity will continue; what's happening now is a metamorphosis. The caterpillar is dying, but the butterfly will be born.'

Naturally, the New York rockers are not going out quietly. Their 129-date farewell tour of America was yet another licence to print money, so now Simmons, Stanley, Frehley and prodigal drummer Eric Singer (original cat person Peter Criss is a late scratching) are bringing their five-year reunion to Australia before hanging up the skyrocket axes forever.

'And then, maybe with dignity intact, we'll get off the stage,' Simmons, the man born Chaim Witz in Israel fifty years ago, says. 'You know, while we've still got teeth in our heads. We would rather leave the stage than have people wondering when we're leaving the stage. I never want to have a fan come up to me all misty-eyed for the golden years. You've got to quit when it is the golden years. You've got to go out on top.'

In Kiss world, this can only mean one thing: firepower.

'Bigger, better,' Simmons says smugly. 'This tour might be called *Size Does Count*. It's going to be more bang for your buck. We'll throw everything, including the kitchen sink, into it. Paul will fly off the stage to the back of the hall and sing "Love Gun" way above your heads. Look to the skies. Not all the action is going to be on the stage.'

Perish the thought. With tickets ranging from \$70 to \$180 and a range of merchandise to put Pokemon to shame, the lion's share of the action will be going down at the cash register, right?

'Obviously this costs a lot more,' Simmons coos, unfazed. 'Look, let's face it. If I was John Farnham or Tom Petty or any one of those guys, you stand on stage and strum your guitar. Thank you very much, here's a song off my next album. And you don't break a sweat. That's fine, but it's not what we do. We're closer to the Olympics, you know?'

And just like Sydney 2000, it can get kind of emotional up on that podium.

'I don't want to be cornball about it, but this is way beyond anything I thought would happen,' Simmons says of Kiss's twenty-eight-year climb into the hearts and wallets of the world. 'On stage, every now and again it hits me like a tidal wave and – nobody sees it, but I can talk about it now – the lump in the throat and the tear in the eye has happened more than once. It just overcomes you: Oh my God! Look what they've done for me!

'The whole family's there this time. Dads bring their kids, telling them, this is what I've been telling you about! There's a kind of . . . I don't know . . . a last time for passing the torch kind of thing. It all seems to mean a lot more than four guys on stage playing guitars and spitting fire.

'I'm a believer,' Simmons concludes, with just a touch of evangelism, 'and this has carried me a long way. I'm a believer in the roar of the greasepaint and the smell of the crowd. I believe that what we do roars and I believe the crowd knows.

'I believe in the American ideal: "Of the people, for the people and by the people." No queens or kings, no backroom politics, no critics, nothing decides for the people except they, themselves. If they like something, so be it.

'French food critics might tell you frogs' legs are great but that's not going to change people's minds. They're going to eat McDonalds hamburgers 'cause that's what they want. You can pooh-pooh it all you want but guess what? They're going to McDonalds. Maybe at the end of the day Kiss have more to do with hamburgers than with frogs' legs.'

As famous last words, they've got to be up there with 'I wanna rock and roll all night, and party every day.'

April 2001. Original text: Michael Dwyer.

The John Butler Trio

Three's the magic number

In 2001, the John Butler Trio won an ARIA for Best Independent Release with the album *Three*. The story was an inspiration for musicians in a changing world. As major record companies were losing a hint of their prior domination, Butler proved that good music could reach a fan base through traditional means like getting in the car and driving miles between gigs. Good songs connect with people and a little radio airplay doesn't hurt either. The commercial success *Three* enjoyed was the icing on the cake following five years' worth of hard work for Butler and his crew. Politically active, Butler never shies away from voicing his environmental concerns. Quite astutely, Butler releases music through his own label, Jarrah, and has tipped funds back into supporting younger artists with his JB Seed initiative.

They say good things and bad things come in threes, but when it comes to John Butler's new album, it's all good. Titled *Three*, it's the first in which the John Butler Trio have truly been able to express their musical style. While they've been playing together for some time now, *Three* has seen the band hit a new level in their development, due partly to the time they've spent on the road, collecting fans at each stop.

The album's evenly paced recording has offered the band a chance to free themselves up, reaching out for sounds they've previously ignored. Having just remastered the album, Butler is happy with the progress.

'We've just touched up the master,' he says. 'On a couple of the tracks, some of the vocals were a little bit too loud, so I've just come into the studio to do a second master of the disc. We've pressed five thousand CDs so far, so the next pressing will be slightly different to the first one. It feels good to be able to press five thousand CDs off the bat, though. We sold something like ten thousand or eleven thousand copies of the last album and about five thousand of the EP before that, so it's good to be that confident that I can press up that many copies.'

Being an independent artist in this position is no small feat. Many major label signings ship fewer copies in their first week than the John Butler Trio have done, so the singer has good reason to feel particularly chuffed. Attributing his success to a small number of variables, Butler concedes that one of the most vital aspects of his success can be traced to the constant touring he's undertaken from day one.

'The radio play has certainly helped too,' he explains. 'That really helped push things over on to the next stage. Mainly before the radio, the touring gave me the opportunity to consolidate the fan base. If you want to consolidate a fan base quickly, you've got to be out there showing people the songs and letting them know what it is you do. If people like it, they'll come back with their friends and that's how it gets started.

'The first tour I did on my own was a bit hellish. It was fourteen shows in sixteen days between Victoria and Byron Bay. That was driving between each show as well. It was a pretty big effort, but fortunately when I wanted to do the first tour with the band the shows allowed me to pay for tickets for everyone to fly, so that made things a lot easier for everyone. Since then, we've always been able to tour like that, so the band have never had to do the driving tour. I did all the hard work myself. They were good times early on and they really helped me get the confidence I needed.'

Confidence has played an important role in how this record came together. Fuelled by the overwhelmingly positive response his music has received around the country, Butler's latest release is the first where he's really felt that there was room for a little studio experimentation. Embellishing the songs with some added acoustic elements, *Three* shows a greater depth to the trio's abilities.

'We're all very proud of this record,' Butler says. 'It was a chance for us to get out a lot of the ideas that we've been working on for the last few months. Gladly, I can say we did that. Because we've been sitting on some of these songs for a while now, when it came time for us to record them, there was a chance for us to get out as many ideas as we could in them. We knew the songs well, we knew the arrangements and we could add stuff into that. There was a bit of double bass and lap steel that we threw into the songs. We just wanted to evolve what we do.'

An evolution has also taken place between the members of the trio themselves.

'It's an evolution of our relationships with each other. We know each other so well now – we've spent a long time together, with all the touring, and from that we've formed a strong bond, both as friends and as musicians. You can hear that on the album too. We really got some good stuff down in the studio and I think you can hear that we've got to know each other very well in the few years.'

May 2001. Original text: Dave Gendel.

Radio Birdman

You're gonna miss me

'Legendary' gets thrown around with abandon these days. Take a memo, Radio Birdman were *legendary*. *Radios Appear*, their debut, was released in 1977. It's one of the great first outings of all time. Famous for their Surry Hills Fun House gigs, the band were influenced by the Stooges and held up as Australian punks. Punk is another word that's become twisted over time. Incendiary hasn't and that's what Radio Birdman were all about. Deniz Tek, an American medical student, played guitar and wrote the bulk of the band's material. Rob Younger, who later joined the New Christs, was the raw energy out front. Radio Birdman had their own symbol, looked like a military unit, had an army of fanatical fans and a very long hiatus between 1978 and 1996 when they reunited for the Big Day Out. A new album, *Zeno Beach*, appeared in 2006, but since 2008 all has been quiet.

It was cosmically planned out.

When he was still in high school, Radio Birdman leader and guitarist Deniz Tek attended a double bill at the Michigan Union Ballroom in Ann Arbor. That night, he saw the MC5 and the Stooges; the same the night Danny Fields signed the Stooges to Elektra Records. Deniz personally sold a guitar to his hero, Keith Richards, during the Stones' 1973 Australian tour. Tek's musical and visual signature remains the late Fred 'Sonic' Smith's white Epiphone, although Patti Smith would like to have the instrument back where she believes it rightly belongs. In the early seventies, he used to pick up any local copies of yet-to-be recognised classics like the Stooges' *Fun House* and the MC5's *Kick out the Jams* from the cheap bins at Ashwood's and Lawson's in Sydney and hand them out as sonic business cards.

These days, Tek's beloved Radio Birdman have virtually come to be seen as contemporaries of their heroes, a fact dramatically demonstrated during the recent string of North American dates Tek did with the Scott Morgan Band. In New York, eight hundred packed into the venue and Tek's background was anything but lost on the crowd.

'The Birdman songs seemed to get the most respect of anything even more than the Stooges or other songs that we were playing,' Tek says from home in Montana after a heavy day working in the emergency room of his local hospital dealing with an endless line of ambulances and the odd helicopter. 'Ron Asheton from the Stooges was with us there too in New York. So we did a main set for ninety minutes and then took five minutes' break and then we came back with Ron and did half a dozen Stooges songs. We ended with "New Race" and it was "New Race" with Ron that brought the house down.'

Now is, as Tek says, the right time for that music once again, as the pace at which tickets have been snapped up for Birdman's third and final reunion tour of Australia unarguably testifies. Last year's overseas release of the Sub Pop compilation *The Essential Radio Birdman 1974–1978*, which is now available locally, appears to have been the catalyst that has elevated the band beyond their global cult standing. The long-awaited reissue by Citadel Records of the classic *Radios Appear* and *Living Eyes* albums – the first thousand of which are available with the *Burn My Eye* and *More Fun!* EPs, respectively – will further entrench the band's place in rock and roll's true hierarchy.

'The only time I actually get those recordings out and listen to them is like this week when I'm relearning the songs for the tour,' Tek says of the original albums. 'It's not something I go back to very often. Personally, I tend to minimise that stuff, but then every time I hear it I think wow, that still sounds really good.

In fact, it sounds a lot better than I thought I remembered it.'

What's also striking is that the albums continue to occupy their own unique musical space. Influences from the Stones and the Stooges to the Blue Oyster Cult are completely seamless.

'Everybody brought their own element to it and somehow there was a cross-section of all those things that became a thing in itself. I know it's been said over and over again in many different ways that there was a chemistry or a whole that was greater than the sum of the parts and all that kind of thing, but it's really true with this music. It ended up being something that none of us have been able to really achieve on our own otherwise. We've all done good things and other types of things, but it had its own thing.'

A new album, however, is a considerably more difficult proposition than simply booking studio time.

'We may get together in the studio and just see what happens, kind of in a demo mode. We've had an offer for some studio time and we're still talking about it. The idea of Radio Birdman doing another album is certainly appealing and holds interest, but to me it also holds potential for a lot of problems. In the old days it was easy because I wrote all the material, almost all, maybe ninety-five per cent of it. Now all of us have developed into good songwriters. Chris writes great songs, Rob obviously has been writing for fifteen years with the New Christs, writing great material. So you'd have all these people contributing to the songwriting and it would be interesting to see how that could all come together. My opinion would be to be very democratic about it and let everybody have roughly the same number of songs and whether it would be unified or not as an album would be a question that I would have.'

May 2002. Original text: Murray Engleheart.

David Bowie

Living in the moment

David Bowie remains rock's greatest chameleon. After a hiatus of two decades, Bowie reconvened with producer Tony Visconti to create two fine albums, *Heathen* and *Reality. Heathen*, the first Bowie–Visconti collaboration since 1980's *Scary Monsters (and Super Creeps)*, was released in 2002 and went on to sell over two million copies worldwide. Largely recorded in upstate New York, the period saw Bowie turn out a flurry of cracking tunes as well as covering material by the Pixies, the Kinks, Neil Young and Jonathan Richman. With no real guise to hide behind, Bowie described subsequent live dates to promote the work as a 'jeans and t-shirt' tour with an emphasis squarely on the songs and away from theatrics.

David Bowie is relaxing in an armchair overlooking midtown Manhattan. New York is the city he calls home these days, and, reading the apocalyptic lyrics that accompany his new album *Heathen*, you'd be forgiven for assuming the work was written and recorded in the wake of September 11. In fact, the album was largely concluded in upstate New York in August last year.

The release of *Heathen* has had press and public reaching for superlatives. Co-produced with old sparring partner Tony Visconti, *Heathen* is Bowie's best since *Scary Monsters*. After two decades of not quite getting it right, *Heathen* rests alongside *Low*, *Diamond Dogs* and *Young Americans* as one of Bowie's finer works.

Prior to recording, Bowie had been tinkering with forty or fifty ideas. By his own admission, these fragments were largely chord structures, phrases and half-songs. Starting work four hours before Visconti and the musicians arrived at the studio each day allowed Bowie the chance to turn his ideas into something more discernable.

'I was very isolated during the recording,' Bowie explains. 'It was so serene and tranquil. It was almost like the dawn of time. I'd get at up 5:00am. I'd be alone in the studio with these huge twenty-five, thirty-foot high windows. It was overlooking maybe fifty miles. It was like this,' his hand spans the NYC skyline, 'a water reservoir there and mountains over there. It was just extraordinary. There were deer grazing, wandering down to the reservoir. The words just came. It was so easy to write. That definitely put me in the place. It was a bit of an epiphany.'

Bowie resisted polishing his ideas too well. Often a session professional would add a part, only to have Visconti and Bowie remove it after the player had left. Bowie was even reluctant to work out his own ideas too thoroughly prior to recording.

'I know if I finish things off too soon before I get into the studio, I'll start finessing them,' he explains. 'I'm in danger of crushing the stuff that makes them interesting. I'll start to get too sophisticated about how things are written and what the chords should be. I stop at a point where I know the direction it's going, then I pick it up and finish it off quite quickly, so I won't have finessed it too much.'

Alongside Visconti, *Heathen* saw Bowie bring out a few old 'friends'. First, there was the stylophone first used on 'Space Oddity' and then there was Brian Eno's old EMS synthesiser that featured so prominently on Bowie's mid-seventies German trilogy.

'You wouldn't dream of taking one through an airport these days,' Bowie says. 'It's a really smashing briefcase synthesiser. We used it for the first time on *Low* and then consecutively on *Heroes* and *Lodger*. The EMS definitely has a sound. You don't hear the whole Moog sound from the seventies too much these days. They're not quite as controllable as modern machines. Today's synths, I find, can get too finessed. The sound can get too sophisticated.'

Alongside Bowie's own tunes, *Heathen* features three covers:

'Waiting for You' from Neil Young's first solo album, the Pixies' 'Cactus' and 'I Took a Trip on a Gemini Spaceship' from the Legendary Stardust Cowboy.

'He was the greatest clatterer on earth,' Bowie explains of the Stardust Cowboy. 'In the late sixties, he was instrumental in me coming up with the name Ziggy Stardust. I read on his site that [adopts southern accent] "David Bowie took ma name, he really should've done one of ma songs". He made me feel so guilty. I thought "You're right, I really should have." That's why I did it.'

'Cactus', a genuine highlight on *Heathen*, sounds positively more Bowie than Bowie.

'Yeah, I was quite happy with that. He's a very good writer, Frank Black. The three things I did as covers were in a way a homage to the people who've written them. It was like "I really must do a song by this person because they're just terrific." I thought it was a hell of a shame that America didn't recognise its own with the Pixies. They broke up virtually penniless. I mean, they were so important, but they never meant a thing outside of New York and Los Angeles. I always thought "Cactus" was a real cracking song. I played drums on that one.'

A strong influence on *Heathen* was German composer Richard Strauss. 'Last Four Songs', written towards the end of Strauss's life in the 1940s, moved Bowie to the extent that he felt he should 'try to capture some of the gravitas and spiritual weight' of Strauss's work in a pop/rock way.

'When I was living in Berlin, I really listened to a lot of his work,' he continues. 'There were all kinds of German music I listened to at the time, not just Kraftwerk. Strauss was always . . . I was going to say I liked the stuff he wrote for Kubrick!' he laughs. 'I liked the stuff Kubrick used in *A Clockwork Orange*. It's funny isn't it? [Adopts American accent] "Who's that writer?" "Strauss, sir." "Did we sign him?"'

Prior to recording *Heathen*, Bowie switched off the radio and retreated to his own artistic enclave.

'I've got my own little world: books that I read, things that I look at and things that get me going,' he explains. 'The kinds of music that gets me are always very obscure things, stuff that doesn't put me in a contemporary frame of mind too much. I was listening to things like Strauss, Speedboats for Breakfast and a group called Godspeed You! Black Emperor. They're an extraordinary French Canadian group of violinists and tin can bangers . . . really strange neo-classical anarchistic clatter. I love interesting clatter.'

Despite the instrumentation and the presence of Visconti, *Heathen* is hardly revisionist. If anything, Bowie has reused techniques from the past to create a contemporary piece of work. Looking over his shoulder is hardly a Bowie trait.

'In my Buddhist way of thinking, you cannot be controlled by the idea of a past or the idea of a future. If you're not taking significant notice of the now, of this moment in time, then you have no life at all. The moment is all. It's best not to neglect that.'

July 2002. Original text: Sean Sennett.

Paul Weller

All hail the Modfather

During his years with the Jam, Paul Weller was dubbed 'spokesman for a generation'. Next came the popstar years with the Style Council, followed by a slew of acclaimed solo albums. Along the way he dodged the slings and arrows of Dad Rock and became a major influence on Britpop. With a lifetime achievement award at the Brits, the Modfather is a music lifer whose creative output shows no signs of waning. For years, speculation was rife as to why Weller hadn't visited Australia since the mid-eighties. It was assumed he couldn't go the distance without a cigarette. When he did return in 2008, he proved the fire hadn't gone out. Earlier, with 2002's *Illumination*, he scored top spot on the UK album charts and returned to Australian radio with 'It's Written in the Stars'.

Paul Weller has been recording music for the best part of three decades. His new album, *Illumination*, proves that age has barely wearied him. With the single 'It's Written in the Stars' doing big business in the UK, Weller is back on top of his game. *Illumination*, which was recorded in Surrey and at Noel Gallagher's Wheeler End Studios in Bucks, has Weller plying his well-worn trade with a new upbeat bent. Possibly the result of coming to terms with his own unique legacy, the album sees Weller embracing the 'Weller' of old, while still forging new ground.

'It's Written in the Stars' is a collaboration with Noonday Underground's Simon Dine. The song grew out of Dine's sample, with Weller adding further touches. The result is the most refreshing Weller single in half a decade.

'It wasn't as if it was totally revolutionary,' begins Weller. 'I can't say it was a brand new way of working with somebody, because I've worked by building tracks up through samples in the past; and later replaced them with live playing. The fact it was someone different [to work with] was good. We did a couple of tracks for the album, and we did a B-side for the new single as well. Whoever you work with is always going to bring something different to the table.'

To work on *Illumination*, Weller called upon Carleen Anderson, Steve Cradock (Ocean Colour Scene), Kelly Jones (Stereophonics) and Noel Gallagher to lend a hand.

'We spread the recording over quite a long period of time,' he explains of the process. 'We'd only go into the studio for like three days and put down two or three tracks. We did quite a lot in a short period of time. Then, we'd come away and take a listen and fix bits that we needed to do.

'If you put all the time together, it probably took less than two months to do the whole thing. It took so long, because all of last year I was on the road doing this solo acoustic tour. So, we had to record around that. We finished in June, but April and May were our most intense periods.'

Weller's acoustic tour led to the live album *Days of Speed*. Armed with an acoustic guitar and a set list, Weller traipsed around the UK and Europe and fell in love with a few old tunes again. The Jam's 'English Rose' was one; the Style Council's 'Down in the Seine' was another. It's been suggested that the time spent reliving old songs lit a spark for his recent work.

'A lot of those songs from the Style Council days were written really quickly,' he continues. 'I'd literally write the night before, and we'd go into our own studio the next day and put them down. Having our own studio gave us freedom. That kind of happened at least for the first two albums and that run of singles. It was very fresh at that time. I still think of it as an exciting golden time for me.

'I think all the songs on *Illumination* were written quickly [too]. With me, I'll start them and get an idea and then I'll put it down for days or weeks or whatever and come back to it. They're done in stages. It's similar to what I was saying about the recording really.

'With previous albums, I've been in the studio for weeks on end . . . which can be productive. I don't know if I can do it anymore. I've got other responsibilities and stuff. I don't like to be away from home for too long anyway. For me, it was best to get in for a few days, do as much as you can and then come away and listen to it. I didn't want to be on top of it all the time. Mixing as well was really . . . we got a rough mix up on the desk, and if it felt good we went with it. A lot of the material is live; it's first or second takes. There's at least four tracks that were demos and we couldn't really think how we could improve on them. We kind of kept them as they were really.'

It's been suggested that the upbeat nature of *Illumination* might have something to do with the fact that Weller has become a dad again.

'I think it's the way I feel generally,' he explains. 'Obviously, all my children make me feel that way. You have to be positive for your kids' sake. For me personally, it's the kind of record I want to hear as well. So, it's for me and everyone else really.'

These days, Weller spends time with his family, rehearsing, writing and touring. There's half a chance he may even make it to Australia early next year. The rest of the time, he's listening to music.

'I never shut myself off from listening to things,' he considers, 'but I don't listen to things that I think are going to directly inspire my music. I think it's more an overall "inspiration" I'm after. I've got really eclectic tastes. I can listen to Indian classical music. I might play some African music; some reggae . . . whatever's good at the time. It's not as though I'm listening to one form of music. I can't say anything has a direct influence, apart from the fact you just get inspired when you listen to great music.'

September 2002. Original text: Sean Sennett.

Eels

Accentuate the positive (and avoid the whorehouse)

The American writer Kurt Vonnegut once said, 'I'm whistling as I walk past the graveyard and I'm whistling as beautifully as I can.' It's a line that could easily have come directly from the voice of Mark Oliver Everett.

Life has been a long and bumpy ride for Everett, otherwise known as E, the leader and only constant member of languid Los Angeles rockers the Eels. In a career that now spans fifteen years, E's many triumphs and successes have always been offset by tragedies, both large and small. And E has poured both into music that can swing wildly between aching beauty and loud, dirty rock (or is it loud, dirty beauty and aching rock?).

'So what's the future got in store for me? What have I got to look forward to?' a nervous voice croaks down the phone. The Kermit-the-Frog-style mumble belongs to Eels front man Mark Oliver Everett, or as most people know him, E. It's 8:00pm on Thursday night in Los Angeles, but at the *Time Off* office, Friday afternoon is already being ushered in.

Unfortunately, if West Coast America's weather patterns mirror Brisbane's, shitty weather's about the only thing E can expect when he wakes tomorrow.

'Oh great,' he moans.

E is, to borrow the title from the Eels' debut long-player, a beautiful freak. He's frustratingly difficult to talk to, but in an endearing kind of way. He even apologises shortly after the interview gets underway for his introversion and claims, 'nothing in my life is easily explained'.

He doesn't mean to be rude; it's just how he comes across. He's shy and unwilling to delve too deeply into any subject, refusing to be drawn even after considerable prodding, although he does reveal the biggest compliment anybody's paid him is to tell him they listen to his music during sex. But, by his own admission, E's 'a miserable old bastard'.

Really, you can't blame him. He experimented heavily with drinks and drugs during his teenage years. He found his father dead when he was nineteen years old. And then came his sister's suicide in 1996 and his mother's loss to cancer two years later. It doesn't stop there. When Flight 77 crashed into the Pentagon on September 11, 2001, E's cousin and her husband were both on board as flight attendants. Neither survived.

So what about now, in 2003? Where's his head at?

'It's a struggle to be positive sometimes,' he admits. 'At different points in my life, it's been a struggle but you've got to try. I wouldn't still be here if I hadn't tried so hard. Anyway, being pissed off . . . it's not a fun way to live your life.'

Eels' latest offering, *Shootenanny!*, is certainly a poppier and more uplifting affair than much of what's gone before. Sure, it's up and down and there are definitely some dark moments (for example, 'Restraining Order Blues' and 'Agony'), but tunes like the undeniably catchy first single, 'Saturday Morning', ooze sunshine and smiles. So what sets E's pulse racing? What makes him happy?

'Well, I just came home from practising with the Eels and it was a great day. I got to sit around and play music all day. I used to hate touring but as you get older you learn what to get upset about and what to just accept as part of your life. I always try to keep the perspective that there are definitely worse things I could be doing. Before I had ambitions to play music I didn't have any ambitions at all, so while it's not an easy life you do get to rock each night and that's pretty good.

'I never thought I'd make a living as a musician, but, when I was about twenty-one, I realised there was nothing else I had any passion for. Everyone I knew was going off to college and I didn't have any direction. All I did was write and record onto four-track tapes. I had hundreds of songs and I was always making these albums on cassette tapes. Every month I had a new album.'

These days, the process of releasing an album takes a little longer, although E admits he's still an alarmingly prolific writer. And while we only get to hear a fraction of the work he produces, it's not for the reason many other artists prefer to keep certain songs locked away (otherwise known as the 'oh, I only wrote this one for myself' excuse). E says there's no such thing as writing too honestly or getting too personal.

'When I write a song it's always an intimate and lonely process,' he says. 'It never occurs to me that one day this will be on an album and lots of people will hear it. I'm just not concerned what people think about it. The Eels were designed to just let me breathe and let me grow. I don't care about alienating fans. I mean, it's nice to have people listening, but I'm happy if I just get to make the next record.'

So what about reviews? The new record received a scathing 2.8 out of 10 from Pitchfork Media recently.

'I've heard about that one! They're like the indie poseur guys, aren't they? Those kinds of people, the so-called indie people, are just the emptiest people I can imagine. The worst part about being in a band is I hate being lumped into the alternative music scene because it's all bullshit. It's supposedly rebelling against something but there's no such thing as an alternative scene. It's all for sale and it's all bullshit and a bunch of people acting cool and missing the point about being an individual and what it's meant to be about.

'I try to avoid reviews but someone always seems to stick one or another in my face. Sometimes they make good points, but so often they don't. I really think the whole idea of rock criticism is kind of ridiculous.'

That's a funny thing to say coming from someone who once tried his hand at music journalism. But, like E says, nothing in his life is easily explained. He recently hinted that the next Eels album might well be the last. So is this where the sunshine ends?

'Well, that's how I feel right now, but that's also probably something of a defence mechanism. I really want to pour everything into the next album and the only way to do that is to look at it like it's your last. You know, live every day like it's your last day. Well, you have to make every album like it's your last one. But maybe it really will be. I don't know.'

And which incarnation of his famously itinerant band should Australian audiences expect to see on their next tour?

'Well, we've been playing as a four-piece rock combo, but by the time we get to Australia you never know. They're musicians, so they're naturally flaky. Musicians sometimes just disappear and end up dead in a whorehouse, particularly when they go to exotic places like Europe, Japan or Australia.'

Let's hope E doesn't go the same way.

'Oh, I can go to the whorehouse,' he chirps. 'I just can't die there! I've got shows to play!'

June 2003. Original text: Nick Coppack.

Metallica

Back to basics

With the release of *Some Kind of Monster*, Metallica lifted the bar on what was expected from a rockumentary. The film took us inside the mildly dysfunctional unit that created 2003's *St Anger* album. With a therapist on the payroll to help navigate their problems, front man James Hetfield attempted to kick an addiction, bassist Jason Newsted had left the fold and the controversy with Napster wasn't that far behind them. At the time, it was six years between drinks for the band: their previous effort *ReLoad* was released in 1997. Produced by Bob Rock, who also played bass on the album, *St Anger* debuted at number one on the American charts and saw the band return to touring with new member Robert Trujillo (who was famously given a million dollar 'sign on fee').

Metallica's first official shows with former Suicidal Tendencies and Ozzy Osbourne bassist Robert Trujillo were a symbolic homecoming in the form of four nights at the legendary Fillmore in San Francisco.

While Trujillo sat and quietly learned an unfamiliar song a mere hour before hitting the stage (these are the very qualities that landed him the job), guitarist Kirk Hammett had a more stressful evening under the gaze of an unexpected observer.

'There was a picture of Jerry Garcia staring at me the entire time we were on stage last night!' he says after the first show, which they opened with the early classic 'Hit the Lights'. He then adds dismissively, 'I'm not a Dead fan.'

That was kids' stuff. A few weeks earlier, on Thursday May

1, Metallica performed at the notorious San Quentin Prison after shooting a video there the day before for the title track of their new album, *St Anger*. For a band out to re-establish their attitude credentials it was the ultimate launch pad. Not to mention it's also the hallowed ground where Johnny Cash – singer and guitarist James Hetfield's hero – legendarily performed.

'Once I got around the concept of actually going into San Quentin, the dreaded prison that I can see from the freeway when I drive to our studio, it was fine,' Hammett reveals. 'And there were a lot of inmates there that were just total Metallica fans. We signed a lot of autographs for a lot of guards and some of the inmates we were actually able to interact with. But for the most part there were a lot of boundaries that were put down right away!' he laughs. 'Actually, the only thing keeping us separated was a yellow line painted on the ground that said "Out of bounds",' he laughs in disbelief. 'That made me nervous but there were guards everywhere.

'At one point we played with a bunch of prisoners above us. That was pretty scary. They're in a cellblock and they were five storeys up just leaning over watching the band. It was a bit intimidating but we got through it.'

Put in perspective, the San Quentin experience was a picnic compared to the challenges Metallica have faced over the past three years or so. Their trials were twofold: the departure of bassist Jason Newsted and the somewhat surprising personal difficulties of Hetfield that led to a stint in rehab that, at one point, placed a question mark on the band's entire future. Now, all that seems nothing more than a rite of passage.

'When I look back at this time last year, we hadn't played a note since James had come back from rehab,' Hammett says. 'Now we have a kickarse album, a kickarse tour, we're playing our hometown tonight and we have a great band and a new bass player that we love who's just an incredible human being. It couldn't be more the polar opposite of where we were a year ago and I'm just so thankful it's gone this way. It feels like a rebirth of the band.'

The flagship for that reawakening is the hotly anticipated new album, *St Anger*, which is destined to reclaim Metallica's crown as the biggest metal band on the planet. Statements of intent and purpose come no stronger or more forceful. Earning its title from a manic renaming of Hammett's St Christopher's medal by Hetfield, the name's more than appropriate for what the band are offering up musically, even if the back-to-basics classic Metallica sound isn't intentional.

'It just kind of happened that way,' Hammett admits. 'We wrote a bunch of songs and at the end we all got together to vote on what songs should be on the album. Out of thirty songs, only four got all four votes. That was clearly telling us something: that we all agreed on a certain kind of direction because these songs were very different than the other batch and that kind of set the tone.

'It wasn't something that we thought we should just revisit old memories. I don't think it's that at all. I really think that it's more like us just harnessing aggression and power again, and energy and dynamics again, like we used to. It felt good, it felt fresh to us.'

But most powerful of all is the knowledge that the band now recognise and appreciate their own collective magic.

'You know, it was something that we all kind of took for granted. Now there's a greater appreciation for our chemistry that we have and for each other as individuals. I mean, mentally as well as, you know, lovingly and physically. Metallica in 2003 is just a wonderful place to be. In the past it's been a very turbulent thing to be holding on to . . . at times by the skin of your teeth.'

June 2003. Original text: Murray Engleheart.

Marilyn Manson

Step right up to the Marilyn Manson circus

Courting controversy is Marilyn Manson's modus operandi. A former music journalist, Manson has made a career from cleverly pushing the cultural envelope. Like Alice Cooper before them, Marilyn Manson are a band, though it's their darkly enigmatic leader who captures most of the attention. The image of Manson as a simplistic OTT shock rocker with little substance was challenged by Manson's thoughtful and measured turn in Michael Moore's *Bowling for Columbine*. An accomplished artist, Manson has also acted in over a dozen films and was allegedly used by Johnny Depp as the basis for his Willie Wonka character.

Simulated sex acts, fake blood and crucifixes made from guns proved a bit too much for the Six Flags amusement park in Darien Lake, New York, which banned 'shock and roller' Marilyn Manson from performing on its grounds.

Highly publicised at the time, Manson was due to play at the park as one of the headlining acts on the Ozzfest tour. But, instead, on the day thousands of fans put the roar of a roller-coaster to shame, he found himself in a New York hotel room on the phone to an Australian journalist. The amusement park deemed Manson's act 'not appropriate' for the venue. This, Manson found comical. The irony of the situation made him laugh anyway, even if the fact of his fans' disappointment didn't.

The singer, whose live shows are notorious for their graphic political and religious statements and absurd imagery for shock's sake, spoke nonchalantly about the ban.

'Well, you know, it's unfortunate that some people in Buffalo still think we're living in the middle ages,' he says in a monotone, considered and slightly croaky voice.

'They seem to find my ideas, my songs, my aesthetic and my performance more offensive than what the President may be doing on any given day. But that's okay. I'm going to go back and do my own show on my own terms after Ozzfest. And after I come to Australia of course.'

Manson promises to stalk Australian stages with a typically sordid show featuring all the childish, sometimes scary, elements of Disneyland – women baring flesh-coloured fake breasts, butts and genitals – inspired by the politics and decadence of Germany's post–World War I Weimar Republic. That period of artistic and cultural revolution is also the basis of Manson's latest album, *The Golden Age of Grotesque*.

The sultan of the surreal didn't choose the period to play history teacher for his faithful, but for its impact on expressionism as an art form. He insists what he does is art, not just music.

'You know the clichés,' he begins. 'Obviously history repeats itself, you can't see where you're going unless you see where you've been and it can't be modern unless you look back to the past. Expressionism is what this album is about and expressionism was born in that period. The people took a time of political upheaval and turned it into one of the most creative periods of all time.'

The Golden Age of Grotesque's connections with pre–Nazi Germany, the McCarthyism of the 1950s and the present world's political climate are clear.

'I just wanted to depict the spirit of that time. It's such a visual era. Be it fashion or the military or in art and films. The world was changing in so many ways that it was hard to avoid that inspiration. It is still something that fascinates me. It's a time that we will never get to be in, probably never wanted to be in. But we can learn from it, we learn from mistakes.'

Often perceived as a sideshow or just an act, there is something eerily genuine about Manson. Brian Warner, as his name would have appeared on school class lists, is a being of the past. He lives a life of decadence with his long-term partner, popular burlesque artist and leading fetish model Dita von Teese, and takes pleasure in absinthe, his tipple of choice. But he strangely admits to liking Chevy Chase movies. As Warner, Manson once worked as a music journalist. He began Marilyn Manson & the Spooky Kids with a mission to 'explore the limits of censorship'.

'I think I became a music journalist because I was a big fan of music. And I think I became Marilyn Manson because I was a big fan of music. There wasn't anything filling a void that I was looking for, so I had to fill it for myself.'

Last year, Manson attracted an army of appreciators following his appearance in Michael Moore's Academy Award–winning documentary *Bowling for Columbine*. Conservatives blamed Manson for the 1999 shootings at Columbine High School because the kids that committed the crime listened to his brand of music. But when Manson appeared on screen, dissecting the 'fear and consumption' at work in American culture, he proved himself an informed, intelligent, articulate and controlled individual. He admits his appearance changed the way he was treated by many people, although he publicly stated that he did not appreciate the film's overt political agenda.

'It's another part of me that I think some people didn't know. Partly the timing of that became a challenge for me in creating *The Golden Age* . . . I wanted to make an album that contained all of my personality, one that had my sarcasm, my wit or my bitterness or my vitriol, or my love: all of it. I wanted it all in there.'

Manson would like to think that like the black and white make-up he adorns, there is no grey area in his music.

'I've come to realise that what I do cannot be misunderstood because I want it to be understood by everyone differently. So for someone who thinks it's rubbish or satanic or just nonsense, that understanding of it is just as important as someone who finds a philosophy, or a beauty behind it. My understanding of what I meant when I wrote it is always going to be different when other people listen to it.

'On *The Golden Age of Grotesque* I wanted to point out not what I see is wrong in the world but what I feel is right as well and show people my world. It is my amusement park.'

September 2003. Original text: Mick Gadd.

Jet

Fasten your seatbelts

Success of bands like the Vines heightened international interest in Australian music. Jet's first EP was reviewed by the *NME* and picked up by a major label for re-release. Attracting not only an American studio producer for their debut album, the band were also able to enlist rock keyboard virtuoso Billy Preston (who had worked with Sam Cooke, Eric Clapton and the Beatles among others). Such was the hype surrounding them, Jet were offered a support slot for the Rolling Stones' Australian tour while still recording the album that would become *Get Born*.

This interview from 2003 pre-empts that album's phenomenal success around the world. The Hottest 100 and iTunes commercials were still a while away, but the indications were already there that this was a band capable of something spectacular, however briefly.

Like anorak-clad trainspotters diligently recording locomotive numbers, the music purist can be an obsessive breed. Sure, there's no harm in a game of spot the riff, but when music zealots delve into classicism – the world of 'we've heard it all before' – they might as well pack up their eight-track and head home.

Jet are set to know all about the dismissive music purist, the kind of party-pooper who'll dismiss the band's jukebox-fuelled rock and roll as overtly derivative. Not only are such naysayers missing out on the fun, they're entirely missing the point.

As vocalist and guitarist Nic Cester admits, the boys from Jet aren't afraid to wear influences on their collective sleeve. He agrees it's the way Jet combine influences from the Beatles and the Rolling Stones to AC/DC, the Kinks, and the sounds of Motown that makes things interesting.

'We could have tried to dull it down a little but that's not what we wanted,' Cester says resolutely. 'We know we're going to cop shit for it but we really don't care.'

Neither should they. Jet's debut album *Get Born* is cracking good fun, offering up songs like 'Are You Gonna Be My Girl', a song that neatly segues the Supremes' 'You Can't Hurry Love' into Iggy Pop's 'Lust for Life'.

'I'm glad you said the Supremes because everyone's talked about the Iggy Pop reference but for us it was always more a Motown kind of thing,' he says of the single. 'We love these bands so much we just wanted to combine them. Part of the fun for me is to wonder stuff like "what would happen if the Who, the Stones and the Beatles got together and wrote a song". They're all my favourite bands and with the benefit of hindsight, you can really have fun with that.'

Jet recorded *Get Born* in early 2003 at a handful of Los Angeles's finest studios, including the legendary Sunset. Behind the mixing desk was producer Dave Sardy (the Dandy Warhols, Supergrass), selected for his broad artist resume.

'We went to a couple of studios but we started there,' Cester beams of Sunset. 'Just for us to be in a studio knowing the Stones had been there and so many of our heroes have recorded there . . . There were photos of them there but I think the rooms have been changed around so much it now looks nothing like it did. Aside from that, having access to all this gear was just incredible.

'As for producers, we pretty much had our pick of who we wanted. We kind of whittled away at this enormous list for about a month until we got it down to a small enough list of people we could actually start ringing and talking to. That's when we decided to go with Dave. He's really well known as a "sound guy" and probably better known as an amazing mixer.

'We knew what sort of sounds we wanted to get and we knew

he was capable of getting those sounds. Also, he'd worked with such a wide range of artists and we thought one of the problems with our songs might be that the style kind of varies throughout. We wanted someone who'd be capable of treating all those songs as individual songs as well as putting them together into a cohesive album.

'With the people we've worked with, one of the things we've found is that everyone likes our influences. Working on these songs is kind of fun for them because we wanted to achieve some really classic sounds. For people who are really into music, they generally share a love of those sounds. I think it was kind of fun for Dave.'

Is songwriting more a band effort these days?

'It depends. Songs like the ballads, because they're more personal, it's probably best they come from the one person and that's generally the case. It's different every time and there really is no one set way. Maybe that's why there are a lot of different things going on there. Sometimes you might just get on a roll and do a whole song from start to finish as a band or someone might have a riff and you jam on it. It might start with a groove, chorus or verse. It's different all the time.'

Indeed, when *Get Born* turns sweet for ballads – 'Look What You've Done' and 'Come Around Again' – it plays its strongest cards.

'Originally it was just an acoustic song,' Cester says of 'Look What You've Done'. 'Obviously now it sounds like a fuckin' Beatles song but originally it was kind of more Neil Finn. We could have done it more acoustic and not made it sound so Beatles, but that was part of the fun for us. We've always loved the *White Album* drum/snare sound. One of Ringo's tricks was to use a packet of cigarettes filled with nuts and bolts on his actual snare, so we had fun doing that on that song. I think the piano makes it sound pretty classic as well.

'"Come Around Again", that's my favourite one on the album, I think. That's probably one that doesn't really wear its influences as much as some of the others. It started off with a sort of country chorus that I had and I think Cam [Muncey, guitar] had a verse – they were a perfect match. We knew we needed a bridge and it kind of all happened in a couple of minutes and it was done. But I don't think it really shone as a song until Billy Preston played some fucking amazing stuff on it.'

September 2003. Original text: Matt Connors.

The White Stripes

It's been a bad year for the White Stripes' bones

Using basic raw blues as their template, Jack and Meg White have, as the White Stripes, fashioned a sound at once modern and retro and entirely their own. The band are unusual in that they are defined as much by their self-imposed limitations as their sound or their image (seemingly lifted directly from bullseye lollies). On their fourth album, *Elephant*, the band broke through to an international audience, earning them both critical acclaim and a legion of young fans that evidently made them slightly uncomfortable.

About a year ago, the door of the White Stripes' dressing room in San Francisco opened with a quiet ceremony and in walked Tom Waits and his entire family. Jack and Meg White had been warned about a possible audience with the retiring Waits, but they still weren't properly prepared for his actual presence, particularly in their honour. The pair wasn't so lucky when it came to crossing paths with the late Johnny Cash and they have been suitably outraged by the massive, populist outpouring of 'respect' for the man in black since his death.

'I think in Vancouver, Jack awarded him video of the year [for the equal parts harrowing and majestic 'Hurt'] because MTV neglected to do so,' Meg says with a delightful giggle that's every bit in keeping with her ponytail and teen looks. 'It was just at one of our shows; we were kind of upset that he didn't get anything, you know. I mean, he should have got every award that he was nominated for. It's an amazing video! Not that he really would care, but it was just rude, I thought. But then he dies and suddenly everyone has all these retrospectives on him and it's like *fuck you*! You don't have the . . . you've ignored him until now, don't fucking . . . I don't know . . .'

The White Stripes were in Portland on the fourth show of their tour after a period Meg describes as 'a long break'. No pun is intended, but it's a term that certainly suits their circumstances of late. Meg broke her arm in February after slipping on an icy surface. Then, just as the *Elephant* album was kicking into full gear, Jack broke his left index finger in three places after an airbag did what airbags do in car accidents. They were off the road for about two months.

'He's still getting back into it,' Meg says. 'He doesn't have full use of his hand yet, but he's trying! It's been a bad year for bones! I guess we didn't have enough calcium when we were children or something.'

Jack's plastered hand ruled the band out of the UK festival season in August, although Meg made the trip to Reading where her boyfriend was appearing as a member of the Soledad Brothers. Nonetheless, she was still in the limelight and, at one point, found herself posing sweetly with a teenage fan while her beaming dad took a photo.

'I can't specifically remember that one, but I have my picture taken with little kids a lot actually!' she says, slightly embarrassed. 'I think the thing is, when you get a little more popular, of course you get more mainstream attention and that's where a lot of kids are watching. So I think it tends to kind of go that way. We have kind of a wide spread but it does seem like more kids now.'

As was the case with the Stones and their use of the blues early in their career, few of the younger members of the White Stripes' audience are likely (and reasonably so) to be aware of the pair's enormous passion for such classic musical touchstones as Son House, the Stooges' *Fun House* album (the Whites' all time favourite), Captain Beefheart or Tammy Wynette.

The impact of *Elephant*, which has the same gritty rock and roll appeal as the Stones' *Sticky Fingers* or *Exile on Main Street* – albeit with MTV-type smarts – has broadened the pair's potential instructional demographic enormously. Kids, school is now in session.

'I guess sometimes it feels a little like that,' Meg admits. 'If we play Son House's "Death Letter" and there's a fourteen-year-old girl singing along, you hope she might look at *Fun House* too and buy that album. That would be a good thing.'

Strong sales to one side, in a recent breakdown of the 100 Greatest Guitar Albums, respected UK magazine *Mojo* ranked *Elephant* alongside such modern-day masterpieces as My Bloody Valentine's *Loveless*, Nirvana's *Nevermind* and Radiohead's *The Bends*. Acclaim like that, along with the general critical reception the album's received around the world, has all been a very pleasant surprise for the White Stripes.

'We didn't really know what was going to happen, if people were going to love it or hate it. But we loved it so we thought however it would be is how it would be and that was fine. We're still doing our thing. Whether it becomes huge or just a bomb, it doesn't matter to us.'

That same take-it-as-it-comes down-to-earth attitude has been the ballast steadying the band's good ship over the past year or two.

'We're very private people and try to live our life,' Meg says. 'If somebody comes up to us you try to absorb it without thinking about it too much.'

October 2003. Original text: Murray Engleheart.

Public Enemy

Still fighting the power

Uber-producer Rick Rubin first heard Chuck D rapping on the track 'Public Enemy No 1'. Rubin was so impressed he offered a recording contract. Reluctant initially, Chuck signed on the dotted line once he'd lined up Flavor Flav, Professor Griff, Terminator X, S1W and the Bomb Squad. In 1987, they released *Yo! Bum Rush the Show*, their label, Def Jam's, lowest-selling release to date. That all changed with *It Takes a Nation of Millions to Hold Us Back* and *Fear of a Black Planet*, both of which helped usher in the golden age of hip-hop.

Beneath the beats there's always politics. S1W stands for 'security of the first world'. In Chuck D's words it 'represents that the black man can be just as intelligent as he is strong. It stands for the fact that we're not third-world people, we're first-world people; we're the original people [of the earth]'.

Besides his work with Public Enemy, Chuck D, who follows Islam, is an author, publisher, lecturer and vegetarian. You can also hear his sports commentary on PlayStation 3.

In 2003, rap music is one of the staples of commercial radio and television, with the vast majority of people enjoying it in one form or another. But it hasn't always been this way.

Without groups like Public Enemy, it's debatable how widespread or homogenised hip-hop would be today. Public Enemy were one of the first rap groups game enough to voice their opinion on anything and everything, without fear of rebuke or reprisal. They quickly established themselves as visionaries and still cling tightly to their freedom.

The group contains two core rappers: the enigmatic and unstoppable Flavor Flav, somewhat responsible for the 'bling-bling' styling in modern hip-hop fashion (although he often prefers clocks to chunky gold chains), and the silky smooth and fervently political Chuck D.

Today, at half past one in the morning, it's Chuck D who comes down the phone line from halfway around the world.

'I'm in Rio de Janeiro, Brazil,' a very relaxed sounding Chuck D says in that instantly recognisable voice. 'I never for a moment thought Public Enemy would be turning in their fiftieth tour in such a wonderful place. Yes sir, it's our fiftieth world tour! There's a big awards ceremony tonight – we're doing some songs there – and then we're doing a proper show in São Paulo. We're really very happy to be here as ambassadors of hip-hop.'

It's a statement that's loaded with meaning, and indeed Public Enemy are worthy to be one of the worldwide ambassadors of hip-hop. From their first work back in 1987 with *Public Enemy #1* the group have been outspoken and challenging while still block-rockin' the party. The band's consistency owes something to the stability of their line-up.

'The line-up of the band hasn't really changed too much since the turn of the millennium,' Chuck explains. 'Last time we were in Brisbane we had Terminator X in the house but he retired soon after and we replaced him with DJ Lord, who's a world-class DJ all by himself. He's actually toured to Australia himself on numerous occasions. He's a brilliant drum'n'bass DJ.

'So then we've also added a band component to the group called PE, which are a band consisting of a drummer, bassist and guitarist. Of course, there's also myself, Flavor Flav and the S1Ws, and that's the whole group. It's a combination you've never heard or seen before and it's really very hard to imagine what it's going to be like. We take the dynamic elements of both a great DJ and a great band and combine it in an awesome fashion. It's something you've just got to experience for yourself. I call it ferocious soul,' Chuck says, painting a picture that's not altogether easy to decipher.

But considering these boys have toured the world fifty times now, including a little outing with U2 for the *ZooTV* tour, it's bound to be pretty mesmerising.

'It's easily the greatest hip-hop show on earth,' Chuck D proclaims. 'It's more than that, though. It's like the Grateful Dead meets the Dave Matthews Band meets the Rolling Stones meets James Brown meets Rage Against the Machine, all rolled into one. We present an event. When we present an event you really can't replace it. It's beyond top ten shit. It's a total event.

'We draw on the whole period of our work when we play live. We would disappoint so many people if we didn't play some of our tunes. When I go and see the Rolling Stones I want to see Keith Richards going *yang yang yang a yang* . . .' Chuck says, launching into 'Jumping Jack Flash' down the phone. 'I want to see that!'

On their more recent albums, the group's anger at America has broadened, holding a mirror to popular black culture as well as denouncing the recent actions of President George W Bush.

'My whole thing has always been say something or say nothing,' Chuck says. 'We have made sure with the loud music and soundscapes we put together that our voice can always be heard and both myself and Flavor have something distinctive to say.

'We've always had a totally global point of view. When you limit yourself to an American kind of view you really limit the kind of discussions you can enter. And yes, we are black men inside this world, so we know that world opinion is more relative about what we mean when we say "Fight the Power", as opposed to just having an American state of mind.

'From day one it was our goal to have a worldwide point of view, to have a global hip-hop message. America treats itself like it's the only place in the world, that it's far more important than anywhere else. I think becoming an American is increasingly becoming a smaller part of world opinion.

'We have to think globally,' Chuck concludes. 'We have to work out how we all live in this world together, considering that governments are the cancer of civilisation. It's going to take a bit of work.'

Maybe so, but God knows it'll be worth it.

November 2003. Original text: Matt Fraser.

Missy Higgins

Girl wonder

There are few better indications of how far Australian music had progressed and grown in confidence over the previous thirty-odd years than with this short, but sweet, interview with Missy Higgins. The accumulated effect of strong local independent venues, street press, and radio can be found nowhere better than in the fortunes of the various artists who have been 'unearthed' by Triple J. That Australian artists can talk of pushing into the United States market – without a hint of sarcasm or bitterness – speaks volumes for the confidence and strength of the artists this decade has produced.

Forget *Australian Idol* and the likes of Anthony Callea: the biggest Australian artist of the past six months is undoubtedly Missy Higgins.

On its release last September, her debut album, *The Sound of White*, flew to the top of the charts and has since sold more than 350,000 copies. Recent weeks have seen the long-player top the charts again, eclipsing sales for the likes of Robbie Williams, Green Day and Gwen Stefani.

Not that the laidback Melbourne singer/songwriter gives a toss. Talking sales percentages and celebrity status just isn't her style. When *Time Off* spied Higgins and fellow hot property Pete Murray being accosted by camera-toting fans at Wave Aid, the pair seemed equally bemused.

'It's funny,' Higgins admits of her growing fandom. 'I find it really hard to believe that I'm on that side of things now, that people want to get a photo of me. It's just very . . . strange.'

She'd better get used to it. Her performance at Wave Aid in late January elicited arguably the day's biggest crowd reaction, despite sharing the bill with the likes of Powderfinger and Midnight Oil.

'I was really happy with that,' she says of Wave Aid. 'The sound was so bad when I got out there because obviously no one had any time to do soundchecks or anything. It was just so loud! But it was amazing to play in front of so many people for something like that. It felt so amazing to be on the bill with so many great acts and I had to keep mentally pinching myself.'

Higgins is again in the spotlight this month with a national tour that sees her jump from medium-sized venues to theatres and large-scale entertainment centres.

'That should be fun,' she says of the tour. 'It's a pretty big deal for me because it's the first time I've done such big venues headlining. Six months ago I was the support act in these venues where people were just wandering in and not really listening to what I was playing. Now I've actually got my own shows there, so it's pretty exciting for me.'

Higgins will tear into the tour just days after returning from the United States, where she's starting to make solid inroads with select showcase gigs. She's signed to Warner Bros Records for the rest of the world, who have just released the *All For Believing* EP in the States.

'They're all very supportive and passionate about my music, so I think they're going to get behind it. They all said that you've really got to put in the hard yards in America; you've just got to tour your arse off because it's so much harder to crack than somewhere like Australia. I guess I've just got to spend a lot of time over there and put in a lot of hard work. I'm not expecting it to be easy.'

Missy Higgins's ever-growing US commitments are likely to keep her Australian fans waiting a little longer for a follow-up to *The Sound of White*.

'We're not really planning it yet,' she says of her next album. 'I've not really started in America yet, so I guess it's not something we're going to start talking about until it's quite obvious that we've got to move on from the first album. We haven't even released it in America yet, so it will still be a while.

'It's going to be especially hard since I released *The Sound of White* in Australia months ago and I've had so much time to listen to the album and be extremely critical about it and realise what I want to change about it, what I'm not happy about and how I'm going to do better next time. I'm just about to do it all over again in America with the same album. I feel like I want to do it with a new album and a better album, but what can you do?'

Eager fans clamouring for a fresh Missy fix can pick up *The Special Two* EP, which hits stores this week and features new material.

'That's coming out on an EP with three other songs. I've got the Skyhooks cover that I did for Triple J's thirtieth anniversary and two other songs I wrote a couple of years ago before the album came about.'

So how did Higgins feel about singing 'You Just Like Me 'Cause I'm Good in Bed'?

'When Triple J asked me, I listened to it and thought oh my God! How am I ever going to do a version of this song?' she laughs. 'We did one version which was really rock and it was really fun to sing. *You just like me 'cause I'm good in bed*,' she belts down the line in her best rock voice.

'We were really happy with it but I played it to my management and they told me, "You can *not* release this!" I was like, "What's wrong with it? It's funny!" And they said, "Yeah, but no one else will get the tongue-in-cheek factor. Everyone will think you're trying to be serious."

'Ostracising fans is not the kind of thing I normally would care about but I guess it's the kind of thing management have to care about. So we did another version and it ended up being kind of a cabaret-style jazzy song, which ended up being really cool. I'll save the other version for my own collection.'

The EP also features two new Missy cuts: 'Drop The Mirror' and 'Blind Winter'.

'I've got so many songs so it's good to get them out there and move on. Otherwise they just stay in the vault and no one really hears them.'

August 2005. Original text: Matt Connors.

Arctic Monkeys

The first pinups of the iPod era

When the record company first mooted the idea of a phone interview with the Arctic Monkeys, the promotions manager from EMI wondered if we'd struggle with the band's broad Yorkshire accents. It worked out fine, thanks. The Arctic Monkeys, who formed in school, were famous for 'breaking on the internet'. *Whatever People Say I Am, That's What I'm Not* was the fastest-selling debut album in UK chart history. The band have lived up to the hype with a cache of fine albums, as well as Alex Turner's sublime side project, the Last Shadow Puppets.

The beauty about Arctic Monkeys is not that they've rewritten the rules in cracking the charts or that they're the fastest phenomenon to come out of the British Isles since the Beatles (both from the north of England, by the way) or that the Kaiser Chiefs think they're 'brilliant' and Noel Gallagher – whose records they kept playing – asked to meet them or even that they're all nineteen (except their guitarist Jamie Cook who is a year older) and still live with their parents.

The beauty of Arctic Monkeys is they refuse to play the music biz game. Maintaining they didn't get into a band to become famous, they don't do television, they hardly do interviews anymore, their videos are cheap, and they don't dress up. Their song 'Perhaps Vampires Is a Bit Strong But . . .' about the people in the music industry sums up their disdain. Unlike other bands that hit the top spot, they don't reek of the desperation of wanting to make it.

'We thrive on being on stage,' Cook says. 'That's where we have control. The rest is just propaganda. As the Jam said, it's about being in the moment.'

Their first two singles – 'When the Sun Goes Down' (about hanging in the Sheffield streets at night) and 'I Bet You Look Good on the Dancefloor' (about going to clubs to pull a bird, and failing) – went straight to number one in Britain.

Their debut album, *Whatever People Say I Am, That's What I'm Not*, sold a staggering 360,000 copies in its first week making it the fastest-selling debut album of all time in the United Kingdom.

The band formed three years ago while Cook and singer Alex Turner were at school together. The Christmas before, they were given guitars, so they teamed with Andy Nicholson (bass) and Matt Helders (drums) and rehearsed in a garage. They would cram into their manager's old Saab and ask venues if they could go on first because they had classes the next day.

No labels took any notice, so they burned copies of their demos and handed them out to crowds. The kids would upload them and send them around the internet. The Monkeys' hometown shows started to pack out, and audiences sang along to every line in every song.

'There were times when people would actually jump up on stage when we were playing to ask for a demo!' Cook says. 'It got crazy. People would drive for hours to come see the show.'

Part of their attraction is in songs by ordinary kids with ordinary experiences. 'Riot Van', for instance, is about hanging out together before the cops chase them off.

'When I was fifteen, all I did was hang around the streets and play football with my friends,' Cook says. 'I'd usually be in a football shirt, jeans and sneakers. I remember I shaved my hair because it gave me ten more minutes in bed before I had to go to school.'

A recent magazine article suggested that the new Brit bands like the Kaisers and Bloc Party came together to prove they were as good as the US bands like the Strokes and the White Stripes, but Cook doesn't place the Arctic Monkeys in the same territory.

'That wasn't what got us going,' the guitarist recalls in a strong Yorkshire accent. 'Our friends were in bands. We figured it was fun so we did it too. Our first gig was in a Sheffield pub called the Grapes, with four other bands. There were thirty people there, mostly friends. We were dead scared; we played our songs and covers like the Undertones' "Teenage Kicks" and the Beatles' "I'm Only Sleeping". Our friends were saying wow, you're not bad! It gave us the confidence to carry on. If that first show had been a disaster, we'd have stopped.'

By last March, they'd signed to Domino Records (also home to Franz Ferdinand), Radio One was playing their downloads and the *NME* was writing stories. But essentially, the Arctic Monkeys had exploded without much of the London music industry's awareness. One could argue it's all timing; that Arctic Monkeys are the first pinups of the iPod era, that they got discovered via the internet at a time when legitimate websites were popping up like mushrooms.

But there's more to the Monkeys. Their shows bristle with energy. Their music is as much inspired by indie-gods such as the Smiths as hip-hop acts such as Roots Manuva. Their songs like 'Dancing Shoes' and 'Still Take You Home' have interesting rhythms.

Their secret weapon, though, is Turner, whose lyrics capture what it is to be a teenager in a Northern town. They're little vignettes based in clubs, taxis and the streets. It's about hanging out, watching the poseurs and the hookers, or trying to get the nerve to chat up girls.

He's not only acclaimed as a modern-day Morrissey or Jarvis Cocker but also compared to Manchester punk poet John Cooper Clarke.

'When we first started the band, someone said to him, you remind me of John Cooper Clarke. When Clarke played in Sheffield we went checked him out, and Alex is a big fan now. Everyone thinks our name is crap. But John said, that's brilliant, there are no trees in the Arctic, how would the monkey survive?'

Did Cook realise when they were mucking around at fifteen that Turner was a gifted wordsmith in the making?

'He never showed me his stuff then, but, yeah, he's turned out to be real good.'

Does Cook understand all the words?

'No, but it doesn't matter, does it? You take what you take from it.'

February 2006. Original text: Christie Eliezer.

The Grates

A lack of Patience

Though much had changed, street press in 2006 remained as important a vehicle for championing local bands as it had since its inception. The difference now was in the sheer volume of local music being made. Homemade posters, a handful of venues and the occasional (rare) and celebrated recordings (on seven-inch vinyl) had given way to Photoshop, MySpace and professional-sounding multi-track recordings made in bedrooms and practice halls. Record companies too had woken up to the role of street press in breaking artists. As bands were signed up and touted earlier and earlier in their career, they began making inroads internationally almost as quickly as at home.

Not all championed bands were destined for such a path, but the Grates were always a little different from their contemporaries. Fun, outrageous and poppy, the Grates caught the eye of *Time Off* writers soon after they began performing at Ric's and other stalwart Brisbane venues. This piece from 2006 catches the band a long way from home and in the whirlwind of their first major success.

The Grates are in London, two of them eating square pies at a table next to Har Mar Superstar and having the time of their lives.

Between steamy mouthfuls of steak-and-Guinness, drummer Alana Skyring and guitarist John Patterson talk animatedly about where they've been, what they've done and what lies ahead. Enigmatic singer Patience Hodgson is tucked away in a dressing room, warming her vocal cords with odd exercises that have her sounding like she's doing impersonations of a bird trapped under water.

In an hour the Grates will walk on stage at Koko, a lavish four-tiered venue playing host for three consecutive nights to three kids from Brisbane and headliners the Go! Team. And tonight, just like last night, the Grates steal the Go! Team's thunder with a captivating and energetic performance that leaves both audience and band breathless.

It's a long way from Ric's in Brisbane's Brunswick Street Mall, the cosy bar where the Grates first stepped nervously into a 'red-eye' 2:00am slot in January 2004.

Then, Triple J had just picked up their home-recorded demo and the national broadcaster was spinning the ultra-catchy song 'Trampoline'. Now the Grates are primed to deliver *Gravity Won't Get You High*, a bold and ambitious debut album recorded in America with super indie producer Brian Deck.

'We didn't mind being three people in a shed,' Alana says of the obvious contrast in recordings.

'But you're making an album,' John explains, 'so you want it to sound like one. You don't want to be restricted and think, "Well, we're a band with a guitar, drums and a singer, so that's all we can do." We just wanted to make a proper record, not a crappy DIY one. "Trampoline" is still bare because that's all the song needed.'

'A lot of the time,' Alana says, 'we'd just put on anything and everything we thought might work. And then we started stripping back the tracks. "Inside Outside" was a freaking wonderland when we did it the first time around. You know, all the little bits themselves worked well, but they clashed horribly when they were put together.'

Many fans are anxious to see what time in a 'proper' studio has done to the Grates. It's true the band have broken free from the lo-fi recording techniques that permeated their early demos, but John and Alana say it's merely evolution.

'Our songwriting is a lot more elaborate now because we're more self-conscious,' Alana admits. 'Back in the day, when we were first writing together, we just didn't care and we'd settle for anything.'

'We always try to better ourselves,' John adds. 'We had really simple arrangements in the beginning and we just tried to better them each time. And I think we've got good arrangements now. We spent more time and more money doing things on this album because we wanted to be better than we were.'

Outside the band's trademark tight simplicity, there are horns, splashes of electronic noises and intricate percussion at work on *Gravity Won't Get You High*. But while outside musicians were called in to master some of the more difficult instruments, direction came entirely from the band.

'Brian Deck knew these guys who did horns so we got them in and we talked about what we wanted and where we wanted it,' says John.

'Everything we imagined we told them about,' Alana adds. 'Then we got people in to play the parts. Everything's us, except the horns and the fiddle.'

With the album release just around the corner, John and Alana say they've barely had time to ponder the enormity of the achievement. And they may not for some time. The Grates, you see, are in demand.

In England, music industry insiders are flocking to see the band, with major label scouts and high-profile media personnel all vying for space on each night's guest list. Appreciative of the attention, John and Alana are also quick to point out the other side of the coin.

'It's not all like that,' Alana laughs. 'People from the crowd yell out "Go home!" They yell out "You're fucked!" You just hope more people like you than don't like you.'

Certainly, their touring schedule – England, America, Canada, Australia – suggests there's plenty of interest in the trio. And now, with the Grates finally back on Australian soil and preparing to embark on a massive national tour, fans should expect just about anything from their live show.

'We're just thinking about good lighting and maybe some kind of set. I really want to do a set,' John says excitedly.

'Mmm,' Alana muses, 'even if money was no concern I wouldn't go over the top.'

'I would!' John laughs. 'I'd love to have this over-the-top winter wonderland.'

'Ooh, yeah!' Alana says, warming to the idea.

'And animatronics!' John mumbles, all starry-eyed and lost in his imagination. 'Yeah, I need to find a cheap animatronics guy . . .'

It might sound far-fetched, but don't be surprised if John's dreams come true. After all, it seems gravity's the only thing holding the Grates down right now.

Patience is a virtue

Following her absence from *Time Off*'s scheduled interview in London, we caught up with Patience Hodgson to ask her the really tough questions . . .

If gravity won't get you high, what will?

'Elevators, scaffolding . . . although I do recommend trying to pull a cone of gravity.'

Can you let us in on what 19-20-20 means? Is it true it referred to the band members' ages when you wrote it?

'Close, but no cigar! 19-20-20 was the ages we were when we thought about writing a song about our ages but we were actually 21-22-22 when we wrote it.'

The 19-20-20 film clip looks like it would have been loads of fun to make. What do you remember about that day and what's your favourite part of that clip?

'I remember heaps:

1. We had to get up really early and I was so scared I cried most of the trip. I have trouble in front of the camera because I'm not a model/actress.

2. It was the hottest day ever.
3. The tiger passed out because of the heat.
4. We had a sausage dog dressed up like a hot dog, but we didn't end up using it because it looked so scared.
5. The tiger also threw up after it passed out.
6. There was loads of fairy bread.
7. The house we filmed it at was amazing! There were huge taxidermy animals everywhere!'

I heard you doing some strange vocal warm-ups in London. Can you walk me through your routine and what it's meant to achieve?

'Well, it's pretty complex and involves a few muscles most people don't have. Last night Keith from We Are Scientists tried doing vocal warm-ups and it put him in a bad mood so he's never going to attempt them again. I don't think he was born with the right muscles. To tell you the truth, it would be a crime against nature to walk you through my vocal warm-ups because the only way to get through them is by long jumping.'

It's always seemed like being in the Grates must be like one big party. But with all your extra commitments these days, is it really as fun as it once was?

'It's more fun onstage these days than it's ever been, but if I continue to lose things I might wind up losing my mind as well. When I used to live in a house, losing things was just a game. Now we're on the road, the loss of an object is usually very serious . . . or fatal. That's the worst part: losing stuff.'

Have you ever used your bed like a trampoline?

'No. But I have used Jenny Jones's bed like a trampoline! She was my best friend in grade three and I spent an afternoon jumping on her bed until it broke. I remember I felt so guilty that I then spent the rest of the night crying in the corner until my mum picked me up. Not much has changed: that's still how I react to moments of great shame.'

Alana and John were fantasising about their dream stage sets.

If money were no issue, what would the ultimate Grates live show be like?

'We would be called Josie & the Pussycats and everyone would show up wearing brain-washing headphones. I would then expose a conspiracy and play guitar like a pro to a saved audience of thousands. Everything at our show would be environmentally friendly. Whales would sing.'

Finally, what can we expect from your Brisbane show at the Tivoli? Are you excited to be playing there?

'I'm both crying-in-the-corner nervous and singing-in-the-rain happy anticipating it. Put them all together and what you got? Ding dong, clap-clap, hot dawg excitement!'

April 2006. Original text: Nick Coppack.

The Vines

This year's vintage

The Vines were one of the first young Australian bands caught up in the new decade's relentless hype machine: snapped up, packaged, mass produced in gargantuan numbers and trotted out to a fawning media and a global audience. For a while, it seemed our first exposure to the biggest Australian bands was not at a local pub, but through a television ad for a phone company. After more than six years plugging away in anonymity, the Vines almost became a casualty of the system. Their third album, *Vision Valley*, similarly failed to meet its near-impossible sales requirements and the band found themselves dropped by their record labels in 2006. But away from the glare, the Vines – and front man Craig Nicholls in particular – have found a seemingly more comfortable space to continue plying their trade.

'STAR'S SECRET AGONY' brayed the headline in Sydney's *Daily Telegraph* in November 2004; 'Vines front man has brain disorder'. As a tabloid story, it had everything – except, perhaps, the exclamation mark. In reality, Craig Nicholls's 'debilitating brain disorder' – a form of autism known as Asperger's Syndrome – looked likely to put a final full stop on a band biography that was as eventful as it was short.

In an industry famed for precipitous ups and downs, few have gone from penthouse to pavement faster than the Vines. The Sydney band's debut, 2002's *Highly Evolved*, put Australian music on the front burner worldwide and shipped 1.5 million copies.

An introductory tour of small venues in the UK had one *NME* critic nominating the Vines' show in Brighton as 'one of the most sensational' debut gigs he had ever seen. Manic Street Preachers front man James Dean Bradfield proclaimed them 'absolutely fucking amazing'. The album's breakthrough single, 'Get Free', hit the UK top thirty, came in at number five in that year's Triple J Hottest 100, and caught the ear of savvy ad-execs looking for a product-friendly rebel anthem.

Album reviews flooded in. The *Times* reckoned *Highly Evolved* was based on 'a sound so sexy and sludgy that it makes you want to roll around in it'. *Q Magazine* thought that 'the Australian quartet's debut album justifies the fuss'. The *NME* was moved to run a full page illustration of Nicholls under the heading 'Anatomy of a Rock God', and pondered whether *Highly Evolved* is 'the greatest debut album ever'. They became the first Australian rock band to make the cover of US *Rolling Stone* in twenty years.

It wasn't long before critical opinion on the band seemed to shift. The hosannas were initially tempered by Nicholls's reputation for odd or violent outbursts in interviews. Reviews of live shows featuring Nicholls bellowing into the microphone, falling over and smashing his guitars (he broke *fifty-seven* guitars on consecutive nights) ceased being awestruck descriptions of a tortured genius at work and began to openly question his sanity. 'Witless, dismal, joyless, depressing', complained one critic.

After beginning 2004 with a gruelling US tour with Jet, the Vines' tour of Japan was defined by Nicholls abusing the crowd and gigs falling apart as the band worked out their tensions on stage. It came to a head when The Vines' tour lurched into Sydney for a Triple M-sponsored gig at the Annandale Hotel. You know the story: insults thrown, kicks dispensed, cameras smashed, charges laid, and the Vines found themselves banned from the Triple M playlist 'forever'.

The cumulative effect of all this negative publicity was that the band's sophomore album, *Winning Days*, stalled mid-year after selling a still-impressive 600,000 copies. Bass player Patrick Matthews quit the band, never to return, and the Vines were forced to cancel all touring commitments. Nicholls faced assault charges, underwent psychiatric evaluation, and was eventually diagnosed with Asperger's Syndrome, a neurological condition that leads to difficulties with social interaction and an inability to cope with interruptions to routine. Hardly surprising that the *NME*'s 'Anatomy of a Rock God' missed that.

If nothing else, all of the above makes the Vines' third album, *Vision Valley*, a feel-good story of triumph over adversity. Recorded with one eye on the mercurial Nicholls's mental wellbeing, the fact that it's so damned good is even more remarkable.

'Most people thought the band had broken up,' drummer Hamish Rosser says. 'So the expectation was zero as far as I'm aware.'

Working in a Sydney studio with Australian producer Wayne Connolly (a self-confessed analogue 'fanatic' who has recorded You Am I, Underground Lovers and Youth Group among others), Nicholls, Rosser and Ryan Griffiths (guitar, keyboards) recorded the tracks simply and quickly – no big production values, no hours of overdubs.

Connolly's relaxed style would prove to be as helpful as his expert ear. After fraught sessions in Los Angeles during the recording of the previous albums, it was important for a new protocol to be established if anything fit for release was ever going to make it to tape. Ryan Griffiths says that Connolly's presence at the sessions was 'almost therapeutic – he could calm things down, but he also has a good punk ethic'.

'We commenced the demo sessions in May of last year at Velvet Studios and recorded seven songs,' Connolly says. 'In fact, the first two songs from the album, "Anysound" and "Nothin's Comin", are from the original sessions.'

'Anysound' is a good example of the new Vines modus operandi.

'It was probably the first song on the album that we recorded,' recalls Rosser. 'We did it way back in May. I'd never heard the song before we recorded it on that day and we recorded about five takes of it. We tried to record it again later in about October, but we couldn't beat the original demo so we used that. It was unbeatable.'

Likewise 'Futuretarded'.

'It's basically a mix of what we recorded at the demo session,' Connolly says. 'Two takes of vocals and a bunch of percussion on top of the live band track.'

But it's not all stripped-down, pared-back rock and roll. 'Spaceship' is the most ambitious track the group have ever attempted, with Nicholls in symphonic 'Across the Universe' Beatles mode.

'Craig first played it to me on acoustic and I loved it,' Connolly says. 'After hearing it with the band I thought it was the one that needed the most work. That's why it took the longest to record, but now I love it so.' Connolly takes pride in the song's 'wild, insane sound . . . there's a psychedelic fuzz mandolin. There are hundreds of things like that layered in.'

'It's a six-minute epic,' Nicholls says. 'It goes through a lot of different stages. It starts out very mellow acoustic and it ends up space-rock. It's pretty interesting, I think.'

It makes for a stark contrast with the album's electrifying, you-can't-miss-it track 'Gross Out': seventy-seven seconds of sneering punk aggression that could well supplant 'Get Free' as the band's anthem and calling card.

'When we were trying to get the track listing in the order of the songs for the album, "Gross Out" was the song that no matter where it went in the album, just leapt out at about a hundred miles an hour,' Rosser says.

With the band's touring and promotional schedule strictly curtailed to accommodate Nicholls's needs, *Vision Valley*, more than any other major release of recent times, will have to stand or fall on the quality of its songs and whether it can connect with an audience who may never see the album performed live.

April 2006. Original text: Lorna Macpherson.

The Saints

Halo again

Anyone with a passing interest in the Saints would have been scratching their heads when it was announced that three members of the original foursome were reuniting for what was to be a one-off performance as part of 2007's Queensland Music Festival. Maybe it had something to do with *Pig City*, or the lucre involved but it certainly wasn't for nostalgia. Messrs Kuepper, Bailey and Hay took no prisoners and delivered a set that was nothing short of primeval in its intensity. The truce between Kuepper and Bailey seems to have lasted. More Saints shows followed and the pair has once again begun collaborating on new music.

To many music fans, the thought of a Saints reunion seemed nigh on impossible. Now, the city that gave birth to them will play host to a one-off reunion of the three original members as a part of this year's Queensland Music Festival.

Forming in the western suburbs of Brisbane in 1973 as Kid Galahad & the Eternals, guitarist Ed Kuepper, pianist (and future bassist, then drummer) Ivor Hay and vocalist Chris Bailey began a five-year journey as one of the world's most highly revered punk bands. By 1974, they were the Saints – performing many of the songs that became the basis of their first two albums.

Come October 1976, their independently released single, '(I'm) Stranded' received the 'best single of this week and every week' title in the UK's music bible, *Sounds*. By the year's end, the band had signed to EMI, and within six months they'd relocated to the UK and supported the Ramones at London's Roundhouse.

By the time the band split in mid-1978, the Saints managed to release three LPs and crack the British chart with the single 'This Perfect Day'. Within eighteen months of releasing their debut, the band were history.

Kuepper relocated back to Australia and formed the Laughing Clowns, a band that continued the horn-driven themes of the final Saints album, *Prehistoric Sounds* – steadfastly non-commercial, but artistically gratifying. Bailey, meanwhile, picked up the Saints name and applied it to an ever-changing rhythm section that bore little resemblance to the band EMI signed in 1976 at the height of the punk rock movement.

And now, more than thirty years later, Kuepper, Hay and Bailey are bringing the band back home. The obvious question to Ed Kuepper is: why? Why have the band only now gotten back together?

'Love,' he laughs. 'What can I say? That's my answer!'

Having not performed together since promoting their second LP, 1978's *Eternally Yours*, the band's songwriters, Kuepper and Bailey, both say they mutually feel a great optimism towards the occasion.

'Yeah, I am fairly optimistic that it'll work,' Kuepper confirms. 'Some of it will be a little trial and error – that's why I like the fact we'll be rehearsing so we can see how things go. I've got a good idea of how I want it to sound. Working in any kind of collaborative situation, there's always going to be some give and take.'

'I kind of feel like I'm in the middle of two bands,' Bailey adds. 'It's like having my very own private time machine. Having seen Ed recently, it seems like we haven't lost our peculiar sense of humour. I think it will be interesting, and there's certainly been a lot of talk about the set list.'

What the original band never got around to doing was performing material from *Prehistoric Sounds*. Queensland Music Festival's musical director, Paul Grabowsky, was quick to offer the band a horn section.

'It's not one of my personal favourite records,' Bailey is quick to point out. 'It is interesting that I've done those songs with others, but never with the people actually on the record. Ed's played some of that material and so have I, so it'll be funny in rehearsals seeing which versions we end up doing.'

Bailey's take on the reunion seems to be based purely on the fact that it's in Brisbane, despite offers for the original band to tour abroad and interstate.

'There have been a couple of wacko offers, which I'm not very interested in at the moment,' Bailey says. 'I think it's fitting in some kind of funny way, because this is where the whole thing kicked off. It makes sense, so that's why we're so enthusiastic about it. It's either going to be beautiful or a brilliant disaster. The fact that it's happening now is terrific. I do think I bring a different dynamic to Ed's performance and no doubt vice versa.'

That the band will only play at the QMF comes as a disappointment to Kuepper, who has always left open the possibility of future shows with Bailey and Hay.

'I thought it would have been good to do more,' Kuepper says. 'At least some more shows around Australia. But I've got a new record coming out, so I'll be busy with that stuff anyway. A series of shows after this in quick succession would have been great.'

What Kuepper would like to underline in red pen is that this performance isn't about nostalgia.

'Doing this show is like a thing unto itself,' he says. 'For me, the whole thing isn't an issue. Other people may see it differently. Nostalgia seems to imply that it's Gerry & the Pacemakers or something like that. Even if it's about the band getting back together again and playing songs in their original form, it's not a nostalgic event. How could it be nostalgic if you're supposedly playing with people you don't get along with? I could listen to the records if I wanted to feel nostalgic. How could it be for the audience? How many people will be at the show who would have seen the band in the first place? Not many. It's a new thing for a lot of people. It's something that transcends nostalgia, from my perspective.'

With the show only weeks away, EMI Australia have planned

to release Ed Kuepper's remastered versions of the previously out-of-print albums of the band's late seventies canon – *(I'm) Stranded*, *Eternally Yours* and *Prehistoric Sounds*.

'You've got to hand it to EMI Oz, they're very enthusiastic at re-releasing stuff! I just wonder how many times they could do that,' Bailey laughs.

'The intention always was to put the albums out again,' Kuepper says.

As for the future of the Saints in their original form, Bailey gets the last word.

'Well, I did make a cameo on Ed's new record and it sounds fine. It works. As Sean Connery says, "Never say never." If the spark is there, we should certainly fan it up.'

June 2007. Original text: Donat Tahiraj.

Hilltop Hoods

More strings to their bow

Starting out in 1991, the Hilltop Hoods have been at the forefront of Australian hip-hop for nearly two decades. Hailing from Adelaide, the group turned heads when they released a 'restrung' version of their album *The Hard Road*, which saw their regulation beats remixed alongside string players from the Adelaide Symphony Orchestra. Aware of where they've come from and prepared to give something back, in 2005 they established the 'Hilltop Hoods Initiative', providing both grants and mentorship to up-and-coming Adelaide hip-hop artists.

The Hilltop Hoods have been riding a wave of success for the past couple of years to arrive at their current status as possibly the biggest hip-hop act in the country. It's the kind of wave that their American counterparts would gladly jump on, grandstanding on the crest before washing up on bling-bling beach. But, far from letting success go their heads, the three lads from Adelaide – MCs Suffa and Pressure and DJ Debris – maintain a down-to-earth focus and their legendary work ethic – making tracks, rocking shows and, in their spare time, drinking piss.

Among all that, says MC Suffa (or Matt Lambert when in the presence of his mum), they've been trying to find time to work on a follow-up album to 2006's *The Hard Road* and its orchestral remix album, 2007's *The Hard Road Restrung*.

'We haven't had a great deal of time to write, because we went straight from doing the *Restrung* album and launch to doing the *City of Light* DVD for the last few months, and a bit of touring as well,' a chilled-out Suffa drawls down the phone.

'Since we've finished *The Hard Road* I've produced probably a hundred or a hundred and fifty beats and we've gone through them and chosen three or four for the new album. We're getting producers and writing a lot. I've even recorded a few verses. But it's in the pre-natal stages,' he says with a ready laugh.

One thing Suffa's sure of is that the Adelaide Symphony Orchestra will be sitting this one out. Last year's *Restrung* experience, which saw the boys regularly backed up by swathes of strings and horns, was considered universally positive. Nothing like it had ever been attempted before and the orchestral remixes were adored by fans and lauded by critics. Even the 'tea and scones' gags levelled at the gone-soft Hoods by fellow rappers were good-natured and perhaps born of a tiny smidge of envy. But it was a lot of hard graft.

'Yeah, there'll be no orchestra, that's for sure,' Suffa laughs. 'It was a wicked experience, don't get me wrong, but it's just too full-on; too much work to take on. At the show, we had people coming along who were fans of the Adelaide Symphony Orchestra. I don't know what they made of it, because I can't see classical music fans going nuts over anything, especially a hip-hop group. Apparently we had some there, but I think some people would go just to listen out of interest.'

The Australian hip-hop world is eager to find out just what it can expect from its leading lights later in the year. In a recent interview, Suffa's partner in rhyme, MC Pressure, suggested the new sound would be more stripped-back. Suffa suggests that the process may turn out to be a little more organic.

'Well, to be honest, these albums sort of write themselves,' Suffa reveals. 'We don't go in with a plan like, this is going to be a dark album or whatever because we're too fussy about beats and what we write to ever have a running theme. So, we could never do a whole album of beats that we feel have an early nineties vibe or something like that, because we'd never find thirteen or fourteen beats that we were that passionate about that all have a common vibe.

'A lot of it'll be run-off from *The Hard Road*, stuff that didn't make it on there purely because of time, not because of quality. The same thing happened between *The Calling* (2003) and *The Hard Road*: the production never stops, and the recording never stops.'

2007 saw the band undergo a punishing tour schedule that's made the Hilltop Hoods a household name across the nation. They even dipped a toe in the UK market twice during the year.

'We played at Shepherd's Bush Empire, and packed it out with almost two thousand. There's so many fuckin' expats over there that when you get a crowd it's hard to judge what's what – when you play over there, the flags all pop up and everything. But it's fine; it's cool. They're familiar with the songs and they're getting into it and you're getting the English crowd coming along with them, getting in amongst it, and getting the vibe as well.'

Some artists relish the opportunity to go on tour; soaking up different cultures and landscapes seems conducive to the writing process. For the Hilltop Hoods, however, writing while on tour is impossible – probably because most of the time, a beer is thrust into their hands as soon as the last one's dry.

'I can't write on tour,' Suffa says flatly. 'Every now and then I'll write something on a plane or text some lyrics on my own phone to myself, but to record and really seriously put together and finish a record, we need six months. So we're taking a break from domestic touring from March until late in the year to dedicate to the album. I'm really looking forward to that because we've been touring non-stop for the last two and a half years.'

But before they drop off the radar for the remainder of the year, the Hoods will wave farewell in the presence of Big Day Out crowds all around the country.

'We've got a string quartet with us and a live band; there're going to be eleven of us on stage! We're playing a main stage, luckily,' Suffa laughs. 'But, you know, I kind of prefer the smaller stages, sometimes – just the way the crowd is packed in wall to wall. It's a little harder to catch a vibe like that on the big stadium stages.'

January 2008. Original text: Baz McAlister.

Yves Klein Blue

Seeking your attention

Yves Klein Blue started turning heads in Brisbane almost from their inception. Taking part in an MTV competition, they caught the eye of street press, community radio and finally the record label Dew Process. Their original indie EP was given a makeover with remixes, re-recordings and the necessary amount of rejigging to get the band heard far and wide. Publicists began courting editors over Chinese lunches and YKB were on their way to cover stardom and beyond. Hardly resting on their laurels, the band took the attention by the lapels and they've continued to run with it.

Think about it: how many people can you think of who can claim to have actually invented a colour? French artist Yves Klein can. Classified largely as an enigmatic post-modernist, Klein is still considered an important figure in post-war European art to this day and, among his many lifelong accolades, left his mark by patenting a colour: International Klein Blue.

While they're not reinventing the colour wheel, Brisbane indie rock quartet Yves Klein Blue are pretty much living the rock and roll dream. Kicking around our backyard for only a couple of years, they've quickly built themselves a healthy buzz on the back of their debut EP – *Yves Klein Blue Draw Attention to Themselves* – and a string of excellent shows.

A combination of boyish good looks, switched-on indie smarts, and a penchant for writing hooky pop tunes soon attracted the attention of Brisbane label Dew Process, who immediately funded the remixing of the EP and whisked them off overseas for a number of international dates.

Even as *Time Off* catches up with YKB's charmingly humble front man Michael Tomlinson, the band are in Austin, Texas, and have only just completed the shows for South by Southwest earlier in the day.

'I never want to say anything too brash without touching wood,' he muses, scrambling to a quiet alley to complete our conversation, 'but I think we went really well. All of this, needless to say, is sort of surreal. We went through Los Angeles on our way here and we played three shows there. Then we went to New York where we were playing with the Panics, but more notably – not to take anything away from the Panics – we played with the Vines. That was a real thrill for us; all the high school bands each of us was in all did a cover of "Get Free". Then we're off to London and after that we're returning to Australia for the EP launches.'

The original version of *Yves Klein Blue Draw Attention to Themselves* was released in 2006, and, after snaring the record deal, the band felt it didn't represent them as accurately as they would've liked. They wanted a big, powerful recording. Big guitars, not thin and jangly. Big, solid drums. And the list goes on.

'We really wanted to put the representation of our best, much like we did on the first EP,' Tomlinson explains. 'The songs that we feel show what we are as a band most effectively. It's a re-recording of sorts; it has the same name. Nothing of the old EP is on there, so it's illustrating that it's the same concept as the first EP and how we could've done it with more money, more time and if we were able to play the songs.'

With the EP growing from five to seven tracks, it's more of a mini-album when played in its entirety. Aside from a shiny new production, what's the newbie got to offer?

'I guess you could say there are two and half new songs on there,' Tomlinson continues, searching for the right words to explain the rare scenario. 'I call one a half because "Blasphemy" has a drastically different arrangement, plus there are two other songs. We used a Brisbane producer called Caleb James, who we were really lucky to get on board. He's an incredible musician, a great producer and, really, a guru of sorts. We went down to Byron to record our drums and then went back to his studio to complete the tracking. We had a couple of tracks remixed by Wayne Connolly, who did all Josh Pyke's stuff and the Vines and You Am I. We didn't want to sound produced or sterile in any way; we wanted as much energy as a live show but sounding as strong for the radio. I think we got there in the end.'

As easy as it is to lose yourself with a string of endless accolades, worldwide trips and mingling with celebrities, Tomlinson and the lads are determined to stay grounded and not completely lose themselves within the whirlwind skyward journey.

'It is really surreal, very hard to believe,' Tomlinson says. 'To us, we're still just a local Brisbane band who have a chance to do some really cool things.'

But like every band trying to attract attention from labels and an adoring public, Yves Klein Blue had decided from a very early stage that this little thing called music is exactly what they wanted to do and they weren't willing to compromise to get there.

'We tried a lot of stuff when we first formed,' he explains. 'We'd already had all the time spent jamming and whatever in high school bands, playing just for the love of playing. By the time we were at uni, I was feeling like I really wanted to play music and we met some guys so we thought if we really want to do this, then we really have to step up. So we tried to make ourselves appealing, initially. If you want something like this – without being rude – be good. I just think the best thing is not to behave like an arsehole. If you don't behave like an arsehole, things might turn out alright. Usually.'

April 2008. Original text: Ben Preece.

Angus & Julia Stone

Nomadic lifestyle suits siblings

Angus & Julia Stone were destined for life on the road as performers. Their parents had a band and the kids were always encouraged to perform. Both Angus and Julia write their own songs and lend each other support when it comes to arrangements and instrumentation. An independent EP, word of mouth and good tunes landed them a major label record deal and an overseas release. Famous fans include Travis's Fran Healy, who lent them his studio, and Natalie Portman, who included their song 'The Beast' on a charity compilation. Starting out, 'officially', in 2006, they filled a small tent at that year's Splendour in the Grass and they've never looked back.

For a band on the road as much as Angus & Julia Stone, 'home' can become a very blurred concept. The nomadic lifestyle the siblings have led over the last three years has seen them relocating between Australia, London and New York.

'It's funny, because when you are moving at such a steady pace on the road, you get used to constantly being in the car, on the train or in a motel,' says Angus. 'You tell yourself that when you get home you'll just chill and be in one place, but you get off the road and you've got this gypsy bug in you. Pretty much as soon as I got home, I jumped in my car and hit the road! I just travelled up the coast staying with friends and family.'

'The road' is a concept that runs deeply through the Stones' enigmatic second album, *Down the Way*. Recorded in various studios around the globe, it demonstrates an intrepid sense of journey and demonstrates the pair's newfound worldliness. With the endless months of travelling and the languid days between, there is a lot of inspiration to take in. A number of tracks were recorded at an idyllic studio in Golant, Cornwall – a beautiful country village setting that once gave birth to the Oasis classic *Definitely Maybe*.

'We went to an old sawmill, on the riverside, that has been converted into a studio, and the only way to get there is by boat, or you walk down the railway track,' explains Angus. 'The whole vibe of the place was quite enchanted and it definitely had an inspiring energy when we were in the cave recording songs.'

At twenty-three years old, Angus Stone is as laid back a character as anyone listening to his songs could possibly imagine – quiet, charming and articulate. His voice is soothing, yet his words are thoughtful enough to keep all ears pinned to his stories. Angus's offstage persona mirrors his mellow groove on stage. There is nothing fake, pretentious or typically 'rock star' about this man. For Mr Stone, performing is his bread and writing is his butter, and he never misses an opportunity to put pen to paper.

'For me, writing songs it is an ongoing thing. Being on the road definitely limits certain things to do with writing, but it doesn't limit the inspiration you find in different corners of the world,' he says. 'You find so much in different countries and towns and in people you meet. I can always find time to sit down and write and get these feelings out.'

What separates Angus and Julia from their indie-folk counterparts lies primarily in their differences rather than their similarities. The songs on which the pair collaborates are separate entities, dreamt up and realised in two different worlds.

'The songs that I sing are mine and the songs Julia sings are Julia's. We've always written separately; that is just the way it is, that is the way we are comfortable with,' says Angus. 'We have written together, once, sitting by the creek somewhere in Nimbin. Dad's wedding was coming up and at the time we couldn't really afford a present. We wrote a song and played it together at the wedding in his backyard, I guess that is the only time we have really written as a pair.'

As the Stones rolled through their hectic touring schedule, they became a classic gypsy travelling band gathering and dispersing members as they went. They recorded on and off with different engineers and musicians, each bringing subtle variations to the sound of *Down the Way*.

'On this album there are four different drummers and three bass players. The band I guess are just whoever is in town,' he laughs. 'It's good, though, because you get different colours that you wouldn't have seen otherwise and they really add another flavour to the mix. When we were touring with Martha Wainwright in Europe, we hung out with her band and formed a relationship with their drummer and we ended up asking him to come on the road with us afterward. I guess that is how all the members of our band really come together, we just meet on the road and just ask them if they want to come play.'

This organic process may just be the key to *Down the Way*'s success. The pair's chilled outlook on life and willingness to just 'go with the flow' has achieved remarkable results. Even after experiencing the ritz and glitz the music industry can offer, Angus believes that the best musical moments are the unplanned ones, the ones that can crop up at any time.

'It's like you can go to a real fancy restaurant and have a not-so-good time or you can take your meal out onto the gutter and have a ball. The aesthetics are not always so important to creating something amazing,' he says. 'With *Down the Way*, a lot of the stuff we collected and recorded along the way, just in different countries and towns, at friends' places. It just kind of just happened like that. There was really no direction or time limit on where it would go.'

The sleepy-sounding Mr Stone may seem relaxed enough, but not one aspect of 'Angus & Julia Stone' slips out to the public without his and his sister's consent. From their cover art to their film clips, the pair dictates absolutely every fine detail. The cover art for *Down the Way*, for example, originates from a photo their grandfather took many years ago.

'We are responsible for pretty much everything, we don't really let much go past without us seeing it. It's always been that way since the beginning. Something like cover art is very important. I don't understand how other bands just let go of that, because you're representing how you feel about things in what you do when you release the imagery surrounding your music.'

With *Down the Way* out of the way and the pair refreshed after a lengthy break, the next step is take the new songs out on the road, a task Angus has mixed feelings about.

'I am a bit nervous actually, I haven't played a show in eight months. I'm the only person I have been playing to lately, so it's going to be a bit confusing seeing all these people in front of me again! I am looking forward to hanging out with the old gang and making new friends, visiting different cities, towns and countries, though. That'll be fun. It's great to know that people out there are making connections to the songs; that you are not alone and there are people who feel what you are doing.'

March 2010. Original text: Nolan Giles.